Reggie Martin

*Bayou Farewell*

Also by Mike Tidwell

*The Ponds of Kalambayi:* An African Sojourn

*In the Shadow of the White House:* Drugs, Death, and
Redemption on the Streets of the Nation's Capital

*Amazon Stranger:* A Rainforest Chief
Battles Big Oil

*In the Mountains of Heaven:* Tales of
Adventure on Six Continents

# *Bayou Farewell*

## The Rich Life and Tragic Death
## of Louisiana's Cajun Coast

# Mike Tidwell

*Pantheon Books   New York*

All rights reserved under International and Pan-American Copyright
Conventions. Published in the United States by Pantheon Books,
a division of Random House, Inc., New York, and simultaneously
in Canada by Random House of Canada Limited, Toronto.

Pantheon Books and colophon are registered trademarks of
Random House, Inc.

Library of Congress Cataloging-in-Publication Data

Tidwell, Mike.
    Bayou farewell : the rich life and tragic death of Louisiana's Cajun coast /
    Mike Tidwell.
        p. cm.
    Includes index.
    ISBN 0-375-42076-2
        1. Gulf Coast (La.)—Description and travel. 2. Gulf Coast (La.)—
    Environmental conditions. 3. Coast changes—Louisiana—Gulf Coast.
    4. Bayous—Louisiana—Gulf Region. 5. Gulf Coast (La.)—Social life and
    customs. 6. Cajuns—Louisiana—Gulf Coast—Social life and customs.
    7. Tidwell, Mike—Journeys—Louisiana—Gulf Region. 8. Gulf Region
    (La.)—Description and travel. 9. Gulf Region (La.)—Environmental
    conditions. 10. Gulf Region (La.)—Social life and customs. I. Title.

    F377.G9 T54 2003        976.3'00946—dc21        2002030702

www.pantheonbooks.com

Book design by Johanna S. Roebas

Printed in the United States of America
First Edition

9 8 7 6 5 4 3 2 1

*For Sasha, who is the whole world*

## Acknowledgments

Thanks first of all to Louisiana natives Glen Pitre and Michelle Benoit, who first offered the opinion that an outsider like myself could safely hitchhike down the bayous of Louisiana aboard Cajun fishing boats. In between my boat trips, they opened their beautiful home to me along Bayou Lafourche, giving me a treasured place to rest up, regain my land legs, and feast on sweet blackberries just behind the back porch. Fine writers themselves, Glen and Michelle also offered invaluable comments on early drafts of the book. In a state famous for its warm people and welcoming culture, these two truly stand out. Again, *merci beaucoup.*

Special thanks also to heroic conservationists Mark Davis, Kerry St. Pé, and Windell Curole, who spent hours in the field, on the phone, and in their offices patiently explaining to me the social and scientific reasons behind the rapid disappearance of Louisiana's fragile wetland coast.

Enormous thanks, too, to my agent, Jennifer Lyons, who immediately recognized the importance of this subject and applied great stores of grace and savvy in finding a home for the book.

For help large and small, thanks also to: Craig Stoltz, Edward Kastenmeier, Nick Varchaver, the Melancons of Leeville, Papoose Ledet, Dean Blanchard, Knuckles and Rose Mayeux, Wayne Belanger, Charlie Broussard, Papoose Plaisance, Ricky and Elaine Cutchall, Loulan Pitre Jr., Denise Reed, Peter Vujnovich Jr., Brenda Dardar, Michael Dardar, Lawrence Billiot, Bill Vermillion, Peter Callais, Kirk Cheramie, Kirk Kilgen, Rob Gorman, Father Joseph Pilola, Father Roch Naquin, Chuck Villarubia, Paul Kemp, Glen Thomas, Elam Griffin, Mark Dismuke, John Verdin Jr., Seth Grimes, and Frank Reiss.

Final thanks to my dear wife, Catherine, and son, Sasha, who with great love and patience endured yet another of Dad's exhausting book projects.

*A Note on Accents*

The Cajuns of South Louisiana speak English with an accent as distinctive as any in America. The long history of spoken French in this region means that most Cajuns cannot make the *th* sound, a sound that doesn't exist in French. So when speaking English, "this" comes out "dis" and "brother" comes out "brudder." Elements of French grammar also creep into the English, with some Cajuns saying they have to go "upstair" to find a "pair of shoe." Finally, both the general tones of French and the influence of Deep South isolation color almost every word of Cajun English. A bayou fisherman might say, "Ah don lak ta dance oil de time, me, at de *fais-do-do*. So I deen ween no contest." Translation: "I don't like to dance all the time at the *fais-do-do* [a traditional Cajun dance]. So I didn't win any contests."

Clearly, to write all of the Cajun dialogue in this book in this manner would exhaust the reader and prove, in the end, disrespectful to Cajuns. The true color and dignity of their speech would inevitably be lost in translation. Therefore I've chosen a more limited portrayal, faithfully omitting the *th* sound and including some of the altered grammar without laying things on too thick. This approach serves to consistently remind the reader that Cajuns do, in fact, sound different from most Americans without loading the pages down with an impenetrable soup of dialect.

*Journey Down the Bayous*

## *Prologue*

I can't believe I'm about to cry, but there it is: my eyes well up as I face, one last time, the two Cajun fishermen. They are grizzled men, standing in the thin light of a new moon, standing on a wobbly dock at the end of Bayou Petit Caillou just spitting distance from the Gulf of Mexico. We shake hands goodbye, but the gesture is decidedly awkward and grossly inadequate—and though I dare not hug these men, I want to . . . and perhaps they want to hug me, too. But these are working men—shrimpers—with scars on their hands and tattoos on their arms and cigarettes behind their ears. They are poor men who, on a bad day, will put in twenty hours for just three or four dollars' pay—and yet they've given me everything they have: food, drink, shelter from storm, a ride down the bayou, and a journey through a

Cajun world that is as backwoods and off the trodden path as anything in America.

"What if I want to send you a letter up dere in New York?" says Wayne Belanger, a man with dirty-silver hair and hands as thick as encyclopedias who mixes Cajun French into his English, calling storms *"tempêtes"* and me *"tee frère."*

For the second time I explain that I'm not from New York; I live outside Washington, D.C. But down here in Terrebonne Parish, Louisiana, where three-quarters of the area is water and people live on their boats for days at a time or in bayou "camps" (small houses on stilts) amid a vast landscape of marsh grass and meandering streams and lakes and swamps and bushy mangroves—down here, anyone who's not Cajun and Catholic and a fisherman with mile-deep roots is, it seems, from New York, which is to say that big foreign planet that is the rest of the world.

Big Wayne Belanger, the captain of the *Lady Desiree,* has brought me down this murky bayou by the light of a single candle flickering inside the wheelhouse of his twenty-eight-foot Lafitte skiff. Against that candlelight I now hand him a card with my address on it. Wayne takes it with a hand whose ring finger was lost long ago to a catfish-fin wound. Charlie Broussard, the other shrimper, heads back to the boat just then, threatening once again to load me down with an absurdly huge quantity of fresh shrimp as a parting gift. He's limping slightly on a bum right foot, having stepped on a shrimp *piquant* (the hornlike protrusion above the shrimp's eyes) the day before. He's tried everything to get it out, including the Cajun remedy of tying a slab of pork meat to his foot with a rag.

I protest to Charlie—again—that I can't possibly travel home with such big bags of fresh shrimp in my possession, and at last he agrees.

"Dey might get *beaucoup* smelly up dere on dat airplane, for sure," he says. "So bring you down here a pickup truck next time and we'll fill you up real pretty."

Charlie limps back from the boat, sad he can't offer a gift, and extends his hand for a second, final farewell.

This is it. These barefoot and shirtless men have brought me to the end of my journey, closing out a far-fetched yet rewardingly successful personal experiment in hitchhiking the fishing boats of Louisiana's bayou country. For days I've slowly thumbed my way down two different major bayous and past a half dozen waterside Cajun towns lined with sun-bleached docks and hanging Spanish moss and old Catholic churches whose priests come out to bless fishing boats with consecrated water.

I've traveled aboard rigs ranging from a fifty-three-foot "round-bottom" shrimper to a sixteen-foot chaland crab boat, eating Cajun red beans and rice and shrimp boulettes cooked in tiny galleys by deckhands along the way. I've floated past old bayou swing bridges activated by hand-guided ropes and steamed out into marshland so vast it stretches beyond the earth's curvature with flocks of roseate spoonbills dotting the sunset horizon. I've had one boat captain grab my collar to keep me from falling into a canal replete with ten-foot alligators.

All this I've done without a car, traveling only with a backpack and the loosest of plans, relying on the kindness of locals to let me into their world and onto their boats, one by one, closer and closer, to the Gulf of Mexico. And now the journey's almost over.

Yet more striking than the food and the French language, more unsettling than the gators and water moccasins and "waterspout" tornadoes that occasionally slam into bayou boats like runaway trains descended from jet-black storm clouds—more amazing than all of this has been the unexpected news I've learned along the way: the massive marshland coast of this watery southern state is vanishing from the face of the earth. The whole ragged sole of the Louisiana boot, an area the size of Connecticut—three million acres—is literally washing out to sea, surrendering to the Gulf of Mexico. It's an unfolding calamity of fantastic magnitude, taking with it entire Cajun towns and an age-old way of life.

Yet no act of God has made this happen. There's nothing natural about it, in fact. Human beings have made it so.

From fishermen along the way I learn details of this story of coastal ruin. I learn that the lower Mississippi River, the great creator of land in southernmost Louisiana through thousands of years of flooding and alluvial deposits, is now straitjacketed with flood levees so high—as high as three-story buildings in places—that the river may never jump its banks again. And that, in a nutshell, is the problem. A devastating chain reaction has resulted from the taming of the Mississippi, and now the entire coast is dissolving at breakneck speed, with an area equal to the size of Manhattan succumbing every ten months. It is, hands down, the fastest-disappearing landmass on earth, and New Orleans itself is at great risk of vanishing.

What's being lost is an American treasure, a place as big as the Everglades and just as beautiful, where sky and marsh and wildlife converge, where millions of migratory birds thrive on wetlands that once served as muse to John James Audubon. This world, containing a staggering 25 percent of America's total coastal wetlands, may be totally gone in the next few decades, taking with it a huge part of America's economy and a shield against hurricanes for two million citizens.

Yet almost no one outside the affected area, outside lower Louisiana, knows what's happening here. I certainly didn't,

before wandering—literally—onto this land and this complicated, unhappy tale whose roots stretch back more than a century. "This is, quite simply, the greatest untold story in
America," one conservationist later tells me.

And so there's reason to be sad, even to shed a tear, there on
that bayou dock in Cocodrie, Louisiana (population 600), with
my backpack at my feet and my backwater journey coming to a
close. I can almost hear the Gulf breakers just beyond sight, getting closer and closer, washing away more land every second,
every minute, every hour, fifty acres every day.

"I'm a fisherman, me, like my daddy and granddaddy,"
Wayne tells me. "But de marsh, he's killin' us. He just won't
hold togedder anymore. We'll all be leavin' here soon, just like
de ducks in de spring, everybody moving on."

It makes for an uneasy goodbye—probably goodbye forever—as Charlie limps back into view and I clasp his hand and
then Wayne's hand. Then the fishermen turn and board the *Lady
Desiree* and I watch them fade away, watch the wheelhouse candle flicker to the rock of wavelets as the old diesel engine beats
a slow retreat back up into the ink-black world of the Cajun
night.

# One

"You want to do *what*?" says Papoose Ledet, his balding head sticking out the forward hatch of a whitewashed shrimp boat. He's changing the oil of his 671 Detroit diesel engine—and that's all I see: his head sticking up out of the foredeck.

I stand opposite Papoose on a wooden wharf, my backpack hanging from my shoulders, my sleeping bag held on by bungee cords. I explain my idea of hitchhiking down the bayou on boats just as two of Papoose's sons whiz past me. They're carrying bundles of green shrimp netting and various ropes to be employed during the night's trawling just ahead. A gaggle of laughing gulls hover noisily overhead.

My idea makes no sense at all to Papoose judging by the look on his face. He pulls himself out of the forward hatch and walks slowly toward the gunwale nearest the wharf, eyeing me intently, wiping grease from his hands with a rag. His sun-weathered face squints in the midafternoon June heat, sending remarkable creases from just below his eyes all the way to his jawline. We don't shake hands.

"You ever been down de baya before?" Papoose asks in his heavy Cajun accent. Down here the word "bayou" comes out "baya" and "down de baya" means, in effect, "our home," *chez nous,* that watery rural Louisiana place located at the very end of the world just the way locals like it. Not too many outsiders, lost or otherwise, wander this deep into the region. And certainly none walk up asking for rides aboard working shrimp boats.

"No," I tell Papoose, lowering my backpack to the wharf. "This is my first trip down here."

"What about shrimpin'?" he asks. "You know anyt'ing about shrimpin'?"

"No," I say again, confessing my knowledge of Cajun fishing customs is nil. *"Mais, je parle un peu de français,"* I say, hoping to establish a connection. "And I have a great love of boats and I'm happy to work as an unpaid deckhand."

Papoose's facial expression still doesn't budge.

"I just want to float down the bayou with you," I say. "That's all. It doesn't matter how far you're going. I'm just traveling. I just want to get downstream."

Suddenly he looks a bit less confused. He doesn't exactly smile, but the idea starts to sink in.

"Just travelin', huh? Like a tourist?"

I nod.

"Well, okay den. Why didn't you say so? Put your pack in de cabin."

I see his hand, still stained with engine grease, suddenly outstretched toward mine. I cross the wharf and shake it.

"I can take you as far as Leeville, an hour and a half downstream. I'm going shrimpin' down dere right now."

Papoose is the first fisherman I've met, after a brief search, who's heading my way—and just like that, in the melting swelter of the South Louisiana sun, I have my first ride. Papoose unties from the dock and we begin floating down the sleepy olive-green water of Bayou Lafourche. His quick invitation to board belies the myth of bad-tempered swamp people hostile to all outsiders. In reality, bayou Cajuns turn out to be some of the most hospitable people I've met anywhere.

"Bayou" is a Choctaw Indian word meaning sluggish, slow-moving stream, and this one, Bayou Lafourche, is maybe two hundred feet wide and ten feet deep, situated about an hour and a half southwest of New Orleans. It follows a southeasterly course toward the Gulf, and as it passes through the tiny Cajun town of Golden Meadow, where I met Papoose, it's lined with all manner of fishing vessels tied to wooden docks cushioned with used-tire bumpers. These range from the vaguely tugboat look of shrimp trawlers to the longer bargelike proportions of oyster boats to the quicker, smaller crab boats, many barely bigger than rowboats with outboard motors. Papoose's fifty-year-old wooden trawler has a high, jaunty bow that flares back along softly sloping gunwales to a broad, square stern.

The town buildings, meanwhile, hug the bayou banks like swimmers to a lifeline: a few modern houses, rusting trailer homes on pilings, a Piggly Wiggly grocery store, two gas stations, a tin-roofed oyster bar, some rope swings tied to overhanging willows. Passing the town's main commercial bank, Papoose gives a long, low blow of the boat horn, and his wife, Faye, a teller, comes out the front door to wave goodbye to her husband and sons. The shrimpers are sometimes gone three or four days, and all necessary provisions have been stowed on board. A five-pound bag of red onions hangs side by side with a life preserver from hooks on the wooden wheelhouse wall.

Barely a few blocks back from the riverbank, on either side of the bayou, the town of Golden Meadow stops abruptly, giving way to an endless maze of marsh grass and open water and more marsh grass adorned with statuesque snowy egrets fishing stone-still in a pose straight out of an Audubon painting. The town actually rests atop natural earthen levees created by the Mississippi River when this bayou—Lafourche—was the Mississippi's course to the sea seven hundred years ago.

The forward motion of Papoose's boat creates a cooling, hair-tussling breeze that deepens the exquisite sense of freedom I feel leaning against the port gunwale, my backpack stored away. I'm drifting through Louisiana on the boat of a Cajun I just met, going I know not exactly where. It is, admittedly, a unique feeling seeing my car grow smaller and smaller along the bayou road, not knowing how or when I'll see it again. But I try not to worry, focusing instead on rolling up my pant legs and taking off my shoes.

Shoes seem forbidden here: Papoose and his three sons are barefoot and Papoose actually steers the boat wheel with his toes, sitting on a tall stool at the helm. All afternoon I never see his hands touch the wheel, just his toes, freeing him to operate the two-way radio mike and speak French with his best friend Goo Goo, another shrimper downstream. I have trouble following the conversation, not only because it's *Cajun* French but because there are actually variations of the language from region to region in Louisiana. "The word we use down here on Bayou Lafourche for turtle is de same word dey use up in Lafayette for a woman's private parts," laughs Papoose, who's forty-two years old and has a broad, toothy smile.

Even Papoose's English can be hard to follow. Several Cajuns

I meet later say that when they travel more than a few miles outside Louisiana, other Americans are often baffled by their accents. People ask if they're from the Caribbean, Quebec, South America. Not that your average bayou Cajun travels much, thanks to the region's history of poverty and isolated culture. An amazing number of people I meet over the next few days have never been in an airplane, never owned a credit card, never read a book, never seen a hill much taller than the thirty-foot Indian mounds scattered across the marshland, constructed from millions of discarded clam shells in a centuries-long process.

I ask Papoose what he was talking about on the radio with Goo Goo.

"De tide," he tells me. "Dere's gonna be a strong tide goin' out tonight and dat's good. It flushes de shrimp outta de marsh. But we got us a sout' wind kickin' up too, from de udder direction, and dat can hold de tide back some. So me and Goo Goo, we were tryin' to decide, wit' dese conditions, what's de best place to grab Mr. Shrimp. Maybe a bay. Maybe a bayou. Maybe a canal."

It's a lot more complicated, in other words, than just dropping the nets and gunning the engine.

An hour down the bayou, Papoose announces he's decided to head west along a canal and then push north up into uninhabited Bayou Blue to do some shrimping toward Catfish Lake. This is certified backcountry, accessible only by boat. He'll have me in Leeville, he says, perhaps around 2 A.M. Then he asks if I like Cajun-style venison sausage with red beans and rice.

I tell him I think I do just as pots begin to rattle atop the ship stove behind me.

I'm starting to feel seriously trapped on this fifty-three-foot boat—and the sensation is worth its weight in gold, like the liberating feeling a successful stowaway must feel. There may be many ways to visit the lower third of Louisiana known as Cajun country, home to descendants of French immigrants savagely expelled from Nova Scotia during the French and Indian War in the mid-eighteenth century. But one thing is certain: with America's recent fascination for all things Cajun, considerable authenticity has been lost in the act of translation to mass culture. Overexposure has brought "nouvelle cuisine" gumbo to New Orleans restaurants and given rise across the state to unfortunate "swamp tours" whose often garish roadside signs promise rehearsed hospitality from good ol' boys with trained alligators that rush toward tour boats on command, chomping jumbo-size marshmallows tossed overboard. And with the popular rise of Cajun music, who knows if that washboard player you hear in Lafayette is a local or an enthusiast from the Chicago suburbs who's memorized all the French lyrics?

This is not to say that genuine, down-home Cajun culture no longer exists. It does. In spades. You just have to sidestep the scattered imitators along the way. Which was my goal, precisely, in roaming this far down the bayou and simply hopping on a boat. Just now, as Papoose pulls out the venison sausage and I grab my map to see just where in the heck we're heading, I realize I've tumbled into the committed traveler's ultimate dream: complete cultural immersion. This boat is a floating universe of Cajun bayou life and the only way off is to swim to shore through alligator-infested waters. For the next several days, I'll serve under the command of several Cajun captains, eating from the same enamel galley skillets as my hosts, talking about what they talk about, going where they go, doing what they do. And from them, soon, I'll learn firsthand of the troubling forces, huge beyond comprehension, now bringing their world crashing down upon their heads.

A few miles south of Golden Meadow, as all permanent structures gradually begin to disappear and the bayou steadily
widens in its slow crawl toward the Gulf, I spy a strange sight.
Off to the left, in the distant marsh, a cluster of about two
dozen large oak trees stand leafless and dead in the water, their
skeletal, gnarled branches attached to sun-bleached trunks that
extend directly into the brackish waves. These oaks aren't swamp
trees. They grow on land. Yet there's no solid land within five
hundred feet of them. Farther downstream, there's another odd
sight: a long stretch of telephone poles is submerged in water
along the two-lane road paralleling the bayou. Why sink the
poles in water, I wonder. Isn't there something inherently foolish, even dangerous, about stringing power lines over open water
when solid land is just ten feet away?

But too many other sights intervene before I can put these
questions to Papoose. Soon an imposing sunset finds us motoring up serpentine Bayou Blue, shrimp nets in the water. We're
surrounded by a magical, wide-open landscape of golden-green
marsh grass stretching as far as the eye can see, dotted only
occasionally with the distant outline of other shrimp boats. A
summer thunderstorm has come and gone, interrupting a
sumptuous dinner with raindrops that seep through the old
boat's leaky roof. Porpoises rise and fall in the bayou water
around us, chasing speckled trout just as a rainbow plunges
toward the eastern horizon and the sun sinks toward violently
bruised clouds, billowy in hues of dark purple, indigo, and pink.

In the wheelhouse, Papoose scans the two-way radio and
we overhear fishermen speaking Cajun English and French. We
hear the twang of Texas oil workers heading out to offshore platforms and the exotic language of exiled Vietnamese shrimpers
who've fished these waters since the 1975 fall of Saigon, drawn
to America's own elaborate version of the Mekong Delta. Com-

pleting the ethnic gumbo are French-speaking Houma Indians, driven by European settlers over the centuries to the farthest ends of the bayou country where they now survive as expert fishermen.

Bayou people have a flare for colorful nicknames, and over the radio they go flying. I overhear a fisherman named "Gator" asking another named "Dirt" to come help repair a broken boom. Then "Rooster" wants to know if anyone wants to buy a sack of crawfish from his brother's pond. And "Tattoo" goes on and on, in self-righteous monologue, about how the politicians up in Baton Rouge are once again trying to screw the state's Cajun people out of their fair share of government services.

As darkness descends over our slow crawl up Bayou Blue, Papoose tells me he got his own nickname after being born extremely premature. His mother has a photo of him sleeping inside a shoe box, he says. So common are nicknames along Bayou Lafourche, he says, that phone books are useless to many people, since a man's real name may be completely unknown to his friends.

Papoose tells me all this with a chuckle, but he soon stops laughing as the first catch of the evening comes in. The jumble of armored tails and stalked eyes covering the back deck are Louisiana's famous "brown shrimp," *Farfante penaeus aztecus,* a staple crop for Cajun shrimpers from mid-May to late June. But tonight's first haul is extremely slim, signaling an unproductive evening ahead. Papoose's son Cody ices down the shrimp, then washes off the deck with a bucket tied to a rope and lowered into the bathwater-warm bayou, dark as tar just five feet below us.

Papoose leaves the wheelhouse and heads around back to inspect the catch. Doubling his disappointment, the shrimp are exceedingly small, eighty or ninety to a pound. "I can't even pay for my fuel wit' a catch like dis," he says.

I nod in sympathy, having heard this sort of talk many times before. I've worked on farms in the past and spent time with commercial crabbers. But Cajun trawlers, with their Latin disposition toward fiery emotions, seem particularly given to grousing. And no wonder. Given the vast array of factors large and small completely beyond their control, from cantankerous weather to calamitous markets to craven creditors to a history as an oppressed minority within the state of Louisiana, it's little surprise that the bellies of these men regularly ache with frustration and the fear of bankruptcy.

Yet Papoose's words that night ring with more than just the reflexive grumbling of a man having a bad night in an otherwise routine shrimp season. "We had a great May," he says, "but dis whole mont' of June has been rotten. Every year it just gets harder and harder to make a living at dis."

Indeed, for the past decade Papoose has wondered if each year will be his last. "I love dis life on de water," he tells me. "It's my sanity out here. But dis life is dying. My ancestors, dey were all shrimpers. But I'm not sure I'll finish *my* career doing dis, much less see my sons carry on de tradition."

When I ask why the shrimp industry is in such decline here, he mentions overfishing and cheap imported shrimp, especially from China, which depress prices. But the number one factor, by far, threatening to put Louisiana shrimpers permanently out of business is this:

"De land is sinking," Papoose says.

"Sinking?" I say.

"*Oui, oui.* All dis land around us, as far as you can see, is droppin' straight down into de water, turnin' to ocean. Someday, Baton Rouge, one hundred miles nort' of here, is gonna be beachfront property."

"Why is the land sinking?" I ask him. He's activating a large whirring winch, driven by the boat engine, which slowly drops his shrimp nets back into the water. As we return to the wheelhouse to resume the lumbering push up Bayou Blue, Papoose answers my question by bringing up the Mississippi River.

"De Mississippi doesn't flood anymore," he says. "Dat's why we're sinking. Dat river, she built up dis area wit' flooding. Now de Army Corps of Engineers has got it all penned in wit' levees like a snake in a cage. And wit'out all dat new sediment brought in every few years by flooding, we're going down."

I'm not well acquainted with this phenomenon, at least not on the scale he's describing. "Are you sure it's not just the sea level that's rising?" I say. "You know, from global warming?"

"We're *sinking*," Papoose insists. "Sinking. And not just a little. Dey say every twenty minutes or so, a football field of land turns to water in Louisiana. Every twenty minutes! Most of dat land is marsh and wit'out de marsh grass de shrimp have no place to grow. Dey got satellite photos from outer space showing how much land we're losing every year. It'll make your hair stand up to see it."

He guides the boat around a grassy bend and keeps talking. "You saw part of it yourself today," he says. "Didn't you see dose telephone poles in de water along de bayou? Ten years ago dose poles were in grass. Didn't you see de 'tree cemeteries,' dose clusters of dead oaks in de water? All dose trees were on land twenty years ago. And de big stretch of open water sout' of Golden Meadow all along de bayou? Cattle pastures fifty years ago."

Just then, out of the blue, our bodies lurch forward violently as the boat jerks to an almost complete stop. We've struck something. Papoose abruptly pulls back on the throttle and suddenly we're listing conspicuously to starboard. I rush out on deck and hear the sound of nets and ropes stretching almost to their breaking point and the groan of steel cables and booms nearly being ripped from their anchorings on deck. The starboard net, two hundred square feet in size, has become seriously snagged on some immovable obstruction on the bayou bottom. Whatever the obstruction, it's large and solid enough to nearly flip the entire boat before Papoose, forehead wrinkled in concentration, can throw the engine into reverse and gradually coax the boat free with thirty minutes of back-and-forth engine work and backbreaking efforts to untangle the net and pull it free. We never find out what it was underwater that stopped us cold in our tracks.

In all the excitement, Papoose and I break off our discussion of the mysteriously sinking land, and afterward everyone's too exhausted to talk about much of anything. Around midnight, I drift off to sleep on a bunk bed inside the cabin.


It's 4 A.M. when Papoose wakes me and I grab my gear and we shake hands goodbye. I thank him for the ride down the bayou, then leap onto a boat dock and suddenly find myself all alone in the sound-asleep little town of Leeville, Louisiana, population 60. I find my way, backpack in tow, through the deep darkness to Boudreaux's Waterfront Motel, taking a tin-roofed room on ten-foot pilings. My window overlooks idle shrimp boats whose movements against the dock make my entire room shake.

Unable to sleep, I cross two-lane Louisiana Route 1 to Griffin's Restaurant, right on Bayou Lafourche. Leeville is a small collection of frame houses and trailer homes (most on pilings like my motel room), seashell driveways, scattered palms, annoying sand flies, two gas stations, and Gail's Bait Shop—offering chicken necks and cigar minnows. Most of the townspeople are commercial fishermen or oil workers and most come to Griffin's

Restaurant for morning coffee. I pass the stuffed alligator head by the front door and go straight to the help-yourself coffeepot. Java in hand, I count seven people in the restaurant and suddenly realize they're all speaking French. I'm the only "Anglo-American" in the room. Everyone here is older than forty, which is roughly the cutoff point down here; Cajuns younger than that speak only English. These fishermen with deep tans and dirty baseball caps and cigarette-stained fingers are relics who'll take the Cajun language with them to the grave.

I place my order in French with a cheerful cook named Louella, pausing only to ask for the Cajun word for grits (*la grue*). Around me hang breathtaking wall photos of past hurricane damage to Leeville—Hilda in '64, Betsy in '65, Juan in '85. Louella points to the spot just below the cash register where Juan's floodwaters peaked. Most people this far down the bayou don't dare keep family photographs or other irreplaceables in their homes, stashing them instead with relatives on higher ground, away from the next, inevitable, disastrous hurricane tide.

Eager to continue my hitchhiking journey, I ask around for a fisherman heading down to the town of Port Fourchon, ten miles away, the last settlement on the bayou before the Gulf of Mexico. By midmorning I meet forty-four-year-old Tim Melancon (pronounced Meh-lohn-son), a Cajun shrimper who's come home for a day of rest and to collect fresh supplies. Switching to English for my benefit, Tim tells me his seventeen-year-old son has crab traps strewn halfway to Port Fourchon and would surely take me the rest of the way for a little gas money.

So we pile into Tim's pickup truck, a red Chevy Cheyenne with rust holes so large from the salt air you can stick your finger through the wheel well in several places. Tim's dressed in flip-flops, T-shirt, and cutoff jeans, with dark sunglasses dangling around a neck as rough as worn sandpaper. His Cajun accent is so heavy and peppered with French that at times I can barely understand him.

"Ah cane believe dat boot bag dare need a chune-up ageen," he says, pointing to one of his cousins working on an outboard along the bayou. Translation: "I can't believe that boat back there needs a tune-up again."

Tim's a walking museum piece of backcountry bayou life. He can neither read nor write, got married at age sixteen, built his own wooden shrimp boat with no blueprints whatsoever, speaks French better than he speaks English, and once wrestled—and pinned—an alligator at a bar on a hundred-dollar-dare and lived to tell about it. On his arm is the tattoo "T+P," something he did himself with a sharp needle and black ink before marrying his wife, Phyllis, when she was just fourteen.

"*Mais oui*, dey tried to teach me how to read back in school," says Tim, not a trace of embarrassment on his tanned, unshaven face. "*Mais* book learnin' just didn't stick wit' me. My mind, it was too stuck in de *playree* [marsh] . . . too full of shrimpin' and huntin' and trappin'. Dere was no room left. I could spell 'I' and 'or' and 'and.' But once dey got up to dem four- and five-letter words, it was all over. I just wanted to be in de *playree*, on de water."

While Tim drives and talks in his strange way, I stare out at the equally strange scenery around me. There is very little solid land in Leeville, just a road with water on both sides and a quarter-mile stretch of man-made structures clinging to the road's narrow dirt shoulders. Most of the buildings are at least partially perched over the water on pilings. Tim's house, at the edge of a narrow dirt parking area, is *completely* over the water. It's a two-bedroom affair on ten-foot pilings—a house small enough to be called a "camp"—purchased ten years ago for a grand total of $3,000, much less than he paid for his truck.

We head up fifteen wooden steps to the camp's front door and I notice the whole structure wobble slightly with our steps. Later, when Tim's collie, Simba, scratches his fleas, the house wobbles. It wobbles when the wind blows hard and when Tim goes into his occasional coughing fits from the numerous cigarettes he smokes.

Inside, Tim clears off a dozen wire minnow and crab traps from the living room couch and I have a seat. Somehow this one-story frame structure hovering over the murky bayou current contains a living room, two tiny bedrooms, a kitchen, and a bathroom in an area just twenty-five by thirty-five feet.

Tim's wife Phyllis comes in, a short, attractive forty-one-year-old with close-cut brown hair and freckled cheeks, wearing sandals and a sleeveless cotton shirt tucked neatly into jeans shorts. She lights a cigarette beside the small butane heater that is the family's sole defense against winter, and quickly apologizes for the tight quarters.

"We're poor," she tells me. "Sometimes, when shrimp prices are high, we're middle class for a few months. But den we're poor again."

The occasional boom season has allowed the Melancons a few luxuries—a microwave oven, a new electric range, a Sanyo color TV—but mostly the place has a spare look.

The Melancons' seventeen-year-old son, their only child, emerges groggily from his closet-size back bedroom. His name is Tee Tim, as in *petit* Tim, the Cajun equivalent of "junior." Tee Tim looks anything but petit: his arms and upper body are brawny from lifting 130 crab traps almost daily since the age of twelve. Three hunting rifles hang in his room on a rack above a mattress of eggshell foam rubber, and a passel of *Ducks Unlimited* magazines litter the floor. With a shy smile, Tee Tim shakes my hand, then begins foraging in the kitchen for breakfast in preparation for the day's crab haul.

Tim senior, meanwhile, is keen to show me his shrimp boat. It's a wooden fifty-two-foot flat-bottom skiff moored next to the camp, right on the bayou. We descend the front stairs, then walk *under* the house where a metal dock keeps us above the bayou water. The boat, tied to wood pilings, is an old-fashioned, whitewashed double rigger with fifty-foot booms and the name "Tee Tim" painted on the hull.

"She's got a 671 GM diesel with a four-to-one clutch," Tim says of the powerful engine, chest expanding. "She's made of *cypress*. De frame, de hull . . . all cypress. You can't even find enough good cypress to build a boat like dis today. De boats now, dey're all fiberglass or steel, or if dey do build a wooden boat it's treated pine or Spanish cedar. But not de best wood God gave for boats: cypress.

"Built her myself eighteen years ago wit' my daddy and Phyllis, who was pregnant wit' Tee Tim at de time. We didn't have no written plans at all. We just t'rew away our level and eyeballed ever't'ing. Lot of sawin' real careful and hammerin' away. And no air hammer. Every nail you see, we pounded just like Noah."

Tim's wheelhouse, unlike Papoose's, has no radar or depth finder or Global Positioning System. "Ever't'ing's up here," he says, tapping his head. "De big computer chip."

Tim avoids ocean shallows and other perils using nothing more than his own instincts, a seventy-five-year-old brass compass someone gave him, and a blessed medallion of Jesus walking on water. And in good years he finds shrimp, lots of them, big fat schools of them. He calls it "hittin' de *grosse tallée*," the big tally.

After just one day in the marsh, I'm starting to understand

just how bountiful this waterscape called the Louisiana bayou country really is. Drop a hook off Tim's wharf, he tells me, and you'll reel in a speckled trout or redfish or black drum for the skillet. Lower a baited crab cage and you'll come back tomorrow to find a half dozen of the most succulent blue crabs the world has to offer. From spring to fall you can trawl for brown shrimp, white shrimp, and sea bobs, then hunt to your stomach's content from November to January when the blue-winged teal and gray ducks darken the sky in their annual migration. Not to mention alligator hunting in September, trapping otters and muskrats for fur in the winter, and snagging cocahoe minnows year-round for visiting sportfishermen.

"We're de last of de Mohicans," Tim tells me. "We still live off de land. Ever't'ing we need is right here. To be honest, I never had a job in my life."

By job he means what people down here call "real jobs" or "public jobs" or "pay-by-the-hour jobs." Anything, in other words, other than the hard, independent course of working for yourself and converting sea life into wallet cash.

Yet Mother Nature, which still provides such an old-fashioned livelihood for so many bayou people, also wipes these people out—completely—every few years. This is the Bangladesh of America, flat and watery and horribly exposed to hurricanes. Most insurance companies want nothing to do with property this far down the bayou. If a category 2 or 3 hurricane hits from the right direction, Tim and Phyllis will lose their camp and their shrimp boat, both uninsured and the only things of value they own. Like the land itself, the Melancons are totally vulnerable and exposed.

"She'll take care of you and she'll hurt you bad," says Tim of the natural world upon which he depends.

Phyllis yells down from the camp just then that she's made

a little something for us to eat. When we arrive she's laid out a delicious meal of *boulettes de chevrettes:* ground fresh shrimp mixed with onions, peppers, garlic, and spices, then fried in patties. There's no dining table so we eat with our food in our laps.

"Over here," Tim says, gesturing to the couch. "Come get you some good sit-down right here."

As I dig into the food Phyllis tells me how she has to be resourceful with the household budget. She's a devoted coupon collector, and whenever possible travels up the bayou to the Delchamps grocery store in Larose for their once-a-month triple-value coupon day.

Five years ago, Phyllis went to night school to earn her GED, having dropped out of ninth grade twenty-three years before to marry Tim. She passed the test at age thirty-seven, motivated by the gnawing, terrifying uncertainty of how she'd support herself without a high school diploma if anything ever happened to Tim out there on the boat. Commercial fishermen, after all, are more likely to be maimed or killed on the job than any other profession in America. The work is more dangerous than coal mining, being a cop, or parachuting from planes to fight forest fires.

But the tight family budget doesn't stop Phyllis from stuffing me with food. "Dose boulettes are gettin' lonely on de stove," she says. "Help yourself. Don't stop now."

Like most Cajuns, Phyllis is particularly generous to visitors. "I learned dat from my mama," she says. "She told me, 'You gotta be good to strangers dat come down de baya no matter how bad outsiders treated us Cajuns before.'"

She's referring to her people's past status as the "white niggers" of Louisiana. Given the popularity and respect enjoyed by Cajun culture nationwide today, it's hard for many Americans to appreciate just how much discrimination these people suffered for generations at the hands of Louisiana's English-speaking majority, a majority that looked down on Cajuns for their "foreign" backwoods ways and unintelligible variety/dialect of the French language. As a result, throughout Cajun country, from the Mississippi River west to Ville Platte and Mamou and on down to the Texas border west of Lake Charles, public schools and roads and health facilities were chronically underfunded, and Cajuns were largely locked out of the state political process. Not until the 1970s did Louisiana get its first Cajun governor, despite the fact that at least a fifth of the state's citizens have always been Cajun.

"I remember when I was a girl," Phyllis says, lighting another cigarette and talking about her mama again, "she looked out de house window one day and she seen dese two colored fellas fishing along de baya just next to our camp. And dose fellas, dey had almost nuttin' to eat. Barely a bite all day. So my mama, she cooks up a pot of chicken gumbo and some potato salad and some bread pudding, and den goes out to de baya and tells dose colored fellas to come inside and eat. Dey were polite and said 'No t'ank you, ma'am a bunch of times until she pointed to de camp and said 'Go!' So dey went and had demselves a good meal in our house.

"Not too many white folk in de Sout' woulda done dat in de 1960s—or even now," Phyllis says. "But we know what it's like to be beat down. So Mama made sure dose colored fellas got fed."

Tim passes the plate of boulettes to me again. "Have one more," he insists. "Go on."

The legacy of this harsh Cajun past can still be seen in the Melancon household.

"Here it is!" Tim shouts after lunch, digging through a pile of papers on the coffee table next to the minnow and crab traps. "Here it is! I found it!"

"Found what?" says Phyllis.

"Dat note I wrote down."

"Why, Timmy," she says good-humoredly, winking discreetly at me, "you can't write a lick. Just what kinda note did you write down?"

"Dis one," he says.

He hands her a small piece of scrap paper and she begins to study it intently. It has a crude arrow drawn on it, the kind an archer would use. Next to it is a rectangle with an oval at one end. "Dat's a mattress and pillow," Tim says of the rectangle. "See? Arrow and a mattress. Togedder it's 'Arrow mattress.' It's a brand I seen on TV last night after you went to bed. It's special for bad backs. I t'ink it might help me."

Like commercial fishermen the world over, Tim's back frequently gives out from the strain of hauling nets and lifting 100-pound bait boxes.

"I wanted to get me a new mattress last winter," Tim tells me. "But no one down de baya has any money in de winter. But now dat we're shrimpin' again, I wanna get me one of dese Arrow mattresses."

Phyllis, keeper of the budget, frowns. "Let's see how we do de rest of de mont' trawlin'," she says. "Don't forget de outboard on de crab boat needs fixin', too."

Tim's talk of back pain suddenly explains the mysterious pattern I'd noticed yesterday while driving down from New Orleans. The closer I got to the coast, the more advertisements I saw along the road for chiropractors. Virtually everybody down here in this workaday region—shrimpers, crabbers, oystermen, oil workers, boat builders, everybody—sooner or later needs some sort of back work, it seems. But Cajuns, with their plainspoken manner and penchant for humor in the face of adversity, commonly dispense with the fancy term "chiropractor." To them, these valued practitioners are known simply as "crackabones."

After eating, Tim and I go back down under the house where young Tee Tim is getting his sixteen-foot chaland crab boat ready for the trip to Port Fourchon. The boat has a flat-bottom fiberglass hull with one-foot gunwales and a wooden bait box for a driver's seat.

A thunderstorm has moved in, showering the bayou with big noisy drops and delaying the trip. Tim and I take seats atop upturned buckets placed just below the menacing jaws of a six-foot tiger shark hanging from a rusty nail. During the lull, I mention to Tim the very strange conversation I had had with Papoose Ledet the day before. I describe Papoose's claim that all the land down here is sinking and disappearing at an alarming rate. When I ask Tim if he agrees, his response is emphatic.

"*Losing* land?" he says. "*Losing* it? Hell, here in Leeville we done already lost it. It's done disappeared. Look around." He stands from his bucket and gestures up the bayou and toward the marsh grass and then over to the narrow ribbon of road that runs through town. "Take a few steps off dat road and your foot's in open water. De bayou's so big now it's startin' to look like a lake and all the lakes and bays are startin' to look like de ocean 'cause dat's what dey're becoming. Dere *is* no more land left here in Leeville."

The rain has started to subside and Tee Tim starts lowering the last of his bait fish into the crab boat. He puts on his yellow bib overalls, almost ready to go.

"But when my *grand-père* was a kid," Tim senior says, continuing, "dere was lots and lots of land all around where we're sittin' right now." Indeed, I learn later, cotton was grown in

Leeville as late as the 1920s. And until the 1940s, so many orange trees were grown here that the settlement was originally called Orange City. "But now look," Tim says. "It's just a big salt marsh here. We don't even get many gators no more. Too salty. Yeah, de land's sinkin', dude. But really, we already sunk here."

The rain stops and the sun breaks through clouds of dull pewter.

"Come on," Tim says to me. "I wanna show you somethin'. Tie loose de boat, Tee Tim."

We all pile into the crab boat and Tim tells his son to head down the bayou. A few hundred feet away, just before Route 1 crosses Bayou Lafourche atop the rusting Leeville Bridge, Tim points toward a watery stretch of marsh grass oddly littered with bricks and concrete.

"It's a cemetery," he says.

There, shockingly, along the grassy bayou bank, I can now make out a dozen or so old tombs, all in different stages of submersion, tumbling brick by brick into the bayou water. The rectangular three-foot-tall sarcophagi, each entombing a single human being above the ground in the South Louisiana style, look like slow-motion lemmings dropping over the fateful edge, one after the other. A stone cross atop one sarcophagus sits at a crazy 45-degree angle as the structure slides sideways into watery doom. Another crypt has collapsed completely into a pile of bricks, half in the water, half out. The bayou is swallowing the dead here. I soon find myself scanning the bricks for white flashes of bone.

"Are the bodies still in there?" I ask Tim.

"You leave de dead where dey rest," he says. "No one's touched dem. Dey're gettin' a second burial at sea. Fifty, sixty, seventy years ago, dose people were buried on high ground."

Tee Tim mentions how the half-submerged cemetery is

actually a favored spot for sportfishermen now. The crypts make good hard cover for fish, so people are often seen casting bait amid the bricks and coffins.

I feel my breakfast rising in my throat just then. I sit back down in the boat to steady myself. Tim and Tee Tim, I notice, suffer no such effect. There are two such watery cemeteries in Leeville, and the sight has become commonplace to them, like the drowned oaks and submerged telephone poles farther up the bayou.

"This is happening because the Mississippi River doesn't flood anymore?" I ask Tim. "The levees hold back the river water and all the sediment that once built up this land?"

"Dat's a big part of it," he says.

Reading up on the subject later, I learn that the whole tattered sole of the Louisiana boot was created exclusively by the mighty hand of the Mississippi River and its seven-thousand-year flow to the sea. Draining a vast watershed that includes parts of three Canadian provinces and two-thirds of the continental United States, the world's third-longest river until recently carried rich runoff sediment from as far away as New York State and lower Saskatchewan and deposited it all along coastal Louisiana, its terminus, either through annual flooding along its lower stretches or in classic land-building fashion at its mouth, creating deltas, manufacturing tongues of new land.

Every thousand years or so, when the Mississippi's own sediment load lengthened—and then blocked—the river's route to the Gulf of Mexico, the mother stream would change course completely, finding a shorter route to the sea. Then it would build a new delta, thus spreading the gift of land creation along a wide coastline, fashioning over time the entire bayou region of Louisiana.

But this ancient dynamic of nature was brought to a gradual

halt with the arrival of European settlers—Spaniards, Cajuns, French Creoles, Germans, Englishmen—who settled all across the river's natural floodplain and began to construct rudimentary levees to hold back the river's surge. The floods came anyway, less frequently perhaps, but with a pent-up fury that bordered on biblical dimensions, pouring water tens of feet deep over crops and into towns. Then came the worst deluge of all, the Great Flood of 1927, which killed over a thousand people in Arkansas, Mississippi, and Louisiana. Intending to end such outbursts once and for all, the U.S. Army Corps of Engineers after 1927 perfected the construction of massive, unbreachable levees along the entire lower Mississippi. This has frozen the river in its present course, which streams past New Orleans and out into the Gulf where its sediments no longer create any land whatsoever, tumbling instead thousands of feet over the clifflike edge of the continental shelf. For seven thousand years a builder of rich alluvial land, the river now spills its seed uselessly into a dark, deep, watery oblivion.

Meanwhile, all the bayou land outside those river levees lies starved for the former lifeline of fresh deposits of sediments and nutrients. Unreplenished, this network of wetlands and fingers of flat, solid land under towns like Golden Meadow and Leeville has begun to sink. The soil is soft and unstable, made up of old river silt and sand that naturally compact over time, a geological process called subsidence. Historically, this sinking has been counteracted by new surface sediment from the flooding river. But the Corps has now put a stop to that, meaning that today the punishing waves of the Gulf of Mexico pound Louisiana's lowering barrier islands and make a direct assault into the very heart of this delicate bayou ecosystem.

---

But there's more to the story than this. The levees of the Mississippi River are not the only reason the land is vanishing.

"*Mais* no," says Tim. "It's de big mess left by de oil companies, too, dat's cuttin' ever't'ing to pieces."

We've circled back up the bayou to drop Tim off at the camp. "You'll see what I mean on de way down to Fourchon," he tells me. "You'll see what de oil companies have done."

With that he steps off the crab boat and Tee Tim points us back down the bayou to check on his crab traps. We pass the forlorn cemetery again and then glide under the Leeville Bridge, entering a wide waterway edged by a marsh of thick oyster grass and decorated with a necklace of small white floats, each marking an attached crab trap below.

The morning sun is already turning hostile as Tee Tim, wearing protective gloves, lifts the traps one by one into the boat, then uses metal tongs to sort blue crabs and stone crabs into wooden crates. The frenetic scraping sound of scrambling crab legs fills the air, a minor cacophony punctuated by the sharp click of powerful claws snapping open and shut.

As he works, Tee Tim confirms that he's been a professional crabber since the age of twelve. This in order to buy his own clothes and pull his weight within the family. He literally grew up on the water, he says.

"When I was a toddler, my parents, they would tie a piece of rope around my waist and then tie the other end to the boat winch so I wouldn't fall in the water. Then they'd take me out shrimpin' with them for days at a time on the trawler. That's how I moved around the boat deck: tied to the winch. I started young."

Tee Tim's accent is more conventionally southern, less Cajun. He can make the *th* sound. As for French, he understands it but cannot speak it except to sprinkle his speech with various words and phrases like *mauvais temps* for storm and *bon podnah* for a good friend. He tells me he knows only one kid in his entire high school up the bayou who speaks Cajun French fluently. The gradual "Americanization" of this region, especially since World War II, has dealt blows to Cajun culture independent of the parallel assault on the land.

By now Tee Tim has settled into an almost mechanical rhythm of lifting, emptying, rebaiting, and redepositing crab traps while I try to beat the rising scorch of sun and humidity by slipping into shorts and lowering myself into the bayou water for cooling dips, swimming sometimes within three hundred feet of schools of porpoises. The sleek gray mammals rise and fall with astonishing grace, heedless of my presence, their breathing faintly audible through raspy blowholes. Along the marsh banks, an occasional otter or muskrat appears, seeking out the same profusion of crabs and fish that draws the porpoises this far inland.

Farther up the food chain still, Tee Tim is making out fairly well. Each trap he hauls in contains at least two to three sizable crabs. Before the morning is out, he'll pull in a respectable catch of 120 pounds, part of an annual Louisiana crab harvest that has no equal anywhere in America outside of Alaska. Indeed, I learn later that even in Maryland's Chesapeake Bay region where I presently live and where the blue crab industry is a source of great local pride and eating crab cakes borders on cult behavior—even there as much as a quarter of all crabs consumed actually come from Louisiana during some months.

Yet crabs are just one small part of the take in this massive estuarine waterscape of fresh, brackish, and saltwater habitats spread across endless bays, lagoons, inlets, and marshes shaped by the Mississippi River. Coastal Louisiana, by itself, accounts for an astonishing 30 percent of America's annual seafood harvest, measured by weight.

As the bayou region continues to disappear, so will this remarkable catch. And accelerating the disappearance of both is a ubiquitous and highly destructive underwater creature that Tee Tim and I come across soon after he begins checking his traps.

Barely a mile outside of Leeville, on a body of water west of Bayou Lafourche, we round a ridge of bushy mangroves, startling a regal flock of two dozen white ibis into flight. Then, suddenly, before us is a fifteen-foot-tall wooden sign nearly as wide as a roadside billboard. It sits all by itself atop four wooden pilings, an angular presence fantastically out of place in this backcountry landscape. With two-foot-tall letters, the sign reads:

DANGER:
DO NOT DREDGE OR ANCHOR
TEXACO GAS LINE

"There's a big pipeline right there that carries natural gas," Tee Tim tells me.

"Where's the pipeline?" I ask, seeing only the garish sign.

"It's buried on the bottom, under the water, five feet down."

I knew already there were oil and gas wells all around Leeville and throughout the bayou region. Indeed, we pass a well just moments later, a simple, unmanned affair of high-gauge iron pipe sticking fifteen feet out of the water, capped off with various gauges and cutoff valves. Under a thousand pounds of pressure, oil and natural gas are pushed up from fields a quarter mile below, then routed to various storage tanks and shoreside refineries via an intricate web of underwater pipelines like the one before us now. Intermittent signs, emphatic

and ugly to the eye, mark the pipeline's presence: DANGER: DO
NOT DREDGE OR ANCHOR.

Today, throughout the wetlands of lower Louisiana, more
than ten thousand miles of such pipe lie underwater—crisscrossing, interlocking, overlapping, going everywhere. And to
lay pipe across this ocean of marsh grass, an area so vast it's
often called the "trembling prairie" with its puddinglike mud
below, requires the construction of canals: straight and narrow
streets of water dredged four or five feet deep, knifing through
the grass. Scattered along the canals are the wells themselves,
and at the bottom of the canals lie the interconnecting pipe.

In the 1930s, at almost the exact same time the lower Mississippi River was finally conquered for good with levees, oil
exploitation began in earnest throughout the bayou region. It
was the dawn of a Louisiana gold rush, the infrastructure of
which still produces and/or processes a staggering 18 percent of
annual U.S. oil supplies and 24 percent of U.S. natural gas.
Early on, the big companies—Texaco, Amoco, and others—
launched the practice of extensive canal dredging that continued for nearly half a century. As a result, there are few stretches
of Louisiana marsh today that are not scissored by at least one
or two canals, and some areas—seen from the air—look like
intricate city street maps. Canals intersect, form grids, branch
off into endless culs-de-sac, creating whole subdivisions of
watery roads made possible by the dredge barges that chew
through the marsh with giant mechanical shovels.

Some of this I knew before coming to Louisiana. What I
didn't know was this: canals, once dredged through the marsh,
trigger disastrous erosion.

"We're in a canal right now," says Tee Tim, gesturing with
his crab tongs to the wide waterway around us. "This is a
canal."

"This?" I say. With a girth of about two hundred feet, the water is almost as wide as Bayou Lafourche itself, and I had simply assumed it was another large bayou meandering to the Gulf. But Tee Tim informs me this stretch of water began as a roughly thirty-foot-wide canal dug by Texaco in the early 1960s, just wide enough to lay pipe and allow work boats to pass. Now the canal is more than six times that large—and getting larger—thanks to wave-action erosion from boats and storms that clobber the surrounding marsh grass and its delicate mud base, causing huge swaths of grass to simply sink and crumble into the water, gone forever, the fragile earth dissolved.

"When I was a kid," Tee Tim says, "I remember this canal being so much smaller that you could land your boat on solid ground right over there where that dead tree is." He points, again with the tongs, to a rotting, limbless trunk just up the canal. It's in open water, fifty feet from the bank.

More than the sight of the tree, it's those five simple words that amaze me: "When I was a kid . . ." It makes Tee Tim sound like an old man looking back on a long lifetime. In reality he's seventeen, looking back maybe ten years. It's happening that fast.

I try my best to comprehend the numbers again: ten thousand *miles* of canals, just like this, spread across the Louisiana coast, devouring the land. No wonder the satellite photos—mentioned by Papoose—are so damn dramatic. I keep looking at that stranded tree in the middle of the canal, dead and all alone, so far from the grassy bank, as Tee Tim lifts the last of his 130 crab traps and finally calls it a day.


It's afternoon and the boat gunwales are burning to the touch, pelted by angry sunbeams, when we head back to shore. It's a relief to let the outboard sprint into high gear, cooling us with windy forward motion, as we make our way to a "crab shed" on Bayou Lafourche where Tee Tim sells his harvest—twenty-five dozen crabs—to a wholesaler. Inside the simple cinder-block shop, he pockets forty-three dollars after subtracting for fuel and bait fish. It's a so-so day. He cleans up a little and we continue on down the bayou toward Port Fourchon and the Gulf of Mexico.

The journey, full of sweeping turns and short detours for bird-watching, lasts more than an hour, taking us through a weirdly contrasting landscape that's now becoming familiar to me: long stretches of sinking wetlands, pockmarked with wells and torn up by canals with their hideous warning signs, followed by equally long stretches of intact marsh grass supporting elaborate bird rookeries and marked by a lonely wilderness quietude. Amid the profusion of grass and mangroves, on a small island covered with orange snake flowers, I count fifteen roseate spoonbills, pink as flamingos.

As we travel south I ask Tee Tim about his plans for the future. What will he do after high school?

"Whatever it is, it won't involve crabbin'," he tells me without a moment's hesitation. "Who wants to bait crab traps till he's seventy?"

"What about shrimping?" I ask.

"Too unpredictable. And too expensive to buy a trawler or build one."

Instead, he says, he plans to move "way up the baya" the first chance he gets. "I want me a welder's job or carpenter work. At the big shipyards, they got work like that. The pay, you can count on it day in and out, not like when you're on the water and you might not make even a dollar."

As for his family's long fishing tradition, he tells me he

greatly reveres the past lives of his *grand-pères* and *vieux grand-pères*, men who lived year-round on small, primitive "camp boats" in the far reaches of the marsh, speaking little or no English. These were proud and resourceful people who hunted rabbits with sticks when they couldn't afford shotgun shells and caught shrimp by wading into the water with seine nets and beat back mosquitoes with nothing more than palmetto-frond fans. Tee Tim's father and uncles, now in their forties and fifties, were raised close enough to these old, rugged Cajun ways that they now vow never to leave Leeville, claiming wild horses couldn't pull them away even if the sea *does* continue to advance and their homes become platforms in the middle of the Gulf of Mexico.

"But I've made up my mind," Tee Tim says. "Who needs the headaches of this work, especially with the land bustin' up. I'm outta here after high school."

He acknowledges he's an only child and that his family line will end on the water with him. But there's no remorse in his voice as he tells me this. Just a stern certainty that the point is fast approaching when he'll leave this place forever. He'll just walk away.

Just now, up ahead, rising like a mirage out of the wetland grass, a remarkable tableau comes into focus. It's a small city of giant machines and steel structures and shouting men. Insect-like helicopters buzz the skyline, soaring over gas flares and 500-ton cranes and whitewashed storage tanks holding thousands of barrels of crude oil. To our left and right, fences topped with barbed wire soon replace the previously uninhabited bayou landscape, and hard-hatted foremen give orders from the doors of trailer offices, rolled blueprints in their hands.

We've reached Port Fourchon, the end of the line, where Bayou Lafourche finally spills into the Gulf of Mexico. Boat traffic increases all around us as we reach the port's center, and soon our little sixteen-footer is a mere piece of driftwood jostled in the wake of huge tankers and tugboats and supply boats, some rising four stories out of the water with names like *Fast Cajun* and *Miss Molly,* their massive sides draped with the tires of Boeing 727 jetliners for bumpers.

These supply boats, Tee Tim explains, service oil facilities all along the coast as well as oil and gas platforms as far as 140 miles offshore. Above deck, the boats carry work crews and tools and pipe and casing, and below deck, thousands of gallons of brown liquid mud to pour down offshore drill shafts to control pressure. Along the port's bulkheaded shore, companies with names like Global Envirotech Inc. and Halliburton Production Enhancement edge the water, providing platoons of roughnecks, roustabouts, welders, machinists, gaugers, divers, and fitters to keep the oil flowing around the clock, every day of the year, including Christmas and even through some hurricanes.

Up ahead, we finally see the white foam of ocean breakers, and Tee Tim turns his small crab boat around. We've made our destination: the Gulf of Mexico. To the east, a short distance off, I see a dozen barges purposefully submerged in the shallow Gulf water, two hundred feet offshore in a line that parallels the beach. The barges, filled with giant stones, are meant to slow the pounding of waves against the rapidly eroding Fourchon beachline. Now, as we head back up Bayou Lafourche, passing the last of the port facilities, it's that bizarre necklace of sunken beach barges that I'll remember most. With it comes the supreme irony that Port Fourchon, this busy monument to the forces that have helped wreck coastal Louisiana, is itself being washed out to sea, with billions of dollars of oil-industry infrastructure—all across the state—destined for saltwater burial in the next few years.

In the amber light of late afternoon, we retrace our path up the bayou, glad to be free of the frenetic clamor of Fourchon. The tide has gone out, drawing countless blue herons and snowy egrets to shallow pools scattered across the marsh where small fish lay trapped: easy prey.

We're almost home when, just south of Leeville, the outboard sputters and coughs and Tee Tim starts hissing a long stream of expletives. We've run out of gas. He paddles us to the right-hand shore where, coincidentally, there stands an old and isolated Cajun shack on low stilts where Tee Tim spent his early childhood. The house was left empty and abandoned when his folks chose to move up the bayou to the higher ground of Leeville and their present camp on tall pilings.

Tee Tim tells me to wait by the boat while he walks up the bayou bank to his cousin's trailer home for gas. I watch him negotiate the marsh grass by walking sideways in a curious, gingerly fashion. Like a kickboxer about to deliver a blow, he lifts one leg and, with the bottom of his shoe, meets a clump of grass halfway up the blades. He then pushes the blades down with his shoe to form a thin, grassy cushion underfoot. These cushions barely keep his shoes out of the mud below, that gooey, smelly mess Cajuns call *boue pourrie*, "rotten mud." Tee Tim's technique is not quite like walking on water, but it's close, a skill honed by generations of Cajun life in the wetlands.

Alone now, I try the same sideways walk to reach the abandoned house fifty feet behind me. But my efforts are untutored and clumsy and soon my shoes are caked with mud. I gather a few driftwood planks instead and construct a crude walkway to the house's sagging porch.

There on the front porch of this Depression-era structure, I sit staring out at the bayou, surrounded by ripped screens and rotten wood floorboards and a feeling of ghosts in the air. In the play of sunset light and lengthening shadows a handful of boats drift up and down the water. A tugboat passes by, pushing an oil barge. A canopied oyster boat chugs into view, the deck noisy with the chink, chink, chink of sharp hatchets striking shells as men in bib overalls separate clustered oysters. Next, a steel-hulled shrimp boat rides low in the water, weighed down in a way I've come to recognize means it's had good luck, it's hit the *grosse tallée*.

Despite the massive loss of land in this once boundless estuary system, there remains a staggering amount of life and natural beauty along the coast. But try as I might, I still can't get young Tee Tim's voice out of my ears:

"When I was a kid . . ."

I glance up the bayou to where the water bends north, and can barely make out the outlines of the Leeville cemetery, crypts turning to water, bricks falling into the pale green current. Back at my home in Maryland, a suburban place that increasingly seems a full galaxy away from this land and its culture and its problems, I've attended environmental hearings and written protest letters over the proposed destruction of as few as five acres of wetlands. But in the roughly one hour that Tee Tim and I have now been out of gas, Louisiana has lost almost half that amount. And yet, until the past two days, I knew much more about the appalling ecological collapse of the Aral Sea in the former Soviet Union—ten thousand miles away—than about the vanishing Louisiana coast a few hundred miles from where I was born.

Tee Tim emerges just now from the marsh grass, still in a huff. He broke into his cousin's locked mobile home only to find no phone inside. "No phone!" he says in disgust. "What a loser. No phone!"

But five minutes later we're saved. The bayou has turned calm and glassy in the expiring golden light when we look up to the whine of a green Boston whaler motoring down from Lee-ville. In it stand Tim senior and his nephew Sean Paul.

"We figured de time had come to find out what de trouble was," Tim says in his thick Cajun speech, shooting reproving glances at Tee Tim.

Then, turning to me, Tim says, "So? What? Did ya see all de oil rigs? Did ya see how it all works down here on de baya?"

"Yes," I say. "I saw it."

I then step, carefully, from my driftwood bridge onto the boat and we all head back up the bayou.

# Two

I spend a second night at Boudreaux's Waterfront Motel, looking down on shrimp boats from my room atop ten-foot pilings. The next morning, early, I begin hitchhiking the conventional way, along Route 1, back up to Golden Meadow and my stranded car. I get a ride with a seventy-three-year-old Cajun man whose pickup truck is full of torn shrimp nets. He works at one of several net-repair shops along the bayou, mending all manner of shrimp and fishing nets over a wooden workbench and using a handheld shuttle.

"You like French music?" the old man says, turning up the radio to a local morning program called the *Hot Sauce Express*. Many South Louisianans don't refer to their music as Cajun or Zydeco. It's all just "French music" to them. From the radio now, high-pitched and infectious Cajun lyrics stream forth with accordion and fiddle backup to a tune called "Ma Femme Met Pas la Stepin" (My Baby Don't Wear No Drawers).

During the drive up the bayou the old man, dressed in a baseball cap and camouflage hunting jacket, manages to tell me most of his life story, including the part about World War II. Like many young Cajuns, he was sent to France both to tote a rifle and to serve as interpreter.

"But dey didn't give me no interpreter's pay level," he says. "No sir. 'Cause I couldn't read or write French. Just speak it. But dat's okay. One day I'm a poor kid shrimpin' barefoot in Terrebonne Bay, Louisiana, and de next, just like dat, de war starts and I'm in France introducing big-shot American colonels to French town mayors in funny berets. Even met Charles *dee* Gaulle."

He drops me off and I wave goodbye in Golden Meadow, where I left my car two days before. My goal now is Bayou Petit Caillou, a forty-mile circuitous drive to the east, where I hope to again hitchhike on boats down to the Gulf of Mexico.

I drive north along Bayou Lafourche, heading up Route 1 through the communities of Galliano, Cote Blanche, and Cut Off. I pass pink-blooming mimosa trees, several Catholic churches, a machine shop devoted to oil-field work, a hardware store selling crab traps, and an improbably high number of tattoo parlors. The slower rhythms of southern commerce reveal themselves on a marquee outside one merchant's store: "Gone to see Jessica. Back in July."

In Cut Off, a Kmart and McDonald's restaurant signal the extreme outer fringe of franchised America, and I know I've ventured too far north. I promptly turn west on Louisiana Route 24, a fissured and buckling two-lane road about five years overdue for repaving, its shoulders crumbling.

The land is slightly higher here, no longer marsh country, and a thick forest closes in on both sides. Though only 10 A.M., the sky turns suddenly dark as Spanish moss spreads directly overhead from the branches of stately live oaks. The forest interior is studded with dwarf palmettos and creeping vines hanging from a canopy of honey locust and more live oaks. Patches of mirror-black swamp water dot the forest, supporting stands of bald cypress, water tupelo, and pumpkin ash.

There's no sign of human habitation for several miles, just the dark, gloomy, beautiful jungle pressing in all around, the sort of subtropical bayou forest in which the first Tarzan film was shot, not far from here, in 1916. I finally reach a settlement of Native Americans living in modest frame houses and old mobile homes. Members of the United Houma Nation, they appropriately call the surrounding area Grand Bois (big woods). A nine-banded armadillo crosses the road as I pass through town, and a red-shouldered hawk circles overhead.

Gradually the forest yields to scattered fields of chest-high sugarcane, planted row after row in numbing, leafy precision. I've entered Terrebonne Parish, Louisiana, home to Bayou Petit Caillou (French for small stone), and soon the familiar sight of shrimp boats tied to wooden docks fills my eyes. I drive south along the bayou to the tiny Cajun town of Chauvin and a "shrimp shed" where fishermen are busily selling last night's catch and buying ice for the next run.

I ask a one-armed shrimper with a hook for a hand for a lift down the bayou and he gives me the standard response.

"You want to do *what?*"

I explain again and he apologizes, saying he's got hours of engine work ahead of him before shrimping again. His name is Jacob and he lost his arm ten years ago when it got caught in his boat winch. The arm was torn off completely right there on the spot. Now, with a prosthetic made of metal and plastic parts, and a hooklike pincher for a hand, he still shrimps full-time. When I ask to take a picture of his boat, Jacob says okay but then jumps abruptly out of the way. "A one-armed man messes up a good photograph," he says, averting his eyes. "People'll just look at my arm and not de boat." A sudden breeze elicits the sad, soft clink of boat cables against a boom as I snap the photo.

Behind us, the wholesaler's tin-roofed, open-sided shed is a hive of activity. The smell of fresh shrimp fills the air as thousands of pounds are moved along a clanging steel-chain conveyor belt and weighed on tin-bucket scales. Already the morning is oppressively hot and humid, like "a big old dog breathin' all over you" as one dockhand describes it. Clouds of steam rise the instant spilled ice hits unshaded portions of the concrete dock.

Jacob introduces me to Monsieur Charlie Broussard, a thirty-eight-year-old shrimper who's all iced up and untying from the dock. My instincts are to make excuses and walk away from Charlie and his boat the "S.S. *Minnow.*" It's an ancient, tumbledown "lugger" that resembles the *African Queen* after it's been dragged through hell, replete with chipped paint and rotting gunwales. "But she ain't gone down yet," says Charlie, by way of introduction. He's shirtless and barefoot in wraparound sunglasses, with a frail build, bad teeth, and a thin mustache. He grabs my backpack from the dock before I can decide whether to go, saying "Sure, sure, Cap, I'll take you wherever you want. Hop in." Jacob, meanwhile, waves goodbye from the shore with his hook hand, getting smaller every second, saying "Don't worry! Don't worry!" as we drift out into the bayou.

There's one consolation at least: the bayou here is much narrower than Bayou Lafourche, so I won't have to swim far if we do go down. Indeed I can almost touch some of the oak and willow branches hanging over the banks in this classic scene from the bayou country, this narrow, tea-colored waterway flowing lazily through the nether reaches of Louisiana.

We're headed toward the small town of Cocodrie (Cajun French for alligator) where Bayou Petit Caillou meets the Gulf of Mexico. Charlie says he'll take me almost halfway there with a detour into nearby Lake Boudreaux for shrimping.

Charlie's limping from a shrimp *piquant* that's jammed deep inside his bare foot. The spearlike protrusion above the shrimp's eyes broke off after an unlucky step during yesterday's trawling. Buried in flesh, the serrated, translucent spike is hard to see, much less dig out, and, desperate, Charlie slept last night with a slab of salt meat tied to his foot per the Cajun custom, but that fails to relieve the pain.

To help dull the pain we stop for a six-pack of Budweiser at the Dixie General Store on the outskirts of Chauvin. The store's waterside dock leads past a magical spread of Spanish moss and up to an interior thick with the smell of crab-patty sandwiches and New Orleans-style pecan pies.

But the beer we buy, iced down back on the boat with the same ice brought for the shrimp, can't seem to dull Charlie's other pain: separation from his six-month-old baby boy. Before the shrimping season began in May, Charlie was the primary at-home caregiver while his wife worked at the local Family Dollar store. Now, as we motor past the last homes and docks of Chauvin, Charlie shows me a wallet photo of the little guy. He does this again an hour later. He's miserable without that baby.

Up ahead, a remarkably antique bridge comes into view. It's called a "swing" bridge, and as we draw closer it swings open like a giant gate to let us pass. The single-lane structure of steel and wood sits on a central pivot and is pulled into an open position by a 150-foot-long rope manually guided onto a pulley by a bridge attendant on the bayou shore. The whole operation has a distinctly nineteenth-century feel to it.

Moments later we enter a narrow canal and head west into Lake Boudreaux, soon finding ourselves in a wide-open, six-thousand-acre body of brackish water edged by marsh grass. Charlie lowers the rusted booms of the S.S. *Minnow* toward the water, allowing his nets to sink into the four-foot depth. Charlie's old-fashioned boat, a classic lugger, steams toward the middle of the lake. The vessel has a pointy bow and a round bottom hull and—its defining characteristic—a rounded stern of the sort no longer used in shrimp boats because of the extra craftsmanship needed to create those sharply curved edges.

The first haul, dumped onto the foredeck thirty minutes later, is meager. Charlie squats by the catch and shows me how to "pick" the shrimp, i.e., root out the by-catch of small squid, baby crabs, and fish, and toss them back into the water. The French verb for this is *trier*, from which the noun *triage* is derived, as in what a battlefield medic does, choosing who lives and who dies.

It's backbreaking work, and Charlie, like Tim Melancon, has a bad back to begin with. He tells me he's glad to have me on board as a deckhand. For years he worked as a laborer on an oil-field boat until one day the vessel hit a jetty, going from 22 knots to zero in a split second and slamming Charlie against a chair, nearly killing him. He was able to walk again only after doctors took bone from his hip and used it to fuse two broken vertebrae. He's still damaged goods, though, and no oil company will hire him. So he shrimps, a job he loves despite the sometimes miserable pay and varied dangers. I notice he's frequently lifting his sunglasses and scanning the southern horizon for *tempêtes*, dark clouds that signal a storm might be heading our way.

Lake Boudreaux is famous for nasty waterspouts—tornadoes that touch water and become cones of swirling liquid, capable of lifting boats fifteen feet in the air and dropping them, like toys, upside down. Charlie takes another peek, squinting at the south sky, then drops his glasses back onto his freckled, sun-blistered nose, satisfied we're fine for now.

I notice that Charlie's eyes, momentarily unshaded, are frightfully bloodshot, burnt red like a Gulf sunset. "How much sleep did you get last night?" I ask.

"Sleep?" he says. "*Sleep?* Dis 'ole state of Louisiana, she gives us fifty days to catch all de browns. Fifty days. Not one more. So sleep, dat don't make too much sense."

"You shrimped the whole night, then?"

"Didn't stop," he says. "Over de last t'ree days, I got me maybe ten hours' sleep total. Maybe. But dat's in naps, you know, here and dere, none more dan two hours."

A month before the shrimp season opens, he tells me, he purposefully cuts down on his sleep, going to bed later, getting up earlier, until by opening day he's down to a diet of three or four hours a day, prime shrimping shape. But it's still hard.

"It might be t'ree A.M., dark as de bottom of an outhouse, and you're trawlin' by yourself. De shrimp, dey're out dere so you can't stop. But Lord, at dat wheel, you sure wanna nod off. Dat's when I make sure I got me a cigarette goin' all de time. Dat way, if I conk out, it burns down to de fingers and—shit!—dat'll wake you up."

He shows me marks on his index finger where this happened just the other night.

"But why take the chance?" I ask. "Wouldn't wrecking your boat cost more than whatever shrimp you'd catch trying to stay awake?"

"You're not from down de baya, you, to ask a question like

dat, Cap," he says. "I'm a Cajun. I was born wit' webbed feet. If I took off my boots and socks you'd be shocked. Dis is what I do. If de shrimp are dere, you best stay awake."

We're still clearing the by-catch off the foredeck. I pick up a squid and start to throw it overboard when Charlie says, "Watch out. Dat squid'll shoot you wit' ink right between de eyes."

I turn my face to one side and gingerly drop it in the water.

"I'm wondering," I say to him, returning to the shrimp, "what does it *mean* to be Cajun? I mean, to you personally. What does it mean?"

Charlie goes silent for a moment. He stops cleaning the shrimp and looks at me through those wraparound sunglasses.

"It's a knack," he says. "It's a knack we got. Most people up nort', dey couldn't last a day down dese bayas like us. Dey'd starve, even wit' all de fish and birds and gators around. But a Cajun, nobody gets de catch like a Cajun man. A woman wit' PMS, she's got nuttin' on a Cajun man who can't get out on his boat durin' shrimp season. For me, it's when dat old mornin' sun comes risin' over my boat deck and de boat's covered wit' a ton of shrimp, and den I have me a big bowl of jambalaya wit' de guys at de shed, and we all ever'body got money in de pocket. Dat, to me, dat's bein' Cajun!"

A big smile creeps over his face, but then begins to fade.

"De udder part, for me, is de family. We stick togedder, down here. Nobody sticks togedder like Cajuns. Always had to. We don't move around too much and we don't put no parents in old folks' homes. I got t'ree kids, me—Lane, eighteen, Sara, nine, and Evan, he just made six mont's. Even him, I don't mind tellin', I change his diaper and give 'im de bottle and all dat. But dere's de catch. A bayou Cajun man, he loves two t'ings de most in de whole world: bein' on de water and bein' wit his family.

And you can't do bot' at de same time. And dat tears us up. Tears us up like nuttin' you can speak of."

Charlie reaches for his wallet just then. "Did I show you de picture of my baby boy yet?" Before I can respond he pulls it out and shows me again. Then he stares at the photo himself, one hand pressed against a gunwale, the other caressing the creased and worn wallet shot.

We're almost done picking the shrimp when another somber subject comes up: the vanishing land. News of this phenomenon has deeply colored my trip so far and part of me is still hoping it isn't true, that everything I've heard along Bayou Lafourche is a bad dream and over here along Petit Caillou I'll somehow wake up to find people have no idea what I'm talking about. Everything will be okay. The terrible thing won't be happening.

But of course it is.

"See dis big lake all around us, Cap?" Charlie says, pointing 180 degrees to the left and then to the right using only his nose while his hands continue to throw tiny crabs overboard. "Dis lake, in de 1960s, didn't have no shrimp. De water was too fresh. So when I was a kid you didn't come here. You went furdder sout' for shrimp. Now look."

Again, with his nose, he points, this time to the dozen or so trawlers scattered in all directions, hauling in shrimp just like us.

Charlie picks up a small shovel from against a gunwale. "Nope," he says, scooping several thousand shrimp off his deck and into an ice hold, "not a single shrimp here when I was a kid."

The problem, he says, is more than just the sinking land and the massive erosion spawned by all the oil-company canals.

Those canals also provide highwaylike avenues for the saltier water of the Gulf to travel north through the marsh. This salt-water "intrusion," as it's called, wreaks havoc on fresh- and brackish-water ecosystems, pickling whole forests of swamp cypresses and pushing such species as alligators and oysters farther and farther north. Canals, in fact, are a big part of the reason Lake Boudreaux is now salty enough for shrimp while being inhospitable to the same species when John F. Kennedy was elected president. The entire marine zone is shifting north toward an inevitable collision with higher, more stable, nonalluvial land, where roads and towns and subdivisions and hurricane levees will block any further advance, spelling the death of the entire estuarine ecosystem. If the fantastic land loss continues, the famous ragged edge of the Louisiana coast will simply flatten out, eventually coming to look more like coastal Mississippi, Alabama, and Florida, i.e., made up mostly of narrow beaches with only small pockets of wetlands that produce only a fraction of the fisheries wealth of the current, vast Louisiana system.

Charlie drops his nets back into the water, having just finished icing down all the shrimp below deck. But the haulback twenty minutes later brings almost nothing. "De shrimp have gone into de marsh," he says. "We'll have to wait for low tide, after sunset, to flush dem out." It's only midafternoon right now. "We got some time to kill," he says.

He decides to make an escape into a series of obscure bayous north of the lake. These lead to his favorite resting place: a grassy bend in the middle of nowhere where three idle shrimp boats are already tied together, including Big Wayne Belanger's *Lady Desiree* skiff. Wayne is an exceedingly handsome man with a trim silver beard and silver hair. Over his shoulder, atop the wheelhouse, sits a great blue heron so close it looks like Wayne's pet.

Wayne, forty-six, has the largest hands I've ever seen, nearly rivaling catcher's mitts and inches thick at the palms. The size makes his missing ring finger even more conspicuous. He was picking shrimp one day, he says, when a catfish fin sunk deeply into the fleshy digit. "I did just what de old-timers tell you: make it bleed to get de poison out," Wayne says. "So I bled it and a lot of blood sure came out and I t'ought dat should do it, but damned if my finger didn't turn black anyway and dey finally had to take it off."

Wayne's sun-bronzed face is a study in fatigue from last night's hard shrimping and today's equally long morning repairing his boat winch. He's taking an afternoon break right now, quaffing a few cold Buds. These Cajun shrimpers, away for days at a time in distant waters, rest by tying up together in groups of three or four boats in the shelter of remote backcountry bayous, cooking big communal Cajun meals and drinking beer and talking about shrimp and helping repair each other's boats and talking about women—and that's basically what we do for the rest of the day, hour after unhurried hour. An overflying plane would have seen a knot of dirty boat decks and shirtless men surrounded by a watery world of Everglades vastness with interconnecting bayous and lakes and marshland set ablaze in the gleaming reflection of late afternoon sun. It's something that's almost completely gone in America: the fellowship of working men in a wild place.

At one point a four-foot alligator swims past the boat, and Wayne tells me there are lots more up here north of the lake, some reaching twelve and fourteen feet. Last year he got a five-footer caught in his shrimp net. These cold-blooded reptiles hatch their eggs by cleverly piling big mounds of grass and leaves over them, then letting the heat of decomposition incubate the eggs. People around here still hunt the adults each September, Wayne explains, by tossing out raw chicken parts on huge hooks. They then sell the skins and eat the meat.

"You eat it?" I ask.

"Sure," Wayne says. "A good sauce piquante wit' gator meat over rice? You got Cajuns swear by it. Dere's not much, you know, a coon ass won't eat."

Coon ass. It's a name I've heard Cajuns apply to themselves repeatedly on this trip, a moniker employed not unlike the way some African-Americans use the word "nigger": for years it was employed as a slur against Cajuns until these French descendants claimed it for themselves. Linguists pretty much agree that the word has nothing to do with raccoons, but derives instead from the no-longer-used *conasse,* a French cussword for a prostitute who has not had her regular health inspection. Today, the use of "coon ass" reflects a certain Cajun pride in their traditionally rural and rough-hewn way of life, and it pokes a little fun, expressing Cajuns' own perception of themselves as just a little bit backward. Thus, a beat-up pair of rubber deck boots are called coon-ass Reeboks. A ruler for measuring fish is a coon-ass computer. An elaborately jury-rigged boat repair job is coon-ass engineering. But again, when a Cajun tells you he's an RCA (registered coon ass), he's positively taking pride in who he is. He's not apologizing for anything.

"If you like coon-ass food," Charlie says, turning matters back to cooking, "you gotta come down for de Blessin' of de Fleet. That's when people really eat down here. You got your gumbo, your jambalaya, your shrimp boulettes, your crawfish étouffée, your boiled crabs. It's all dere."

The Blessing of the Fleet, Charlie and Wayne explain, is an old and venerable bayou tradition where a town's Catholic priest, riding at the head of a parade of boats, blesses the community's fishing vessels with holy water just prior to opening day of shrimp season. Before the parade, a mass is held where shrimpers are given blessed medallions to protect them from the season's inevitable storms. Afterward there's usually a feast on church grounds with lots of French music and a traditional Cajun dance, a *fais-do-do*.

The images of holy water and boiled crabs and washboard rhythms resonate in my mind as I sit on Wayne's Lafitte skiff surrounded by prowling gators and Wayne's onboard blue heron. The ceremony these men have just described seems as foreign as anything I've heard so far on this trip. What could be more out of place in a nation where meaningful community rituals have all but vanished thanks to television, the decline of rural America, the weakening of the church in community life, and the generally obliterating sameness of mass culture?

But somehow nothing has derailed the Blessing of the Fleet ceremony in small towns all across Louisiana's bayou country. For many Cajuns "the Blessin'" is second only to Mardi Gras as a chance to throw a party, be with family and friends, and show off valued cultural traits. I keep asking Wayne and Charlie more and more questions about the ceremony until I can almost taste the okra-laced gumbo, hear the pearl-buttoned accordions, and see the parade of shrimp boats decorated in colorful bunting and triangular flags that snap with pride in the salty breeze.

"But you know," Wayne says, "it's all dying down here. De fishing industry and all de towns. Everyt'ing is passing away."

His words draw me back to the blunt facts of coastal Louisiana.

"We've already been talking about it," Charlie tells Wayne.

"So did Charlie show you my favorite tree?" Wayne asks.

I shake my head. "What tree?"

Everyone down the bayou has a favorite land-loss anecdote, it seems, and Wayne's involves a large oak tree near the northeast corner of Lake Boudreaux. The dead and leafless tree, which Wayne shows me later that afternoon, is submerged at its base in lake water, the body a forlorn sculpture of silvery-white branches reaching like fingers toward the sky in a gesture that seems to ask "Why?" Twenty years ago this tree was on a solid bank of land near where Wayne and his brother flipped over in a small motorboat one winter day.

"My brudder, he was being a *couillon* [clown] and turned too fast and we hit de water," says Wayne. "So we went onto de shore, totally wet, and gathered up some firewood, and built us a fire under de shelter of dat tree, which was totally alive, and we had us some sit-down until we warmed up and dried off. Now it's gone, dat land. Twenty years, and de tree is in water where we built a fire. Dere's no more land. I never t'ought I'd live to see anyt'ing like dat," Wayne says.

For more than two days I've listened to dark stories like this, all presented with an air of fatalism, a firm sense of fait accompli, the causes of decline seemingly too monumental and rooted in too many decades of destructive momentum to allow any hope for change.

"Is there *nothing* that can be done to stop all this?" I finally ask Wayne and Charlie. "Is there no way to make the land stop sinking and eroding? To make it stop disappearing?"

"Sure dere is," Wayne says, rubbing his silver beard with his enormous hands as his voice dips into sharp sarcasm. "All you have to do is fill in all de oil-company canals, build up all de barrier islands to de size dey were a hundred years ago, and den let de Mississippi River flood again. Dat's all."

The remedies are fantastically ambitious, of course, each carrying such huge price tags and posing technical challenges as to render them nearly impossible. For his part, Wayne is especially doubtful about letting the Mississippi flow from its banks again. Too many potential flood victims keep the politicians scared.

But I later learn that some isolated efforts *were* under way to fill in certain oil-field canals or otherwise mitigate the erosion they cause. And a few barrier islands *had* been shored up temporarily with new sand and the planting of protective grasses. And, most important, there *was* a plausible plan already developed to let the Mississippi breach its banks in a controlled way, a move that would resume the process of sedimentation and land creation and so save large parts of the coast without flooding homes. But this "controlled diversion" of the river, the Holy Grail of coastal restoration hopes, was expensive and politically complicated in the extreme and time was rapidly running out for it to have any chance of success.

Time was also running out for about two million Louisianans who depend on the state's coastal wetlands as a buffer against hurricane damage. As conservationists, scientists, and public officials make excruciatingly slow progress toward possible solutions, the marsh continues to disappear at a rate of 25 square miles per year. This, Wayne points out to me, means that hundreds of Louisiana towns and cities, all just a few feet above sea level, lie increasingly prone to that deadly wrecking ball of hurricane force known as the storm surge. Coastal wetlands, it turns out, provide more than just a critical nursery for shrimp, crabs, and fish. Every 2.7 miles of marsh grass absorbs a foot of a hurricane's storm surge, that huge tide of water pushed inland by the storm's winds. For New Orleans alone, hemmed in by levees and already on average eight feet *below* sea level, the apron of wetlands between it and the closest Gulf shore was, cumulatively, about 50 miles a century ago. Today that distance is perhaps 20 miles and shrinking fast. With very slow evacuation speed virtually guaranteed (there are only three major exit bridges that jump over the encircling levees for central New Orleans' 600,000 people), it's not implausible that a major hurricane approaching from the right direction could cause tens of thousands of deaths.

This is to say nothing of the literal disappearance of entire towns like Leeville and Chauvin and Golden Meadow which have even less—dramatically less—marsh protection. After the Really Big One hits and drifts up the Mississippi Valley, spending itself over land, there might be nothing left behind under the clearing skies except a sunny expanse of open water and bright waves where bayou people and houses once stood, the land finally battered and scoured of every last handful of ancient and fragile Mississippi soil.

Then the tortured process, at long last, would be complete. Or, as one shrimper tells me, "Dere won't be no more nothin' left anymore, forever."

And then there are the birds to consider.

We're less than two hours from sunset now, the hazy afternoon heat slowly yielding to a cooling, honey-hued air. In the marsh grass around Wayne's and Charlie's boats the bird life grows more active as many species begin their evening search for food. Others, like the white ibis, are returning in flocks to nearby rookeries, their black wing tips sharp against the mellowing sky.

I grow a bit restless as the day winds down, reminding Charlie of his pledge to return me to Bayou Petit Caillou, the main waterway south, so I can resume my hitchhiking trip down to Cocodrie before it gets too dark. Already I notice Wayne has broken out a thick white candle inside the wheelhouse by which to navigate once darkness falls. He places the candle in a glass holder next to the throttle. The sight prompts me to again drop hints to Charlie about heading toward the bayou.

"No problem, Cap," he says. "Right after we fix Wayne's winch."

Despite Wayne's best repair efforts earlier that day, the winch controlling his right boom has gotten jammed again during a test run. So Charlie, bum foot and all, climbs up the raised vertical boom like a sailor up a mast and finds a mess of tangled steel cables that keep the winch from turning properly. What happens next I can scarcely believe. While Wayne activates the electric winch from the deck, Charlie plucks dangerously with his bare fingers at the grinding, spinning loops of knotted cable, trying to get the cables straightened out and back on track. The slightest errant move and those cables will act like scissors, relieving Charlie of several digits.

Not eager to watch this happen, I move up to the bow, sequestering myself. There I find the winch commotion has sent our on-board heron back into the water. He's now two hundred feet away, getting supper beside a spread of lithe green cordgrass. He stands absolutely still, watching the water, his sensuous neck extended, his long beak pointed forward and downward. Then, swifter than a snake, the head descends and a fish goes visibly down the gullet.

A flock of roseate spoonbills float into view and I grab Wayne's "captain's" binoculars from the wheelhouse in time to see three of the birds land in a pool of water a hundred yards away. Their feathers—pink, pinker, and almost orange—are virtual reflections of the evening sky's shifting colors. As soon as they land the birds bury their bare heads in the water and move their long, broad-tipped bills sideways through the muddy muck of the bottom in a crude manner that seems out of place on such imperial creatures. They are stirring up their food with their "spoons," exposing aquatic insects, shrimp, snails, and small fish that live in the shallow water.

This odd eating method joins others I've seen so far, like the ring-billed gulls dropping clams from the sky to crack them open on hard ground near Port Fourchon and the once endangered brown pelican out in the Gulf which dives suddenly, takes in the typical three gallons of seawater in its mouth pouch, gargles and spits the water out, then swallows a drumfish still flapping conspicuously on its way down the gullet.

Wetland habitats hold title as the most biologically productive areas on earth, and the great range of plant and animal life found within Louisiana's coastal zone provides food and protection for no fewer than 353 species of birds residing here at some point during the calendar year. Wading birds, waterfowl, songbirds, raptors, shorebirds, colonial nesting birds—they're all here. From the screeching swoop of red-shouldered hawks in the swamp forests to the furtive diving and darting of clapper rails and purple gallinules in the marshes; from the awkward takeoff of double-crested cormorants in the lakes and bays to the six-foot wingspan of brown pelicans nesting on the barrier islands, southern Louisiana is a veritable avian dreamland.

Yet Wayne and Charlie have already told me that the many species I'm seeing now, in June, are nothing compared to what's on display in the spring and fall when the migratory birds are on the move. Twenty percent of all the ducks in North America—four million of them—overwinter in coastal Louisiana. These wetlands are located right in the heart of what ornithologists call the great "Mississippi Flyway," the principal travel route used by millions of migratory birds traveling within North America and between North and South America. Birds making the latter journey, known as neotropical migrants, include species as common as the magnolia warbler and as rare as the swallow-tailed kite, with its brilliant yellow torso and nests made with Spanish moss. There's also the hard-traveling Arctic peregrine falcon which spends summers on tundra nesting grounds and passes winters as far south as the tip of South America.

The diverse estuary system of coastal Louisiana couldn't be better located for these species, sitting as it does right smack in the middle of America's Gulf Coast. From this enormous, food-filled habitat it's a straight shot down to Mexico's Yucatán Peninsula and points south, making Louisiana a convenient jumping-off point for birds headed down to Latin America and a lifesaving point of return for those coming back. Indeed, the Louisiana wetlands seem less a fortuitous accident of nature than a place specifically designed by a fastidious army quarter-master whose knack for stockpiling food is matched only by his genius for seizing strategic ground.

Each spring, for example, the common yellowthroat, a deli-cate warbler noted for its bold black mask, arrives in Louisiana after wintering in the moist lowland forests of Venezuela, Ecuador, and Colombia. Exhausted and half starved from the nonstop fifteen-hour Gulf crossing, having lost as much as a third of its body weight along the way, the first landfall many of these yellowthroats see is coastal Louisiana with its great penin-sulas of deltaic land jutting out into the Gulf like outstretched hands of welcome. The birds wearily land and gorge themselves on insects and berries along the forested bayou banks and in the moist thickets of the wetlands, tanking up for the continued journey north as they've done for thousands of years. Others stay behind to breed, building nests in the sedges and grasses of the marsh, well protected from predators.

But each year, spring gets a little quieter in Louisiana and the skies a little less crowded. Each year, the common yellowthroat finds that once food-rich forests have collapsed into water and fewer marshes exist in which to take cover and build nests. So each year fewer of the birds survive the trip to and from Latin America, and their aggregate numbers continue to tumble.

Data collected over the last several decades have shown serious population declines for many migratory bird species like the common yellowthroat. Forest-dwelling songbirds alone are disappearing at a rate of 1 to 3 percent per year. And over a ten-year period, at least nine types of Gulf shorebirds declined to half or less of their former numbers. Most disturbing, the total number of birds detected by radar crossing the Gulf of Mexico each year has decreased by *half* within the last twenty years.

Habitat loss throughout the Americas tops the list of factors precipitating this decline, with Louisiana representing a particularly agonizing blow. If the wetlands here continue to decline, experts predict major losses for scores of migratory species— many of them already rare, threatened, or endangered. For these magnificent flying creatures, the fastest-disappearing landmass on earth doubles as a place of unbearably fast-sinking luck: it couldn't be happening at a worse time. It couldn't be happening at a worse place.

Finally, Charlie and Wayne have fixed the winch and Charlie has retained all his fingers in the process.

"Now where is it you want to go?" Wayne asks me, wiping grime from his colossal hands with a rag. The roseate spoonbills beyond the bow have gorged themselves and moved on, replaced now by a lovely tricolored heron at the same spot.

I tell Wayne I need to head east to the main bayou, then hitch down to Cocodrie.

"Hmmmm," he says. "I can take you to Cocodrie myself, if you want."

Neither he nor Charlie plans to shrimp till after sunset, he explains, plus Charlie's got a sister who's a restaurant cook down in Cocodrie, and he hasn't seen her in a long time. So the two volunteer to take me all the way down the bayou in Wayne's skiff, the *Lady Desiree*. It's an exceedingly generous offer, one that confirms something Tim Melancon had said to me the day before: "A Cajun will give you de hat off his head on a hot sunny day if you need it."

After grabbing my pack from the S.S. *Minnow*, I insist on returning the favor as we steam across Lake Boudreaux and into Bayou Petit Caillou. I politely order Wayne to pull up to the Dixie General Store where I spring for more beer under the store's whirring ceiling fans. We ice the beer down back on board, then untie from the dock and float away.

The journey down this last narrow stretch of bayou has the feel of an epic storybook drawing to a close. Outside, atop the wheelhouse roof, I sit cross-legged amid hanging shrimp nets, following the flight of wood ducks with Wayne's binoculars as the sun lowers over mythic features: glass-smooth water, more overhanging trees, intermittent Cajun camps made of rusting corrugated tin. Kids fish with rods for speckled trout on one dock, drinking Kool-Aid from mason jars while swimsuits dry on clotheslines behind them. On another dock, an old man carefully sews a shrimp net onto a *paupière,* a special stationary frame he'll lower into the bayou later that night for a shrimp catch driven by the tides.

At dusk, I slip down to the wheelhouse as Wayne lights his candle in the swelling darkness. As in a car, any light brighter than this makes it hard to see out the cabin. Wayne's silver hair and beard seem to glow in the flickering dimness of candlelight, and Charlie, grabbing another beer, his foot still smarting, stares out at the dark bayou bank and again wonders aloud how his baby boy is doing back home.

Wayne's 210 Cummins engine rumbles on until the scattered lights of Cocodrie come into view: a shrimp shed, a few fishing camps, a waterside motel. We've arrived. The Gulf of Mexico is just a few more minutes down the bayou, the waves barely beyond earshot. I hop off on a dock and Charlie throws me my pack while Wayne ties up to some pilings. Then both men join me on the weathered planks, facing me. It's time to say goodbye.

The tourism bureau of this great southern state has a slogan—"Louisiana: Come as you are. Leave different." Well, I certainly didn't have an aching and sunburned neck and arms when I arrived three days ago, nor did I have these extra pounds of flesh from all the rich Cajun grub. But below the surface, who was I when I came? I was a cynical traveler convinced it was no longer possible to fall completely off the map in America, to get lost in an unfamiliar land among people barely recognizable as my countrymen. But hitchhiking through the bayou country, atop boat decks and with few concrete plans, has changed all that. It's proved my assumptions wrong and, at the same time, stripped me of my innocence. Like the rest of America, I had *no idea* what was happening along this coastline. Knowledge, it's often said, is power. But sometimes it just brings deep, deep sorrow.

Mine is the sorrow of saying goodbye to one of the last interesting regional cultures surviving in a nation once full of them, harking back to a time when "diversity" was much more than just a hip slogan we mumbled on the way to the same melting-pot mall. It's a sorrow for wilderness landscapes everywhere which once survived intact, free from assassination by greed and thoughtlessness, supporting both wildlife and working people of integrity.

So, yeah, I get misty-eyed there on the Cocodrie dock, bidding farewell to Wayne and Charlie. Maybe I've inflated them to heroes in my imagination, but they feel like friends, people I respect, people I'd swap lives with, maybe. And I feel somehow left behind as they motor back up into their bayou world in the glow of that one cabin candle.

And different is certainly the way I feel as I make my way up to a bar in the town of Cocodrie, unprepared for the shock of what I find. This small settlement is a Mecca for sportfishermen from all over America who come to splurge on expensive Gulf charters, casting Technicolor lures with graphite rods and fifty-pound test line.

Sitting on my barstool, unshaven and salty with sweat, my backpack stained with grease and smelling of fish, I survey the crowd of CEO automatons dressed in chinos and yuppie-style pastel shirts. They're gathered around the bar's ridiculous indoor thatch roof, drinking light beer and listening to Garth Brooks, while next door an upscale bait shop chimes with the beep of bar-code scanners.

"Hey, man, did you walk down here?" the bartender asks me, noticing my backpack.

"No," I say. "I hitchhiked."

I stare down at my beer and just leave it at that.

*Return to the Bayous*

# Three

Ten months later, standing on a shrimp boat in Bayou Grand Caillou, I watch as Father Joseph Pilola, clad in a billowing white robe, prepares a wreath of flowers for the two dead fishermen. It seems far too beautiful a day to pause and acknowledge the black fact of mortality. The late April sky is sparkling blue like Arctic ice, the humidity mild, the wind a brisk and blustery caress, generously spreading the rich aroma of boiled and pan-fried seafood from out behind the wheelhouse.

But death intrudes anyway. Father Pilola asks Cajun captain Terry Luke to shut down the thunderous diesel engine and turn off the country western music wafting dolefully down from the top deck. Suddenly quiet prevails. Only a few distant gulls and the ceaselessly blowing wind can be heard. It's such a windy day. From stem to stern, decorative triangular flags flutter insanely, sounding like a million muffled hands applauding the fine weather. Hats repeatedly go their merry way and people chase them across the decks or fish them from the bayou with gaff hooks.

The boat has paused here because fishermen live tough and dangerous lives; and because, forty-five days ago, a particularly sad tragedy struck this community of Dulac, Louisiana, located just west of Lake Boudreaux. Now, wreath in hand, Father Pilola asks the dozen or so shrimpers and their families to move in closer for the special ceremony. On wooden tables across the middle deck and atop the wheelhouse roof sit trays of steaming crabs and shrimp and crawfish and jambalaya and gumbo and corn on the cob—all momentarily abandoned. Adorning the boat's hull are cardboard cutout shrimp figures and Christian crosses, dozens of them, side by side, each about three feet tall and sprinkled with gold glitter.

Behind this boat, in single file, sit dozens of similarly decorated vessels overstuffed with people and Cajun cuisine. One boat has a live band on board playing "swamp pop" music with electric guitars and a full set of drums. But the band has stopped playing now out of respect for the wreath-laying ceremony. The Coast Guard escort boat has turned off its flashing lights, too.

This parade of shrimp boats has just traveled ten slow miles from the front steps of Holy Family Catholic Church, way up Bayou Grand Caillou, the starting point. Along the way, Father Pilola, leaning over the lead bow, has dutifully performed the annual Blessing of the Fleet ceremony for this community of a thousand or so Cajun and Indian fishing families whose main street is called Shrimpers Row. Reaching into a ceremonial shiny pail filled with blessed water and held by a robed altar girl in pigtails, Father Pilola has delivered holy liquid onto docked trawlers before crowds of people cheering along the banks and making the sign of the cross.

But here, near the bayou's end, where it widens greatly before flowing into the Gulf through a salt-marsh maze of tall cordgrass, all the cheering and applause have stopped. Father Pilola emerges from the wheelhouse with a wreath of two dozen red and white carnations while bespectacled Father Jerome Weber, a second priest, turns to all of us gathered at the stern in the hushed and breezy stillness. Bowing his head, Father Weber asks for a moment of silence.

It is not, perhaps, so remarkable that one of my very first acts upon returning to Louisiana is to attend a ceremony like this, one organized to commemorate a truly terrible ending. Given what I now know about this land and this culture, death—of the tragic, untimely sort—seems more or less central to everything here. It's what makes a visit to this coast as exhausting as it is exhilarating: beauty and death, inseparably bound, in states utterly extreme.

"Let us pray," says Father Weber.

And so we pray because local shrimper Mike Parria left Dulac that night forty-five days ago, headed for the Gulf, and found more trouble than one man can expect in a lifetime. Three and a half miles out into the sea, out beyond the mouth of Oyster Bayou, he was about to drop his nets for jumbo white shrimp when his sixty-foot boat collided with an unmarked gas well sticking ten feet out of the water. Instantly upon impact, the sickening hissing sound of escaping natural gas filled the pitch-black night air, gushing 150 feet skyward under a thousand pounds of pressure. The rule in such cases is simple: leave your boat immediately. Dive into the water and swim away as fast as you can. Do not pause to grab a life vest. Do not pause for anything. One spark from the boat engine can trigger a massive explosion at any moment.

Mike, a muscular forty-one-year-old with handsome, dark looks, was madly treading water two hundred feet from the wreck and screaming his head off when his brother Gillis, shrimping just ahead of him, finally turned his boat around and plucked Mike from the water after first almost running him over with the engine propellers. A few calls on the radio got the well shut off from a central control station, but the boat was too damaged to operate or move.

The next morning, back onshore, Mike called Coast Guard officials who refused to help salvage the slowly sinking boat, saying they were too busy. Instead, they said, it was Mike's responsibility to return and place a hazard light on the boat immediately. So the next morning, despite a gathering storm of severe proportions in the Gulf, Mike persuaded his old friend T. C. Fazande, a heavyset, aging Cajun, to take him out in T.C.'s thirty-foot Lafitte skiff. Another friend, Perry Falgout, thirty-seven, known as "the nicest guy in Dulac," came along to lend another hand.

The rain grew to a torrent soon after the men left town, and the seas had reached four-foot intensity as they entered the Gulf. Worse, according to the latest reports, tornadoes were in the forecast. For two hours, battered by wind, waves, and rain in the small skiff, the men searched unsuccessfully for Mike's boat. Convinced the vessel had by now sunk completely, the men finally turned back toward shore, with Perry driving and Mike and T.C. huddled at his feet, trying to stay dry in the small, open-sided wheelhouse.

Five minutes later, it happened. The entire boat began to shudder and convulse violently. Perry, still driving, gripped the wheel with all his might and, without turning to the others, suddenly yelled *"Hold on!"* Mike and T.C. never saw the monstrous waterspout that smashed head-on into the bow, but they felt the boat being lifted up out of the water and turned on its side, fifteen feet in midair, throwing the men against equipment. A second later the boat went into a free fall back to the water where it then kept on going, sinking like a stone fourteen feet to the bottom of the Gulf, all hands on board.

To his horror, Mike discovered that in the chaos of the sinking he had been caught in a tangle of the boat's shrimp-net ropes. For what seemed an eternity he struggled to free his arms and legs before finally kicking loose to the surface. There he gasped for air and found T.C. already swimming, wide-eyed and struggling in the noisy maelstrom of pouring rain and crashing four-foot swells. The boat was gone. Just men battling waves now. Both Mike and T.C. had instinctively reached for life preservers right before the collision, and they were using them now. They were sure Perry, the driver, would surface any moment. Mike grabbed a piece of floating wood from the sunken vessel and pushed it toward T.C. to help him stay above the white-capped waves.

Perry, meanwhile, still hadn't come up. He was still down with the ship.

Only one of these three men would eventually survive, and that by a miracle. The other two would be dead, by different means, in the next few minutes.

It's for these dead men, more than a month later, that I now find myself standing, head bowed, with thirty citizens of Dulac, Louisiana, at the stern of Terry Luke's trawler. Father Pilola has just placed the wreath next to the boat's gunwale, where it rests attached to a three-legged metal stand.

It's surely my imagination or a trick of the wind, but already the wreath seems to be leaning toward the sea, straining to go, as if the ghosts of the dead men were impatiently pulling it toward them. Father Weber, dressed in a tidy short-sleeved shirt with clerical collar, says a final prayer: "We deliver this wreath in memory of those who perished at sea. May they have eternal rest in the heavenly mansion God has prepared for them."

He then tosses the wreath overboard, where a strong outgoing tide carries it straight out toward the Gulf of Mexico.

My only souvenir from that first hitchhiking journey with Papoose, Tee Tim, and the others was a delicate swatch of Spanish moss plucked from an overhanging bough along Bayou Petit Caillou. Returning home, I hung the moss above a calendar on my office wall, and for months its fragile, ghostly beauty reminded me of a trip that had haunted me like none other I'd taken in my life. Every time I checked a date on the calendar I saw the moss again and I thought of another fifty acres gone that day. I actually needed the moss, something I could touch and hold, as proof that the story was true, that I had really been to this place, because no one else seemed to believe me upon my return to the Washington, D.C., area.

Not one of my friends or colleagues who listened to my stories—not *one*—responded by saying, "Oh yeah, Louisiana. I know all about that surreal mess down there. It's amazing how much land is vanishing." Instead they said, without exception, something like, "You *can't* be serious. A Manhattan of wetlands lost every ten months? Is that possible?"

These were mostly smart, well-read people, several of them professional environmentalists or volunteer activists who could cite chapter and verse the details of wetlands loss in the Everglades or the case for breaching dams out west to save California salmon and Idaho steelheads.

But Louisiana? Blank stares. Twenty-five percent of America's coastal wetlands vanishing? Forty percent of the nation's total salt marsh headed for destruction in little more than a life-time? Irreplaceable bird habitat gone? A nursery for myriad aquatic species obliterated? Blank stares.

All of these people were just like me, of course, before my bayou odyssey, and now I felt like a Cassandra whose monstrous story, buried somehow for generations, was just too damn big to be believed.

For the *Washington Post* I wrote a long essay about my hitch-hiking trip and about Louisiana land loss, but the piece ran way back in the Sunday travel section, diluting its punch, I felt. Yet by coincidence, Mark Davis, a Baton Rouge-based conservation-ist, was in D.C. and read the piece and rang me up. "The great-est untold story in America," he said, describing Louisiana's coastal demise. I was glad to learn that at least one organization had been formed to fight the problem. Davis was the head of a nonprofit called the Coalition to Restore Coastal Louisiana, and he implored me—with the urgency of a captain radioing Mayday from a sinking ship—to come back down for a closer, longer look at the problem.

For months Davis's invitation mingled in my mind with Charlie and Wayne's invitation to attend a bayou boat-blessing ceremony before that tradition—and the culture upon which it was based—was gone forever.

So I finally made up my mind. In April 2000 I began pack-ing, filling my car with a backpack, sleeping bag, fishing gear, binoculars, cameras, rain gear, mosquito repellent, sunscreen, a Cajun French dictionary, and a small library of maps and books about the bayou region. My goal this time was not simply to wander as a hitchhiker (though there would be more of that too) but to hang around long enough to carefully document as much of this world as I could before it departs, seeking deeper answers not just from shrimpers and crabbers and oystermen but from scientists, environmentalists, public officials, clergy, and others I met along the way. If one of America's greatest riches was about to perish, I wanted at the very least to help sound the trumpets of its passing and maybe, just maybe, bring into sharper focus the possibility of its last-minute rescue.

But leaving Maryland that first morning of my thousand-mile drive, my mind was less on Louisiana than on the nearby Chesapeake Bay. I passed over the Potomac River just south of Washington, D.C., where the river becomes a tidal stream, widening dramatically on its way to the Chesapeake just a few miles away. Below the bridge, thousands of striped bass were just ending their annual, ancient trip up from the bay to spawn along the Potomac's many tributaries, and fish-hungry osprey flew in low circles overhead.

The Chesapeake, of course, was another enormous estuary system in significant decline. Nitrogen oxides from car exhaust were poisoning its water. Sprawl development was altering watershed flows. Overfishing and habitat loss were decimating the crab population. But the bay, I realized, had two major factors on its side: much of America understood it was a threatened gem, and relatively aggressive programs were in place to try to bring it back to health. Most important, unlike the Louisiana bayou region, the Chesapeake wasn't literally disappearing. The higher, older, and more stable land of this region was subsiding at a tenth the speed of Louisiana, and there were no oil canals eroding the soil. There would be *something* here, in other words, to save fifty or one hundred years hence if human beings continued to care.

Similar thoughts came to mind as I reached North Carolina and brushed up against the Great Smoky Mountains where acid rain was poisoning thousands of acres of spruce firs and northern hardwoods at higher elevations. Again, no matter how bad it got up there in those mountains, the mountains themselves weren't going anywhere, and the conditions affecting them *could* be remedied with time.

The same held for the Everglades, which lay a few hundred miles away as I rolled farther south, edging the Florida panhandle. There, not only was it *possible* to bring back this huge wetlands complex after a century of abuse, but it was actually being accomplished with a recently passed $7.8 *billion* federal and state rescue plan.

Meanwhile, coastal Louisiana continued its headlong sprint toward a point of no return—unsalvageable, perhaps forever—and virtually no one had an inkling. This despite the fact that it provides crucial wildlife habitat and startling beauty *plus* the practical benefits of a fifth of America's domestic oil, a huge amount of its seafood, and hurricane protection for nearly 1 percent of the nation's population. These were all functions neither the Everglades nor the Chesapeake, despite their many merits, could claim.

So why was this one of America's best-kept secrets? How had it been possible to hide for so long this handsome, fragile, and mortally ill patient in the nation's hospital ward of environmental setbacks? "No idea," was the answer I got from every single fisherman I asked in the bayou region. The question dogged me until Mark Davis, from his underfunded, understaffed Baton Rouge office, later offered some theories.

In many ways, he said, it came down to location. The Chesapeake Bay, in addition to being right smack in the middle of the East Coast with its many media markets, was surrounded by several great scientific research universities and stood a mere chip shot from Washington, and the handful of concerned politicians eager to protect this emblem of wildlife and national pride on whose very shore "The Star-Spangled Banner" had been penned almost two hundred years ago.

The Everglades, meanwhile, benefited from South Florida's status as America's number one tourist destination bar none. Proximity to twenty million annual visitors brought attention and much-deserved sympathy. The same for the Great Smoky Mountains National Park, the most visited national park in America.

But Louisiana shared none of these advantages. Tourists didn't visit the bayou region in numbers remotely comparable, and major media outlets could hardly be farther away. The Louisiana state government, meanwhile, compounded the problem by doing relatively little to broadcast the story of coastal erosion to the rest of the nation. This was in part out of fear the attention would tarnish the image of an oil industry which accounted for nearly 20 percent of the state's gross economic product in 2000.

Then there was the outright political corruption woven deeply into the fabric of Louisiana's history, a tradition well established even before Huey Long's name became synonymous with the worst type of Deep South backroom power abuse and malfeasance. French colonial governors in the 1700s were regularly sentenced to the Bastille in Paris for financial scandals in the far-off subtropical territory. The Marquis de Vaudreuil set the standard for "bewigged pomp and be-laced corruption" in the 1740s, granting open monopolies to traders in return for premiums paid to his personal account and blatantly seizing military material for his own enrichment. Historians trace much of the chronic government corruption that would later become Louisiana's hallmark to the French attitude, dominant in colonial times, that office was a form of property from which the holder should profit.

Even after Louisiana achieved statehood in 1812, "democratic" elections were largely mockeries, rigged so wealthy planters and political bosses could have their way through open fraud, intimidation, stuffed ballots, and casting ballots for dead people. When Union major general Ben Butler occupied New Orleans during the Civil War, he too fell sway to the steamy atmosphere of fraud and abuse, closing down gambling houses and reopening them only after a fee was paid to him and his brother was taken on as half partner. The city's prostitutes grew so tired of Butler's reputedly wicked ways they took to pasting his picture in the bottom of their chamber pots. The scale of corruption grew still larger after the war when state treasurer Edward A. Burke brazenly emptied out government vaults in 1887 and took off for Honduras.

And then came the grand master of them all, Governor Long himself, who in 1929 was impeached by the Louisiana House on nineteen counts of wrongdoing ranging from alleged murder, bribery, and misuse of public funds down to complaints that Long had behaved immorally in a New Orleans nightclub. "The Kingfish" was never convicted by the Senate, however, because enough senators signed a "round-robin" agreeing not to convict no matter what the evidence. Long's famous "Share the Wealth" program did bring much needed roads, bridges, and free textbooks to the state, but even these were a form of "patronage bribery" that solidified Long's dictatorial hold on the state to the ultimate expense of everyone.

When an enraged assassin finally took Long's life with a Belgian pistol inside the state capitol in 1935, the scandals only multiplied among Long's surviving cronies, giving way to the notorious "Louisiana Hayride" of the late 1930s. Scores of officials ranging from Governor Richard W. Leche down to low-level bureaucrats were convicted of skimming as much as $100 million in state and federal funds. The schemes ranged from forcing WPA workers to build homes for officials to defraud-

ing the state in the purchase of trucks for the highway department. Louisiana State University president James Monroe Smith
embezzled half a million dollars to support his attempt to corner the U.S. wheat market, then fled to Canada when the scheme
was uncovered.

This long and tawdry parade of wrongdoing has historically
siphoned away attention and energy from the state's considerable social and economic challenges, from public health to education to the environment. As a result, a great many Louisianans
today harbor a deep, paralyzing, and seemingly genetic sense of
cynicism and hopelessness, viewing government as part of the
problem and not the solution to many issues of direct concern
to them.

"A Louisiana politician, he's like the girl you take home from
a bar," one oysterman later told me. "The first twenty minutes
are really great, but then you wake up in the morning and your
wallet's gone and there's no phone number for you to call."

These political woes showed few signs of dying out in the
new millennium. At the same moment my car was finally rolling
into New Orleans, skirting Lake Pontchartrain and passing skyscrapers overshadowing the French Quarter in the sticky heat,
former governor Edwin Edwards was standing trial at a downtown federal courthouse. Edwards and his codefendants were
charged with no fewer than thirty-three counts of extorting pay-
offs from riverboat casinos during and after the governor's last
term, which ended in 1996. Thus my return to Louisiana was
greeted not by newspaper articles detailing how the lower third
of the state was joining the Gulf of Mexico, but by stories of
how jurors had just watched videotaped evidence of a state official stuffing $20,000 worth of payoff money—in hundred-dollar
bills—into his pockets inside Edwards' law firm office.

A week later, while I was back out on fishing boats amid the disintegrating barrier islands and fragmenting coastal marsh, the same jury returned guilty verdicts against Edwards on seventeen counts, ranging from racketeering to wire fraud to money laundering. The verdicts, stacked end to end, carried a maximum sentence of 225 years in prison.

When I pull up to Leeville that late April morning, Tim Melancon is below deck, overhauling the engine of his cypress-hulled trawler. Already the sun is pouring down with conviction, and when Tim sticks his head above the deck to see who's calling, he takes one peek at me with those pale blue eyes on that vaguely Bill Murray face, his chin deeply dimpled, then throws on his sunglasses as if to bring me into sharper focus.

"Holy dog fuck!" he says. "You're back."

Tim leaps up and eagerly shakes my hand even though this is clearly not a convenient moment for him. Down below, he's got the cylinder head and pistons all spread out atop old copies of the *Lafourche Gazette*. His goal is to get this engine revamped and well oiled before the start of the brown shrimp season just a few weeks away. But as hardworking as bayou Cajuns tend to be, visitors seem always to represent a good excuse to take a break, have a smoke, maybe get a bite to eat.

"You hungry?" Tim asks me. "My mom, she's got some leftover jambalaya dat's been beggin' for a fork all mornin'."

And just like that we head up to Tim's camp and I'm back down the bayou, back inside a place and a state of mind.

We step off the wharf as Tim tells me he had a very mediocre shrimp season last year, forcing him into debts he hopes to pay off with better luck this year. He asks how the drive from "up north" went and I tell him I pulled into New Orleans last night after a tiring but problem-free two-day trip.

"Ugghhh. New Orleans," Tim says. "I been dere t'ree times and hated it every time."

New Orleans is two and a half hours away by car. Tim is forty-five years old.

"Just three times?" I say.

He nods. "Once for a marriage certificate. Once for a commercial shrimpin' license. And once to see de freaks in de Vieux Carré [the French Quarter]. Dat's enough for me. Who needs de traffic and automatic gunfire? Whatta dey got in New Orleans dat I need? Here, at least, I ain't gotta lock my doors like a prisoner."

His logic is hard to tussle with. About the only recreational trip he and Phyllis take from time to time, he says, is to visit the movie theater in Galliano fifteen miles up the bayou. They do this about once every ten years.

This isolating desire to stick close to home and to what you know is, today, pretty much elective along the bayou. But the mind-set itself isn't greatly changed from the days barely a half century ago—before cars, TVs, and dependable roads—when the isolation was compulsory. Tim later tells the story of his *grand-père* who traveled to southern Mississippi in the late 1930s to buy some cattle and came back with a jar full of red clay. Everyone in town gathered around that jar on his grandfather's front porch and just stared at the clay for hours and hours, talking about it for days.

Maybe, I muse, those same old-timers are seeing more of the world in the afterlife, because their tombs sure aren't staying in one place. On the drive into town that morning I passed the Leeville cemetery, the one by the bridge, and was startled to see only eight crypts still visible above the water. By my count, the crumbling remains of at least four tombs, all barely above water when I visited here the year before, were now gone. Completely submerged. With just ten months separating my two visits, I'm already a veteran witness of Louisiana land loss, equipped with my own startling anecdote to tell: "Why, I remember when a full quarter of the Leeville cemetery was still above water and you could see . . ."

When I mention the cemetery to Tim, he just nods his head knowingly and points to three burlap coffee-bean sacks sitting empty on the bayou bank below his camp. The week before, these huge sacks had held oyster shells which had now been dumped all along the bank and tamped down to create "land." Only now do I notice that a four-foot-wide band all along the bank is actually nothing *but* oyster shells. No dirt. No grass. Just shells. Like most people who live right on the bayou, Tim has had to build a chain wall along the bank behind which he's deposited some seventy-five or so sacks of shells like these, purchased at a nearby oyster shed for a dollar a sack, to keep his camp from joining the water completely.

"And did you see de Christmas tree *carré*?" Tim asks me, catching me up further on recent developments. He points down the bayou to the other side of Route 1 where hundreds of discarded and browning Christmas trees sit in the open water, piled on top of each other to form straight and porous barrier walls meant to protect the shore from erosion. The walls extend out from the shore to form square-shaped compounds, hence Tim's use of the French word *carré*.

"Dey built dose silly t'ings in February," he says.

Since my last visit, a United States AmeriCorps group composed mostly of high school and college kids had been formed along Bayou Lafourche to organize small community projects like this to help stave off land loss. The roughly three hundred feet of Christmas tree walls in Leeville absorb wave energy on their front side and create calm water on the back side, which, in theory, can induce enough sediment fallout from the still water to spawn marsh growth.

But Tim is skeptical, and at first glance the measure does seem a bit desperate, perhaps foolish. Even on a symbolic or experimental basis, Christmas trees are a crude tool for fighting a calamity of this magnitude. I later calculate that all the Christmas trees sold annually in America, set out in walls like this, would protect only about one-thousandth of the total Louisiana land in need of help.

Just seeing the *carré* has a depressing effect on me, and I figure that's what's bugging Tim, too. He definitely seems a little sad. He's noticeably distracted. He seems changed somehow. But it's not the Christmas trees, it turns out.

"Phyllis and Tee Tim have left me," he says as we climb the wooden steps up to his camp. "Dey been gone t'ree mont's now."

"Gone?" I say.

Sure enough, inside the camp, there's only Simba the collie and the usual pile of minnow and crab traps under construction by the living room couch. Over plates of warmed-over jambalaya laced with boudin (a Cajun-style sausage), Tim begins to explain what happened, and immediately I understand everything. Eighteen-year-old Tee Tim had made good on the pledge he'd made in my presence the year before: he'd gotten the hell out of this dying town and disappearing landscape.

Says Tim, "He just woke up one mornin' in January and said, 'Dat's it. I don't wanna crab no more. I'm tired of crabbin'.' It was as if crabbin' wadn't good enough for him no more and he could just quit and dollars would start fallin' outta de sky instead. So I tell him, 'You don't work, you don't live under my fuckin' roof, no sir.' And he says, 'Well, I ain't workin' on de water no more. I want a payin' job. A *real* job,' he calls it. So I kicked his ass right out de door."

Phyllis later tells me she stood by horrified, watching this collision as she folded laundry, trying to stay out of it. But then she watched Tee Tim get in his pickup truck, about to tear off up the bayou, swearing he'd never come back. With just four months remaining in Tee Tim's senior year of high school, Phyllis was petrified he'd make the same mistake she had and drop out, spending his adult life bereft of a diploma and likely underemployed. So over her husband's screaming objections, Phyllis took off with her son. And now she was living with Tee Tim in Galliano, first with her mom, then in a government-subsidized low-income apartment. For money, Tee Tim worked at a shipyard after school while Phyllis, a handy bayou woman, painted and repaired people's houses. Both of them were just hanging on until graduation day when Tee Tim would look for permanent shipyard work even farther up the bayou, severing permanently his ties to the old fishing world of Leeville. At that point Phyllis would have to decide her next step.

"I don't know if she's coming back or not," Tim tells me, pushing back his now empty plate and lighting a cigarette. "She's pretty mad at me for what I done. But what man worth his captain's hat would put up wit' a boy who don't wanna work? But I tell ya, I ain't cryin' no tears over it. Got no time to cry anyhow. De shrimp season is on us. It's time to work."

But Tim can't hide the cloud of grief and fear that's settled across his rough, sun-cured face. He has regrets, I can tell, but he's far too proud to give in, exhibiting a fierce stubbornness for which Cajuns are well known. To him, his son's departure is a rejection of a family way of life that runs bone deep, and his wife's departure is a double rejection.

But, as he said, there was no time to weep. The shrimp weren't going to wait. "Gotta get back to dat boat engine," he says.

We walk out the front door and onto the camp's large wooden porch where I pause for a moment. There, ten feet off the ground, elevated on pilings above the makeshift bank of oyster shells, I take a long and thorough look at the fishing docks of Leeville, Louisiana—and the sight is remarkable. Everywhere, all around us, up and down the bayou, fishermen like Tim are getting ready for the new shrimp season. Here a man is caulking his hull. There a man is painting his wheelhouse. From every direction a symphony rises: hammering, sanding, scraping, sawing, welding. Human beings are in constant motion, gliding across gangplanks, disappearing down hatches; arms are lifting, carrying; backs are bent. And all minds are thinking one thing: May 15th, sunrise, the shrimp season begins.

Out in the Gulf of Mexico, a man can shrimp year-round with no seasonal restrictions. But almost half of Louisiana's shrimp are caught "inside," meaning inside the barrier islands, in the marshland lagoons, lakes, bays, bayous, canals. In this interior landscape there are two seasons: the brown shrimp season running for usually fifty days beginning in early to mid May; and the white shrimp season running from mid-August to early December.

A majority of bayou shrimpers own boats in the twenty-five-to-fifty-foot range, too small to comfortably handle the rough seas (and often modest catch) of the Gulf of Mexico in winter. So most shrimpers take the winter off. They crab instead or do odd jobs for pay like carpentry, welding, oil-field work, tugboat work. But come April, everyone reports back for duty, and activity redoubles along the bayou as the entire local fishing fleet undergoes a makeover in preparation for May's opening day. Nets are checked and repaired, engines are tuned or overhauled, all cables, pulleys, and ropes are tested, because once on the water, everything must work as planned.

This is what Tim and I see as we stand there on his camp porch, looking down on a panorama whose energy is infectious and utterly hopeful. Someone tests a boat horn just then, letting go three deep blasts, robust and cheering. On this lovely spring day, a feeling of renewal and resurgence fills the air courtesy of nothing more complex than the reassuring joy of age-old routine.

But the scene is confusing, too. Looking out, I feel almost like I'm standing in a strange body of water where a fierce undertow lurks just below. On the surface, all is calm, the weather fair, the tide coming in as the Louisiana fishing industry busily and happily hangs on for one more year or maybe five more years or maybe twenty-five. But underneath, the current is going in the opposite direction at a much, much faster speed: Tee Tim's gone, the cemetery's gone, the land's almost gone, and the Christmas trees aren't making a bit of difference. It's all slipping away very fast.

Sooner or later there was going to be a reckoning of these two opposing currents. Then all previous arrangements would end. Then everything would be pulled apart.

Just like Tim and Tee Tim.


"After de waterspout hit, de boat sank so fast I don't t'ink Perry ever had a chance to get free of de boat," says Harry Pellegrin, standing in the middle of the Catholic cemetery in Dulac, Louisiana. "T.C. and Mike, dey waited dere on de surface of de water, tryin' to keep dere heads above de waves. But Perry, he never came up. He died down dere wit' de boat. He never came up."

Perry Falgout was at the helm that day last month when the cyclone of water slammed into the Lafitte skiff, sending him, Mike, and T.C. to the ocean bottom. I'm standing now next to Perry's marble-fronted tomb, a mausoleum adorned with dangling rosaries and fresh-cut cemetery flowers behind Holy Family Catholic Church, way up Bayou Grand Caillou. Harry Pellegrin, fifty-four, was Perry's stepfather, and Harry's verging on tears behind bifocal glasses, his unruly hair grayer than it was a month ago, as he leads me to Perry's shiny new crypt. Harry raised that boy from age seven and loved him very much, and nearly had a stroke—literally—when word came that following morning that he was missing and feared dead.

It's Sunday morning, the day of the Dulac boat-blessing ceremony, but the ceremony hasn't started yet. The parade of boats hasn't departed down the bayou to dispense the holy water and the memorial wreath. That's all ahead of us still. Right now, Harry Pellegrin, a shrimper and otter trapper himself, is simply explaining to me why there's going to be a wreath-laying ceremony at all this day, telling how the men died.

Mike and T.C., it turns out, spent ten long minutes waiting for Perry to surface that cold and stormy March morning. They waited long beyond the point of reasonable hope. T.C. was in a complete panic. He was a man of frail health, with a history of heart problems, and it was his boat that was now gone, lost for good. T.C. spent those desperate moments after the sinking praying out loud, begging God to save him from the storm as water repeatedly broke on top of him, soaking his head and face. He'd go silent, break into a fit of coughing, then begin praying again, trancelike.

As more minutes passed, Mike was about to suggest they give up and try to swim to shore when suddenly the praying stopped completely. Mike looked over to see T.C.'s face in the water, his head slumped forward and bobbing in the waves. He was dead. A heart attack. He couldn't be revived.

That's when Mike took off, swimming as best he could in

the turbulent sea, leaving behind his friends—T.C. above water, Perry below. For six hours, across three and a half miles of open sea, Mike struggled toward shore, his life preserver tucked under his body for buoyancy while he stroked. Just before sunset, shirtless, shoeless, dehydrated, and shivering, he finally crawled onto a narrow strip of uninhabited beach backed by miles of impenetrable marsh grass.

Wondering how anyone would find him in this remote spot, he began constructing a crude shelter under some mangrove bushes when he heard a noise. Against all odds, an offshore oil-rig helicopter was flying overhead, low enough and close enough for the pilot to make out a waving dot of a man on the beach below. The chopper had just enough room to land, and Mike was rescued, his ordeal finally over except for the nightmares he continued to have every night, reliving the incident over and over again.

"And de bodies," says Harry Pellegrin, swatting mosquitoes in the morning heat of the Holy Family cemetery, "dey found Perry a day later a mile west of Oyster Bayou. On de beach. He still had on his yellow slicker. Dey found T.C.'s body near de same spot."

The battered remains of the boat hull, meanwhile, would not be discovered for another several months, tangled up in a shrimp trawler's nylon nets.

"I'm not sure we'll ever get over dis," Harry says, his heavy Cajun accent now echoing softly against the whitewashed tombs all around us. The tombs, which spread back from the bayou to a distant stand of willows and an earthen flood levee beyond, bear names like LeBoeuf, Domangue, and Voisin; Boudreaux, Portier, Pitre, and Verdin.

And now: "Perry J. Falgout, March 5, 1963–March 16, 2000."

"He was always helpin' people," says Harry, adding an impromptu verbal epitaph. "He volunteered for charities and he died doin' a man a favor."

But as we talk there's no somber organ music floating down from the stained-glass windows of the old frame church behind us. There are no funeral bells pealing from the pine-board steeple. Instead, incongruously, our cemetery tour is animated by a bright stream of lively Cajun and country western tunes that fill our ears, spilling from the church's flung-open front doors. Inside those doors half the town is dancing and eating and dancing some more. There's bliss inside that building.

That's because this day is devoted to much more than just saying goodbye to Perry and T.C. Along the narrow, tea-brown bayou flowing just three hundred feet away, a shrimper is whistling to himself while putting the last decorative strips of bunting across his boat for the parade. He's wearing an Italian-made necklace medallion featuring a large anchor against a background of calm seas. Father Pilola distributed these during "the fishermen's mass" an hour ago. Another shrimper, with thick sideburns and cowboy boots and the same medallion around his neck, comes out of the church for a smoke, perspiring noticeably, then goes back in for another Cajun two-step.

After a long winter of typically lean times up and down the bayou, the shrimp season is finally about to reopen. Everyone, soon, will be working again. Money, sorely lacking from December to April, will flow once more. And thousands of bayou men across Louisiana will have the pleasure of doing what they do better than anything in the world: finding and netting shrimp.

That's why, this very same week, in towns throughout the bayou region, in Dulac and Chauvin and Golden Meadow; in Grand Isle and Lafitte and Galliano, the Blessing of the Fleet is greeted with such great cheer despite the looming dangers of the work and sad reminders of past losses. It's the last time many shrimpers will see their friends before heading out for months, usually by themselves with a deckhand or two, occasionally with wife and kids and even infants on board, into the backcountry for the age-old hunt. It's the last time they'll set foot in church too, there to receive the blessed bronze-colored medallions to protect them from storms, because after the season starts, Sundays will be spent on the water. For nearly a century, the blessing ceremony, "la Bénédiction des Bateaux," has helped bind these communities together, a ritual introduced from Europe by a French priest in Golden Meadow homesick for the familiar maritime ways of his fishing village back in Brittany.

Harry himself, a dedicated church volunteer, has been cooking Cajun food since four o'clock that morning in the church kitchen, stirring fifty-gallon pots of shrimp gumbo with a hand-carved wooden paddle, his eyes tearing up from dicing dozens of pounds of creole onions. He's still wearing the black bow tie and long green apron of the church serving line. The apron has a crawfish on it, saying *"Laissez les bons temps rouler."* Harry, despite everything, is trying his best to celebrate too. He really is.

"Come on," he says, pulling me away from the stony cold feel of the crypts. "Let's go get somet'ing to eat."


We head into the church, where a sensory mix of strumming guitars and aromatic food hovers over a wide wooden floor. The pews have been removed to make room for a dance floor, and dinner tables have been arranged in fifty-foot-long rows with folding chairs. Sunlight streams in through the arched stained-glass windows of this aging sanctuary, built just after the great Mississippi River flood of 1927. The church roof is a checkerboard of tar shingles and the building's foundation rests on two-foot-tall concrete stilts.

A stage has been set up where a pulpit and altar once stood, and a group of four musicians—all retired shrimpers—are playing an upbeat Cajun waltz below hardworking ceiling fans. An older couple have the dance floor to themselves at the moment, twirling their way across the room, arm in arm, the man's cheek pressed delicately at all times to the woman's, his legs in western-cut jeans, his arms adorned with various sailor tattoos. The band's missing an accordion player this morning, so there's just the two acoustic guitars and an electric bass and a pedal steel guitar, giving a twangy, soulful, and decidedly country feel to the French lyrics.

*"Et tu m'as quitté, et j'ai perdu mon idée,"* croons the lead singer as the old couple keep on waltzing and everyone else keeps on eating.

"Get you a plate of dis here," says Harry.

Across two long tables set up just in front of the musicians are pans full of shrimp boulettes, white beans and rice, shrimp jambalaya, chicken gumbo, and shrimp gumbo. Harry's pointing to the latter, and I grab a bowl and the serving ritual begins. First one woman piles a heap of fluffy white rice into my bowl, then another ladles on the gumbo: shrimp, peppers, celery, and onions in a deep, rich roux. A third server then sprinkles on a spoonful of filé, a thickening powder of dried sassafras leaves taken from a tree in Harry's backyard and first introduced to Cajuns generations ago by Choctaw Indians.

With a side order of potato salad, I sit down at one of the fantastically long tables and dig in. The rice is tender, the shrimp young and tasty, but what makes the dish a toe-curling experience is the broth, the roux. A mix of flour and animal fat and/or oil, it's cooked slowly, with regular stirring to prevent burning, until a nutty brown color and complex flavor emerges, serving as the canvas upon which so much Cajun artistry is then painted: gumbo, étouffée, sauce piquante, fricassee, soups.

Though primarily associated with Cajuns, gumbo is a dish evolved from many influences, reflecting the ethnic mix and shifting empires of Louisiana history. The very name, gumbo, is derived from the West African word *guingômbo*, meaning okra— the popular southern seedpod vegetable added to most gumbos. The filé, again, is an old Indian spice. The hot peppers and Tabasco sauce commonly served with gumbo evolve directly from the early Spanish colonizers of Louisiana. And the roux, the soul of the dish, is, of course, French.

I head back for seconds, adding a dollop of white beans for good measure, when one of the servers reminds me to save room because there will be lots more food on the boats. "We eat big," she says. "Your average Cajun recipe, it feeds five coon asses or three hundred regular people."

More people are dancing now, husbands with wives, grand-parents with grandchildren. The band pays token homage to American pop with the slowest rendition of the "Electric Slide" I've ever heard. Everyone sits down except a dozen women who launch into a bizarre, slow-motion version of line dancing.

Everybody else, meanwhile, is "visiting": lots and lots of talking over empty plates, people fanning themselves with church programs. This old sanctuary is used mostly for church functions now, a place to socialize, while formal Sunday mass is held next door in the larger, modern, blond-brick sanctuary. That's where Father Pilola handed out the medallions that morning amid a perfume of burning incense and pews lined with miniature wooden shrimp boats.

Having finished his own bowl of gumbo, Father Pilola, an Asian-American priest relatively new to this community, is now asking everyone to head toward the bayou to begin the parade.

Folding chairs begin to rake across the wood floor as the congregation slowly drifts out the front door and across the two-lane road to the bayou and the boats waiting on the other side. A dozen black-clad members of the Knights of Columbus, that curious Catholic fraternity of cape-wearing, saber-toting escorts in plumed hats, lead Father Pilola from the church steps to the parade's lead boat, the *Randy Boy,* captained by Terry Luke.

There at the bayou's edge we all gather around the priest: deacons, altar servers, babies in strollers, women carrying more pots of gumbo, boat captains with their new medallions around their necks.

"Let us pray," says Father Pilola, bowing his head in his white robe. "Today we gather to bless this lead boat and those who will use it for work or pleasure. The Lord calmed the Sea of Galilee and brought his disciples to safety. We commend those who sail this craft into his care."

The father then dips the vaguely mushroom-shaped metal aspergillum into the pail of holy water and sprinkles the *Randy Boy*'s hull amid the decorative and glittery shrimp and cardboard crosses taped there. With the lead boat now properly sanctified, Father Pilola boards and prepares to bless all the other vessels down the bayou. I join a couple dozen people pouring onto the *Randy Boy* and then watch as all the boats behind us fill up too along a bank fringed with canebrake and scattered live oaks veiled in Spanish moss.

Ahead of us, a Boston whaler Coast Guard vessel starts its engine and activates its flashing lights for escort duty, and we're off. Father Pilola plants himself at the windy bow, aspergillum in hand, and begins tossing water onto docked vessels of every shape and size that pass into view. Many of the boats are decorated and full of people and food just like the *Randy Boy,* and they join the tail of the parade as we pass, eventually expanding the chain to more than thirty vessels.

Onshore, people absent from the church feast are now waving and cheering and crossing themselves from under umbrellas in the intense sunshine and from the shade of back-porch rocking chairs. Parties and picnics abound atop wooden docks and across the grassy banks, each a composite of beer coolers, charcoal smoke, iced tea, and people looking up from plates of *cochon de lait* (roast suckling pig) or the ubiquitous steaming gumbo. We pass dirty, barefoot children outside doublewide trailers and wealthy oil-field workers barbecuing beside multistory brick homes with satellite dishes.

Father Pilola and his pigtailed altar server, Linzey Foret, wave and smile at the crowds and keep the holy water coming. Several times, in the brisk breeze, some of the water lands in a bracing mist across my face and arms, persuading me to leave the bow to liturgical doings. I head to the stern where the "swamp pop" band, three boats back, can be heard, led by head singer Joe LeBoeuf, who sings Hank Williams and Bob Seger in English and love ballads in Cajun French.

Across the *Randy Boy*'s middle deck, under a canopy of shrimp nets, sit myriad pots of food covered in aluminum foil, and thirty-gallon coolers keeping boiled crabs, shrimp, and crawfish steaming hot. A woman named Michelle hands me a plate of "mudbugs," the local name for crawfish. They're about five inches long and boiled to a bright red color. Michelle grabs a piece of corn on the cob and then shows me how it's done.

"First you tear off the head of Mr. Mudbug like this," she says, pinching the crustacean's neck and pulling. "Then you crush the head real good and squeeze out all that head juice onto your corn like this, and take a bite." She closes her eyes as if about to faint from pleasure, then keeps on talking, mouth full of corn, words muffled now. "Finally, you throw in the mudbug tail and you're done. Mmmmmmmmm-mmmm!"

I follow suit and, once again, my knees go weak from the profusion of flavors that seem to assault from every quarter down the bayou. The rich crawfish juice, laced with a peppery spice called "crab boil," mixes with the butter and salt and sweetness of the corn before the savory tail joins in, a meat so sumptuous a Cajun later describes its flavor as "shrimp meat and lobster meat making love."

I gratefully devour several more mudbug extravaganzas, then head back to the bow to talk to Father Pilola for a while. We've traveled far enough down the bayou that homes and docks are now widely spaced and the father can relax a little between blessings. He's leaning against a gunwale, the wind blowing against his forty-one-year-old baby face and tussling his thick black hair. He tells me he was born in New Jersey, the son of Filipino parents, and he's served as a priest to several bayou churches over the past twenty-three years. I can't help but ask how an outsider like him, one of different physical appearance to boot, has been accepted by this very rural parish. His answer is swift and full of eager sincerity.

"I've never felt anything *but* acceptance and love from these people," he says, beginning a response that dovetails with my own experience. "I mean, you never know what to expect from a new parish. But I was at this parish maybe a week when people started bringing me gifts of shrimp from their trawlers and garden vegetables and eggs from their hens. And I was in South Louisiana itself just a couple of years when the first Cajun family asked me to be a godfather—a *parrain*—to their child. In Cajun culture, that's a huge honor and responsibility. It was very flattering. And now I have *fifteen* godchildren and keys to

the homes of three different families because I've been allowed
to be so much a part of their families. It's been, like I said, total
acceptance. I've been more warmly treated here than back in my
father's native village in the Philippines."

A docked oyster boat drifts by and Father Pilola dutifully
casts water over the bow. He adjusts his windswept robe and
pushes his thick wire-rim glasses back to the bridge of his nose,
and keeps talking.

"What I love and admire about these people is how passionate they are about life. They eat, they drink, they enjoy themselves. It's a joie de vivre you just don't see everywhere. Most
Cajuns are really content with their world and who they are and
their work on the water. They're not trying to make a killing, a
million dollars. They save plenty of time for family and church
and good times. Like today." He motions to the long train of
boats behind us. "Incredible, isn't it?"

Hearing the passion in his voice, I can tell that Father Pilola
is a genuinely loving person and a gifted and dedicated priest.
He tells me that one focus of his work is to minister to deaf
people from throughout this bayou diocese, including those suffering from "Usher syndrome." These people are born deaf and
later go blind as well, an awful condition to which Cajuns are
many times more susceptible than other Americans, probably
because an original Cajun immigrant from France was a sufferer
and passed the condition down through the Cajuns' relatively
small gene pool in the New World.

So whenever Father Pilola gets a request, he travels the towns
and back bayou roads of South Louisiana visiting the homes of
Usher syndrome sufferers and speaking to them in the American Sign Language he's worked so hard to learn. Unable to hear
or see, these people "read" the priest's fingers, lightly touching
and feeling his hands. They then sign back their gratitude that a

father would travel so far to pray with them and share the Lord's message.

I'm moved by Father Pilola's descriptions, but also left curious. Why *do* all the priests down the bayou seem to come from so far away? Days earlier, phoning bayou churches to get boat-blessing dates, I spoke to priests from Vietnam, the Philippines, Ireland, New Jersey (original home to Fathers Pilola *and* Weber), and California. But very few Cajuns. Even the priests native to Louisiana were mostly non-Cajuns.

"It goes back to the history," says Father Pilola when I raise the subject. "You have to remember that for generations Cajuns were the low man on the pole in Louisiana. They were discriminated against, not just by the English-speaking people but by powerful, elite French Catholics in New Orleans who weren't of the same descent. The strange language of the Cajuns and the supposedly backwoods 'voodoo' ways were viewed with suspicion, and so investments in education were minimal here, and even today you find relatively few people down the bayou with college degrees. Men just drop out of school at an early age and work on the water. And unfortunately, without education, there's just no way to become a priest. So we have few Cajun fathers even now."

The oppression, however, didn't begin in America, Father Pilola reminds me. Long before coming to Louisiana, Cajuns were openly persecuted and made victims of the worst sort of ethnic cleansing. Indeed, the appearance of several Canadian maple-leaf flags along the parade route that day speaks to the long and sad migration of these people from the religious upheavals of seventeenth-century France to this backcountry Louisiana parade in the year 2000.

Most of the early Louisiana settlers who would later be known as Cajuns left Europe in the 1630s from an area around the town of Loudun, France, 170 miles southwest of Paris, in the modern province of Vienne. For decades, savage fighting between Protestants and Catholics tormented this region, leaving the population constantly at the mercy of marauding religious fanatics and foraging mercenaries. Famine, epidemics, and eventually witch-hunts compounded the misery until a despairing band of about three hundred Loudunais Catholic peasants boarded ships for a new life in North America in 1632.

Arriving barely a decade after the first English Pilgrims at Plymouth Rock, the Loudunais settled in present-day Nova Scotia, part of a colony founded for France by explorer Samuel de Champlain. The colony was named La Cadie, after the Micmac Indian word for "land of plenty." Later, perhaps because it sounded so similar to Arcadia, the Greek land of milk and honey, the colony came to be called l'Acadie, or Acadia. Accordingly, the industrious and frugal French settlers prospered quite well here as farmers and fishermen for more than a century until the French and Indian War of the 1750s.

When the British triumphed in that conflict, the Acadians (as the settlers now called themselves) steadfastly refused to swear allegiance to the British crown, and were harshly expelled in 1755 as a result. Families were loaded onto ships while their homes and crops were burned and their cattle confiscated. So began years of incalculable hardship and suffering as the British scattered the Acadians throughout the American colonies aboard poor, unseaworthy ships where disease took a terrible toll. One vessel departed Nova Scotia with 417 Acadians on board and arrived in South Carolina with only 210 still alive. On another ship, in Philadelphia, the Acadians were forced to stay on board for three months in the middle of winter.

At least 200 perished from smallpox and other diseases during this period.

Those who did survive faced religious and political persecution wherever they were sent, including the faraway West Indies and Falkland Islands. But when a small group of Acadians reached New Orleans in 1765, they discovered a rich land hospitable to French-speaking Roman Catholic settlers. Over the next thirty years, word of this new home spread among the scattered refugees. From across the hemisphere, Acadians painstakingly made their way to Louisiana, welcomed by the Spanish colonizers of the time, who saw the settlers as a much needed buffer against British encroachment.

The Acadians brought with them a tenaciously held sense of group identity spawned by the intense cooperation and mutual aid required by the Canadian wilderness experience. Having left France as a group, having been expelled from Nova Scotia as a group, they now strove mightily to find a new land somewhere, anywhere, upon which to come together once again.

And now they had it. By 1790 more than four thousand Acadians occupied the fertile wetlands along Bayou Lafourche and Bayou Teche where they fished, trapped, gathered Spanish moss, and, with time, raised sugarcane. Eventually they became known as Cajuns (the closest Anglo-Americans could come to pronouncing Acadians) and spread their presence north and west into the Louisiana prairie, raising cattle and planting rice.

Today the Cajun population of South Louisiana exceeds three-quarters of a million people. Close to half of those still speak or at least understand Cajun French, that distinct dialect based on Old French with words borrowed from the English, Spanish, African and Indian languages. The strong and enduring maritime tradition of these people—from France to Acadia to Louisiana—is reflected in the language. You "navigate" your automobile in Cajun French, for example. And *amarrer*, the verb for tying your shoes, is used in France today only in reference to the mooring of a boat.

Yet even in Louisiana, well into the twentieth century, Cajuns were treated as second-class citizens, viewed as hicks and swamp peasants across much of the state. This discrimination lessened as the Cajuns gradually became "Americanized," not always by choice, with the discovery of South Louisiana oil in 1901, the imposition of English-only schools in 1916, male service in two world wars, and the arrival of radio, television, and roads.

But the age-old bias and its lingering effects today have never stopped these devout and hardworking people from fully enjoying the milk-and-honey bounty of the coastal land. Few Cajuns may have gotten rich, but they always found fish and gators to catch in the bayous, muskrats to trap in the marsh, ducks to hunt in the fall. It's no wonder car license plates in Louisiana today still bear the motto "Sportsman's Paradise." For people who live directly off the land, that's just another way of saying "place of plenty." And for the past two hundred years, South Louisiana has been exactly that; it's been the quasi paradise those original Loudunais peasants dreamed of when they left France so many generations ago, enduring famine, war, shipwreck, persecution, and endless humiliations along the way before their progeny, at long last, settled here and prospered here, in Louisiana, across this vast and fertile coast, across this New Acadia.

This promised land.


The parade is nearing the halfway point and snowy egrets peek out from thick blades of marsh grass, eyeing us with curiosity as we pass, when someone opens the first huge cooler of boiled blue crabs aboard the *Randy Boy*. A cloud of wispy steam rises up on cue, revealing a dreamlike collection of bright red claws and armored bodies "begging" to be pried open and devoured.

Next comes the lid to the shrimp cooler, pulled back like a raised curtain to show tens of pounds of unpeeled lovelies, a small ocean, boiled and bearing that singular orange tint that alone can make one's mouth water.

Then comes the cooler of crawfish, and another of nothing but corn on the cob and whole potatoes boiled in their jackets. And on the middle deck, across two wooden tables, aluminum foil rattles as pots of gumbo and red beans and all the other dishes are unveiled. Barely an hour has gone by, but here we go again: another feast about to get under way.

It's early afternoon and I'm standing at the stern, glancing back now at the full necklace of colorful floating boats coming up behind us, making its way in the intense and breezy brightness. The parade party seems to be peaking with the overhead sun. People are crowding onto the bows, sitting on gunwales. Bodies dance, beer flows, seafood graces every plate. I see long-hulled double riggers with their high, haughty bows and smaller, more angular Lafitte skiffs, whitewashed and gleaming. I see old-fashioned luggers made entirely of wood, holding young boys on their fathers' shoulders, the boys wearing captain's hats while white-haired grandfathers sit on lawn chairs below shady overhanging nets. In the sparkling water of the widening bayou, scattered dolphins rise and fall as if in salute to this remarkable sight, paralleling the long line of vessels.

But when I head toward the bow, thinking to ask Father Pilola if he'd like a plate of the food being laid out, an entirely different scene, off to port, grabs my attention and slows me down. By now, of course, I'm nearly habituated to the sight: the knobby, leafless branches and sun-bleached trunks standing in open water like unburied bones. There must be a dozen of the old trees before me, the remains of a once green and shade-giving place, a large tract of land completely lost in the past twenty years.

Since the start of the parade, in defiance of the festive air, the evidence has been abundant: the long stretches of riverbank held together only by oyster shells; the eroding oil-company canals crisscrossing the bayou, devouring land left and right; the several forests of sinking trees like this.

And amid the laughter and lively banter of this annual celebration, I've heard the voices off to the side, serious comments made in dark tones. It's a low-frequency background noise of worry, the words spoken not quite loud enough to upset the mood or startle the children, but there nonetheless, overheard in snippets and snatches.

An old man tells another: "I put a 'No Hunting' sign on my property in September, don't you know. Dat sign, it was four feet from de water's edge when I put it up. But when I come back in April, it was four feet *in* de water. De shore moved eight feet in seven mont's."

A young shrimper tells another: "No, listen, you *can* get your boat through that pass now. It used to be you needed a pirogue [a flat-bottom canoe] to squeeze through that small opening. But now it's wide enough for oil barges, I swear."

Michelle, the teacher of mudbug etiquette, draws me to the side and points: "You see those kids swimming along the bayou? We used to play baseball right there. That was home plate where they're swimming."

The irony, of course, is monumental, full of old sorrow and boundless bad luck. After years of painful history, after so many years of searching, the Cajuns of the Louisiana bayou country are being expelled, once again, from their land.

So when Father Weber emerges from the wheelhouse just then, carrying the wreath of two dozen carnations, it's not just the dead fishermen T.C. and Perry who are being memorialized, though the fact goes politely unspoken up and down the boat. By the time I reach the bow where Father Pilola is still standing, I forgo all talk of food and simply ask him the obvious question: How in the world do his parishioners cope with all of this? How do these fishing families, these Cajuns who in the father's own words cherish this life and this landscape with all their might—how do they deal with the fact that it's all sliding toward a memory?

"It's hard on them," he says. "No question about it. Especially the older people who've seen so much of it disappear. Part of them dies every day with the land. But for a lot of people the situation is just too big to comprehend. It's so overwhelming. I mean, the *land* is disappearing. How many places in the world can people say that?"

Captain Terry Luke has begun slowing down his boat engines and turning the *Randy Boy* around. The parade will go no farther downstream than this point. In a moment he'll cut the engines completely so a prayer can be said for the deceased.

"Maybe it goes back to the lack of education here," says Father Pilola, continuing, "but there's a feeling that the problem's so much bigger than the people who live here, and so there's nothing to be done but watch it happen, as painful as that may be. I mean, what can you do to stop a hurricane? It's sort of on that scale in their minds. The big picture just overwhelms people so they just don't think about it. That's how they deal with it."

This sort of mental paralysis—better described as denial—is one of the region's biggest enemies, I learn later, given that several concrete countermeasures to coastal land loss *are* actually in hand, ready to be implemented, waiting only for sufficient funding and the broad-based support of shrimpers and other bayou people to light fires under political leaders.

Moments later, as if he, too, wanted to change the painful subject, Father Pilola abruptly says to me, "Come on. It's time to throw the wreath."

We head to the windy stern where Father Weber, dressed in sandals, slacks, and clerical collar, says his short and solemn prayer below the mad-flapping decorative flags. The wreath then hits the water and begins floating silently away, toward the wide-open sea beyond. Having paid their respects, having uttered a soft chorus of "amens" as the wreath goes overboard, the crowd of families standing near Father Weber now turns to confront the fine array of food laid out before them. Someone flips the music back on atop the upper deck and, just like that, the boat returns to the happy atmosphere of a parade, a floating party.

It's time to slip back into the Cajun spirit, to resuscitate the joie de vivre. The mood on the deck seems to be saying, "Sssshhhh. Don't talk about it. Please don't. Why spoil this fine, fine day? Why not have some crabs and shrimp and maybe a small serving of hope too? Let's just enjoy . . . for now."

And so I head to the tables, too, bearing a fresh appetite born of the fresh and dazzling smells. Immediately I notice that all those large and round serving trays stacked by the dozens next to the tables all afternoon are not serving trays at all. They're plates! Someone hands me one—it has the circumference of a small bicycle wheel—and then a half dozen hands and serving spoons appear from all directions until my "plate" is covered with crab claws and shrimp and numerous other delights piled high.

More coolers of ice-cold beer are dragged from the wheel-house, and I crack one open and watch Father Weber and others do the same, and then I find a seat along the starboard gunwale and begin peeling my shrimp and cracking my crabs and forking my jambalaya.

And that's when, finally, it dawns on me. Something about this daylong ritual has seemed familiar all along, but I couldn't put my finger on it until now: lots and lots of food, more food than anyone can eat, in an impossibly great array of dishes; family and friends gathered together for an all-day custom pegged to the harvest of good food from the good earth. It is, quite simply, Thanksgiving. Up and down the bayou on this late April Sunday, it's Thanksgiving Day.

The music, the beer, the dancing, the cigars that soon will be passed around—they're all acts of gratitude for the age-old bounty of the water and the land and the lives lived here for so long. Thanks for the crabs and the oysters. Thanks for the fish and the shrimp. *Especially* the shrimp, provider of work for the greatest number of families. Suddenly it makes sense to me the verb Cajun shrimpers often use to describe a good catch. "The shrimp were really *giving* last night," a captain might say, standing onshore with his handsome take. Or, out on the water, a man tells you, "Let's not head in yet. The shrimp are still giving nicely."

For as long as anyone can remember, the shrimp of coastal Louisiana have been boundlessly generous, appearing each spring, right on time, virtually without fail, and giving freely to the Cajuns. It's only proper, then, to offer thanks at least once a year with a fervent day of feasting. The shrimp themselves, of course, are here entirely on account of the land: this magnificent artwork of wetlands, this huge ragged sole of the Louisiana boot, itself a gift of the Mississippi River, taken from all over America over the past seven thousand years and *given* to Louisiana. Fecund and handsome, the land offers a cornucopia of nourishment far surpassing the best harvest of Indian corn and butternut squash on any Pilgrim's plate.

So sitting there with my own enormous plate of food, I chase away the bad thoughts, too, and say my own silent thanks and let my mind wander back to the very start of this parade when Father Pilola stood before the congregation, all heads bowed, all boats ready to go, and finished his soft-spoken prayer:

> *God of boundless love . . .*
> *Protect [these fishermen] from the danger of wind and rain*
> *and all the perils of the deep.*
> *May Christ who calmed the storm and filled the nets of his*
>   *disciples*
> *bring us all to the harbor of light and peace.*

# Four

"Let's put it this way," says Kerry St. Pé, steering his pickup truck, "the White Stallion," past a freshwater swamp north of Houma, Louisiana. "If a foreign enemy were taking away twenty-five square miles of American soil from us every year—year after year—just taking it away from this nation and not giving it back, we would certainly go to war to stop it, wouldn't we? *Wouldn't we?*"

He clenches his jaw and shoots me a pinched smile below serious brown eyes. He lets the question hang there in the cab of the truck for a long time. I glance past him at the green water along the road where alligators live and where crawfish have built hundreds of mud "chimneys" at the swamp's edge.

"And yet," Kerry continues, "that's exactly what's happening in Louisiana. Every year, twenty-five square miles of land disappears, simply gone, subtracted from this nation, and we're letting it happen. As a country, we're not fighting a war to stop it. Or if we're fighting a war, we're totally, totally losing it. By no stretch of the imagination are we winning."

Fifty-year-old Kerry St. Pé is a homegrown conservationist and marine biologist, a man of French Creole descent raised in the bayou country south of New Orleans in Plaquemines Parish. He's as passionate as anyone about the region's wonders (he's got a laminated crab in his office painted the colors of Mardi Gras—green, gold, and purple), and today he wants me to step inside a small aircraft and take a trip with him.

"The *only* way to fully comprehend what's happening to Louisiana's coast is to see it from the air," he says in the lush, lilting accent of a southern intellectual. "To comprehend the sheer scale of the situation, you have to look down on it from above."

It's also the only way to get an inkling of how the coast might be saved, he adds.

But before we get to the airfield, we pass through the town of Houma itself, population 37,000. This is the parish seat of Terrebonne Parish and the de facto capital of Louisiana's deep bayou country. Consistent with the watery landscape all around, no fewer than three bayous and one navigation channel converge on this city of bridges, creating "the Venice of America," a place where many streets are two-lane avenues split down the middle by bayous. In Houma one finds scattered antebellum plantation homes built on sugarcane money, downtown banks flush with oil-field earnings, street-corner grocers run by Vietnamese merchants, and an old and pillared courthouse caressed by the serpentine branches of hundred-year-old live oaks.

This historic Cajun city is emblematic of decline, too, of

course. It lies just thirty-five miles north of a seacoast which is moving inland at an average rate of half a mile per year in places. Portions of the city are just two feet above sea level on land that is sinking at a rate of four feet per century. And the city's main source of drinking water is increasingly contaminated by saltwater intrusion, forcing officials to draw water from a bayou north of town which drains a murky swamp.

Kerry St. Pé has dedicated most of his career to trying to prevent exactly these sorts of costly impacts born of ecological collapse. As we pull up to the Houma-Terrebonne Airport south of town, gravel crunching underneath Kerry's truck in a simple parking lot, he tells me that coastal wetlands have always been his first love. He spent a "totally idyllic" childhood exploring the endless marshes around Port Sulphur, Louisiana, hunting doves and ducks, investigating every backcountry bayou, swimming off a wooden dock, and informally cataloging every living creature he could find.

"My dad used to say we never could keep a glass jar inside our house because of all the pets I made out of turtles and frogs and minnows and crabs."

At an early age, Kerry knew he wanted a career working in the marsh, protecting these wetlands from the sort of gross human abuses well established even back in the 1950s. So for twenty-three years after college he worked all along the coast as a water pollution field biologist for the state government. He documented fish kills caused by pesticide runoff from sugarcane fields. He testified in court against corporate polluters, including in a landmark action brought by the U.S. Environmental Protection Agency against a Louisiana company selling hazardous waste as a road-surfacing material.

But his most important targets were the oil companies and their myriad destructive practices. His greatest success came in

1990 when a study he authored demonstrated the marsh-killing effects of the then common practice among oil companies of dumping toxic brine (a by-product of deep underground drilling) into large and unstable waste pits in the marsh. The same year Kerry's report was made public, the state passed regulations banning the practice permanently.

Throughout these many and hard-fought battles, what motivated and sustained Kerry more than anything were memories of his youth. In Port Sulphur in the 1950s, as across much of southern Louisiana still today, young kids anxiously awaited their first boat the way other American children await their first bicycle. When Kerry finally got one at age twelve to share with a neighbor (an eight-foot aluminum flatboat with a 3.5-horsepower Evinrude) he began embarking on epic Huck Finnesque adventures deep into the farthest reaches of the marsh, following bayous so obscure they had no names.

Miles and miles from home, he would camp on small, magically forested islands resting in utter isolation amid the ocean of spartina grass. These were remnants of old barrier islands created by the Mississippi River and left behind long ago when the river delta pushed farther out into the Gulf of Mexico. To a boy's imagination, these uninhabited islands were deeply mysterious places, their interior dark as night from the dense, tangled stands of live oaks hung with Spanish moss and studded with palmettos and creeping vines, the whole place made more intriguing—and slightly dangerous somehow—by the wild cries of unseen birds wafting down to a silty soil said to hold the treasure of long-ago pirates and the heroic dead of forgotten Indian warriors. With a cast net and 20-gauge Mossberg shotgun, Kerry would hunt for food, then watch at sunset from his shoreside camp as brown shrimp and speckled trout boiled the surface of nearby marsh ponds. The golden-green spartina grass, stretching away in every direction, seemed to obliterate all sense of time and space before slowly bursting into flames before his very eyes, a billion trillion delicate blades erupting in the orange and rose-pink light of a dying sun, creating each time the most beautiful painting Kerry St. Pé had ever seen in his life. And he was sitting right in the middle of it.

But today, on this first day of May 2000, as Kerry sits in the cab of his truck describing these wonderful playgrounds of his childhood, the places themselves no longer exist, having all turned to open water years ago. The bayous, the lakes, the forests, the magical islands—all gone. It's not unlike having your house burn down with all your childhood mementos in it, he tells me. Baseball cards, photographs, trophies. The loss is absolute.

Which is one of the reasons he accepted, in 1997, the position of director of the Barataria-Terrebonne National Estuary Program (BTNEP). This cooperative local-federal program, launched in 1990 under the U.S. Clean Water Act, is charged with assessing problems and finding solutions related to land loss in what's known as the Barataria-Terrebonne basin. This vaguely triangular swath of land is bordered by the Mississippi River to the east, the Atchafalaya River to the west, and Pointe Coupee Parish to the north. With nearly four million acres spilling down toward an outer coastline two hundred miles wide, this vast area includes all of Bayou Lafourche, Bayou Grand Caillou, Bayou Petit Caillou, Terrebonne Bay, Barataria Bay, more than ten barrier islands, and hundreds of towns including Leeville, Golden Meadow, Dulac, Chauvin, and Houma. At least 85 percent of Louisiana's total land loss is occurring within the Barataria-Terrebonne estuarine system, and Kerry calls BTNEP's educational, scientific, and community-organizing components "the last, best chance to save what's left of the Louisiana coast." Today, in a borrowed plane, he wants to give me an aerial inventory of just what he and his organization are up against.

Of course, no one can save the marshland of Kerry's child-hood. His hometown, Port Sulphur, still exists, huddled behind massive levees, but the marsh beyond is all gone. Yet as we get out of Kerry's pickup truck and begin walking toward the air-port terminal—made of bricks and tin siding—Kerry mentions that his daughter is having a baby in July. It's her first child. His first grandchild. And boy or girl, that child's going to want a boat to explore the marsh that remains in Louisiana. So there's lots of work to be done, Kerry says. Lots and lots of work.


Once inside the terminal, my immediate concern is the orange wind sock I see in the distance, edging the runway. It's main-taining a mostly horizontal posture, changing directions with each erratic gust of wind. The morning air is very sticky, the humidity almost 100 percent, the sky a jumble of low-lying clouds. The radio on the way over warned of heavy storms and "tornadic activity" approaching from Texas.

Having just attended a memorial ceremony for two men killed by a waterspout, I can't help but pace the terminal lobby, a frown on my face. But Kerry, in his conservative wire-rim glasses and preppy button-down shirt, assures me we'll be fine. He's got a top-notch pilot on the way and we won't be up in the air more than an hour anyway, well ahead of any storms.

When the pilot, Bruce Stamey, arrives a few minutes later, he's completely calm and turns out to be a real joker. Kerry tells Bruce I'm interested in writing about coastal land loss and Bruce deadpans, "You better hurry!"

We walk out onto the tarmac, passing an emergency fleet of oil-industry planes ready at a moment's notice to spray chemical dispersants on any oil spills occurring offshore. This airfield was first built in 1943 to accommodate bomb-laden American blimps hunting Nazi submarines in the Gulf of Mexico. Now it's a hub for oil-field helicopters and airplanes.

As I climb into the cockpit of Bruce's plane, a small twin-engine Aerocommander, he apologizes for the absence of a stewardess. "She sprang a leak," he says. "And I haven't been able to patch her yet."

He then points to my seat belt and adds, "Make sure you buckle up tight. It's the difference between a closed and open casket." The joke has its intended effect: I lose my jitters in a burst of laughter.

Once we take off and the plane roars to a low cruising altitude of 750 feet, there are fewer opportunities for humor. I peer out my side window as the runway falls away, replaced by a wetland world stretching in almost every direction. Three blunt adjectives describe the unfolding scene below. It's flat. It's green. It's vast. Unfathomably vast.

"Amazing, isn't it?" Kerry says. He's seated just behind me in the tight fuselage, speaking to me through the radio headsets we both wear. Together we look out at a network of forested swamps and a full prairie of marsh grass stretching to the horizon, interspersed with winding bayous, shallow lakes, canals, inlets, ponds. Though we're pointed south, the Gulf of Mexico cannot yet be seen, just this gigantic tabletop, this fantastic pale green plane, which is both land and water, vegetation and liquid, all at the same time. The dramatic visual data gives weight to the implausible statistics: from the Mississippi state line to the faraway Texas border, beginning just below us and stretching in both directions, lie 20 percent of America's total coastal wetlands and a full 40 percent of its salt marshes.

Just now, in the far distance, I can make out the shape of

Lake Boudreaux, where I trawled last summer with Charlie and Wayne. Kerry points out a freshwater swamp directly below us, its glassy black water seen in glimpses between the obscuring crowns of cypress, swamp maples, tupelo gums, and wax myrtle. Somewhere down there may even be the increasingly rare alligator "loggerhead" snapping turtle, some of which grow to two hundred pounds, live 250 years, and are occasionally found even today with arrowheads and Civil War-era bullets lodged in their shells.

But these visual pleasures don't last. For a good five miles to the west, almost to the horizon, stand the bleached and blackened trunks of long-dead cypress trees protruding from the water. When a navigation channel was dug in 1962 between Houma and the Gulf of Mexico, salt water rushed into this vast sweet-water swamp, killing all freshwater plant life in its path and leaving these ghastly remains.

"Such a waste!" Kerry says through his headset. "A complete waste of a God-given gift."

Louisiana's mammoth salt marsh now begins to dominate the landscape below. With the Gulf just coming into focus to the far south, I suddenly recognize Bayou Grand Caillou and the spot where we laid the wreath yesterday. On either side of the bayou, in various lakes and inlets fringed with grass, long-hulled oyster boats can be seen working these lonely backcountry wetlands, harvesting from rich beds which produce more oysters than any other state in America: ten million pounds of oyster meat per year.

We also see small crab boats with outboard motors, each vessel following its own connect-the-dots maze of floats attached to underwater traps full of bait fish and scurrying blue crabs. In a week, these same waters will be chock-full of shrimp boats as the "inside" shrimping season begins.

The health of the marsh grass, meanwhile, varies markedly

from area to area. In some places, a rich green-gold carpet of waist-high blades expands unbroken for hundreds of yards, interrupted only by the natural flow of a meandering bayou or a scattering of marsh ponds dotted with herons and glossy ibis.

But these areas form a distinct minority. Most of what we see on this cloudy prestorm morning, traveling 160 miles an hour above the mind-numbingly flat expanse, is marsh grass in varying stages of a slow-motion march toward death.

"See that right there?" Kerry says, pointing down. "See how that big area of grass is starting to fragment and break up? See how the stalks are growing in clumps and tufts and in little islands surrounded by water? That grass is dying. It's drowning. Wherever you see that sort of fragmentation in what should otherwise be a continuous expanse of grass, the marsh is succumbing."

Unfortunately, this pattern of fragmentation—albeit in varying degrees—is practically everywhere. I look up from where Kerry is pointing and suddenly this entire wetlands complex takes on the appearance of a colossal piece of cloth bearing the same unending design: solid grass, fragmentation, water. Solid grass, fragmentation, water.

And as each square foot of grass dies, so does the root system holding together the delicate soil below. Once the roots decompose completely, erosion quickly follows and another square foot of America has converted to open water.

"And why is the grass breaking up and drowning in the first place?" Kerry asks, reviewing the basic dynamics of coastal decline. "Because all this land, as far as you can see, is sinking. It's subsiding. And it's an entirely *natural* process. This coast has always been sinking."

This is because the sand, silt, and clay deposited by the

Mississippi River for the past seven millennia is still settling. Organic material trapped throughout the soil is still in the process of decomposing and water trapped in the soil is being squeezed out by natural compaction, causing the whole land-mass to shrink in volume. In the past, this was counterbalanced by the spring floods of the Mississippi, bringing new sediments from as far away as the Black Hills of South Dakota and the coal-mining regions of Pennsylvania.

"This estuary system is simply starved for sediments," Kerry says. "Literally starved. It's that basic."

According to one estimate, the Mississippi deposited an average of 85 million tons of sediments across coastal Louisiana each year until the river was shackled for good in the 1930s. That's enough in a decade to cover almost half the state of Delaware with a foot of soil.

"So how do we get sediments on that scale back into the system?" Kerry asks as another blur of damaged marsh passes below. "There aren't enough dump trucks and barges in all of America to bring soil like that into these wetlands. We've got to turn to the Great River itself again."

He's referring to what may be Louisiana's only hope: a proposed ninety-five-mile-long "controlled diversion" of the lower Mississippi River—essentially an earthen ditch on a colossal scale which would bring as much as a third of the lower Mississippi's flow straight down from a point north of here, starting at a bend in the river near Donaldsonville, Louisiana. Nearing the coast, this man-made river, larger than the Mississippi itself where it passes St. Louis, Missouri, would bifurcate, dumping its water on either side of Bayou Lafourche, straight into the vast but receding wetlands north of Barataria Bay and Terre-bonne Bay. This, theoretically, would save hundreds of thousands of acres of marshland now at risk while creating even more marsh over time, forming two new surgically engineered "subdeltas."

This new source of sediment is needed not only to counteract the subsiding land but to help heal the wound of the oil-industry pipeline canals and navigation channels. From the air, the presence of these man-made waterways—I've counted dozens since we took off—is almost surreal. There are no straight lines in nature, so the runwaylike precision of the canals is startling to the eye, wildly incongruous amid the natural curves of the bayous and lakes. The canals, of course, are like poison to an already ill patient, so deadly is the erosion they cause. Scientists at Louisiana State University (LSU) estimate that no less than a third of the total coastal-zone degradation can be traced directly to canals, and note that, once dug, these canals tend to *double their width every fourteen years.*

Many oil-company waterways are no longer used, abandoned long ago as thousands of oil and gas wells have gone dry. But without new sediment to fill them in, the canals just keep growing. Combine this with the already sinking and deteriorating marsh, and suddenly—as our plane begins approaching the state's apron of barrier islands—there's more open water below us than grass. The balance has tipped and the marsh has become the Gulf.

Kerry shakes his head at all the water down below. "And I don't need to remind you," he says above the roar of the propellers, "that without the marsh there *will* be no fishing industry in this state."

A full 95 percent of all the fish and shellfish caught commercially in Louisiana depend on the wetlands as a nursery and/or source of food at some point in their life cycles. "Take away the marsh and you fatally disrupt the life cycle of all those species—shrimp, crabs, oysters, fish. That's not only an ecological disaster. It's a billion-dollar annual fishing industry gone. A *billion* dollars—with untold working families wiped out."

But Kerry has saved his most dramatic image for last.

We're almost to the Gulf of Mexico when Bruce begins to circle around, taking us on a course almost due east. Up ahead, the first of Louisiana's major barrier islands comes into view, a three-mile-long uninhabited strip of sand, marsh, and bushy mangroves roughly paralleling the mainland, called Raccoon Island.

My first thought as we draw closer is to wonder why the whole island doesn't sink just from the weight of all those birds swarming its surface from tip to tip. Below my window are thousands of them: brown pelicans, sandwich terns, roseate spoonbills, black skimmers, several species of herons and egrets, including the uncommon reddish egret. No fewer than thirty-thousand pairs of adult birds nest on this small island alone, creating a tight, Manhattan-like puzzle of neighborhoods: terns nesting in the marsh, pelicans with eggs near the dunes, roseate spoonbills parenting in the bushes.

"And we're not even seeing the migrant songbirds from Central America," says Kerry. "They literally fall out of the sky here in the spring, exhausted and starving, this being the first land they see after their flight over from Mexico. They've all moved on to the mainland now."

This island scene is at first quite encouraging: critical bird habitat well utilized and seemingly well protected, far from any human disturbance. But the situation *around* the island dampens the optimism. For several miles to the rear of Raccoon Island there's no marsh at all, nothing but open water, part of the ever-growing expanse of Caillou Bay.

"There are older people alive today," Kerry says to me

through the headsets, "people still living along the coast, who could once ride horses out to barrier islands like this one. The marsh extended all the way out here, and you could follow on foot or on horses along forested ridges of land. People still breathing have done it. Now it's water."

The situation is even more unsettling on the island's front side, where a thin strip of white beach faces the Gulf. Pounding that beach at the moment are white-capped waves rolling in relentlessly from an ocean made frothy and angry by the fast-approaching storm system from Texas. It's hard to describe just how bullied and vulnerable Raccoon Island looks below the plane's wings. With an entire ocean on one side spoiling for a fight and the expansive bay just behind offering no supportive cover whatsoever, this long, thin island is caught in the middle, barely one hundred feet wide in some places, looking as lonely and fragile and overwhelmed as a matchstick in a roaring river.

The situation is fatal, in fact. Due to the lack of new river sediment flowing down from the mainland and the battering effects of hurricanes and lesser storms, plus other factors not yet fully understood by scientists, Raccoon Island—like all of the state's barrier islands—is eroding and disappearing at a rate just as alarming as that of the marshland behind it. Beaches and barrier islands worldwide tend to move and change shape, of course, disappearing here only to reappear elsewhere in a natural migration of coastal sand and silt. But Louisiana's beaches and islands are situated on rapidly sinking land, so there's little or no chance to re-form.

"Tens of feet per year," Kerry tells me. "That's how much the beaches on these barrier islands recede on average each year. Tens of feet. It doesn't take long to vanish totally at that rate."

After we pass over Raccoon Island and its magical mosaic of

bird life, we see up ahead in the open water a conspicuously large area of white-capped waves breaking with uniformity over an area that appears to be an unseen shoal of sand. And that's exactly what it is. "That used to be an island right there," Kerry says. "What's left is under the surface. We've lost it already."

Bruce, the pilot, such a card back on shore, has been mostly silent. But now his voice fills my headset. "I've been flying out here for twenty years and I can't even begin to explain to people what I've seen. It's like a different place each time I fly over this coast. It just leaves you speechless."

Kerry's not even sure of the name of the next barrier island we come to. "These islands keep fragmenting with each big storm, and the new pieces are given new names and it's hard to keep up."

As it turns out, the next three islands in the chain following Raccoon are called Whiskey, Trinity, and East Islands. They are spread out over a twenty-mile arc, and at the beginning of the nineteenth century, all four islands were *one* island—one long, continuous apron of land called Isle Derniere which guarded the fragile wetlands to the rear like a wall. Today that original land area is 78 percent gone, with the four ragged offspring islands hanging on for dear life. Without some sort of major human intervention soon, most estimates are that almost all of Louisiana's dozen or so major barrier islands will be gone in fifty years. Which is bad news in more ways than one.

"There's a reason they're called 'barrier' islands," Kerry says. "This is the first line of defense against hurricanes. Without these islands, a hurricane's storm surge will slam right into the coast unchecked. Then it'll meet the remains of our shrinking marshes, facing little resistance. Then it's straight into the population centers. The next time a direct-hit hurricane comes, I'm afraid it might be really, really ugly."

Without the islands the fishing industry will be finished as well, its nursery grounds and critically important brackish bays done in by the saltier water of the inrushing Gulf.

All of which, again, is why Kerry has remained in the field all these years, as close to the front line of this battle as possible. The high-stakes implications of everything we've just seen are why he's turned down myriad job promotions offering him desk work up in Baton Rouge, overseeing various environmental programs. He's said no again and again out of fear of being silenced by the blizzard of paperwork, slowed by the bureaucratic pressure to compromise and proceed cautiously, if at all. He's made it a point, instead, to keep his home and office within walking distance of Bayou Lafourche all these years, right in the heart of the estuary system, so he can be a "swamp agitator," able to scream and shout in a way that policymakers can't easily ignore.

It's not been easy, though. He's depended on his wife's salary as a Catholic school teacher to help cover the bills of two growing children and a mortgage as he's turned down promotion after promotion and all the attendant pay raises. "She's basically helped finance my career," he says. But the decisions themselves have not been hard, the sacrifices worth bearing, for one simple reason:

"Time's running out on us," he says.

Another vanished barrier island passes below us, its location marked by the sudden appearance of rows of whitecaps passing desolately over the resultant shoal.

"The final calamity is coming," Kerry says. "It's breathing right down our neck and we have very, very little time to do something to keep it from happening."

By "calamity," he means the obvious: the collapse of fishing, the death of endangered birds and habitat, the drowning of human beings by hurricanes. And by "doing something" he means a radical, massive human intervention which protects and restores existing landforms before they disappear almost entirely.

"There's no way we can let it all disappear, *then* decide to save it," says Kerry. "We can't go out and rebuild from scratch ninety miles of barrier islands out in the open water of the Gulf of Mexico. We can't let our last three million acres of wetlands vanish, let the shrimp and crab populations collapse and disappear, let the birds become extinct, and *then* start diverting the sediments and nutrients of the Mississippi River into the wide-open Gulf. It won't work. It'd take too long to bring the system back. There's a point of degradation beyond which resuscitation in any meaningful sense is made essentially impossible, according to our leading geologists and biologists. And we're fast reaching that point. It's right on top of us."

To support the claim, Kerry and others point to the geologic record showing it took the Mississippi River seven thousand years to create the six thousand square miles of Louisiana wetlands known to have existed as late as the 1880s. Then, in the blink of an eye, in just over a century, almost a third of that land—1,800 square miles—disappeared due to human interference. Simply put: the land disappears much, much faster than it can be re-created even with the most ambitious restoration plan. Many factors work against quick restoration, including the new burden of the Gulf's rising sea level—triggered by global warming—and the fact that no more than 40 percent of the lower Mississippi can be diverted into the coastal marshes for land-building purposes, the rest required to flow past New Orleans and out the river's mouth to sustain ship navigation. Add to this the fact that the sediment load of the Mississippi itself has dropped dramatically—50 percent since 1950—due to the construction of sediment-trapping dams along the Missouri River and upper Mississippi. Most scientists believe that even a massive diversion of the Mississippi would take well over a thousand years just to re-create the 1,800 square miles of coast-land lost since the 1880s.

The goal, then, restoration advocates say, must be to pre-serve what land is left through conservation measures proven through experimentation to stabilize and gradually expand the currently deteriorating grasses. But because the disappearing act is happening so quickly, and because it will take some time to implement a full restoration plan and more time still to pro-duce major results, most advocates believe the state has only about ten to twenty years to really get things under way, after which there just won't be much land left to save.

Suddenly, on the plane, there is a new level of urgency in Kerry's voice. He's like a pastor now, reaching the climactic moment of delivery. He unbuckles his seat belt and leans for-ward, his head now poking between the two front seats occu-pied by Bruce and myself.

"Seven thousand years it took the Mississippi to build everything we see around us." He gestures out the windshield. "Seven *millennia*. Seventy *centuries*. And now it all comes down to just ten or twenty years if we really want to save what's left. That's our window of opportunity."

He leans back in his seat, having made his point, sighing audibly into the headsets. He rebuckles his seat belt and adds, "If we don't do something really, really big—really, really soon—that narrow window closes. It slams shut. And that's that."

Way back in 1718, Jean Baptiste Le Moyne, sieur de Bienville, knew nothing of the seven-thousand-year history of the Mississippi River and the uncompromising dynamics of river delta formation. So he had no way of realizing what he was setting in motion when, acting on behalf of the king of France, he chose a looping bend of the lower Mississippi as the site of what would eventually become the city of New Orleans. Le Moyne's engineers, recognizing the hopelessly flood-prone nature of the site, immediately began throwing up crude levees to hold back the current.

So began nearly three centuries of human struggle against the formidable river: the fashioning of ever more elaborate levees, spillways, locks, jetties, and other structures designed to completely corset the lower Mississippi. For the region to prosper, it was considered absolutely critical to protect crops and settlements from inundation and to maintain safe and dependable navigation routes.

But never in the history of humankind, stretching back to the ancient delta civilizations of Egypt and Asia, had a river this big been controlled to this degree. Southern Louisiana was to be a grand experiment. The closest example of modern man dominating so large an estuary system was the Netherlands, a nation whose very name means "lowlands." Over the centuries, this European country had leveed the estuarine lower sections of the Rhine, Meuse, and Scheldt Rivers, then carried out the systematic conversion of immense wetlands to farmland, pumping out water with windmills as far back as the sixteenth century.

Over the years, Louisiana adopted core aspects of the Dutch model: flood-control levees, dredged canals for navigation, forced drainage of swamps, large-scale marshland elimination. And eventually Louisiana got exactly the same results: the land began sinking.

The first faint signs of the environmental impact came in the 1890s when oystermen near the mouth of the Mississippi began complaining that the leveeing of the river was raising the salinity of nearby marshes, decimating salt-sensitive oyster beds. A subsequent government report unsuccessfully recommended that gaps be made in the levees to revitalize the affected beds with fresh water.

A few years later, in 1905, came the first apparent connection between flood levees on the Mississippi River and land loss beyond its banks. Civil engineer E. L. Corthell produced considerable data suggesting that the marshlands at the river's mouth and all along the coast were subject to significant subsidence, particularly now that the river had stopped depositing sediments through spring floods. The lowering of an old Spanish building near the river's mouth led Corthell to believe that a sinking of one-twentieth of a foot per year was taking place. At about the same time, the Army Corps of Engineers reported similar sinking in the same vicinity.

But a 1914 report by the U.S. Department of Agriculture concluded that "except for this relatively small area, near the mouth of the river, the remainder of [coastal Louisiana] shows no change in elevation." These findings were greatly reassuring to both commercial interests and the scientific community, and were quoted in papers and books all across America and abroad.

For the next fifty years, leading geologists at several Louisiana universities held on to the notion that the coast was in a state of "quasi equilibrium." The dynamics of delta-building had long since come to be understood: the state's southern boundary was a sculpture of thousands of years of sediments spread over a wide coastline by a river regularly changing its path over the centuries to find the shortest route to the sea.

The very *existence* of southern Louisiana, so the thinking went, the very *fact* of all that alluvial land, argued strongly that the "depositional" forces of the river far outweighed the "erosional" forces of the Gulf of Mexico and the natural process of subsidence. Thus, even with the river leveed, whatever land loss took place would surely be slow and insignificant for a long time. The river had left so much to begin with.

Then, in 1927, something happened to alter the fate of the coast forever. That year the lower Mississippi flooded for the very last time, ripping apart miles of levees in Arkansas, Mississippi, and Louisiana, covering 27,000 square miles of those states (roughly half the area of New England) with up to thirty feet of water. At least a thousand people died, the homes of one million were inundated, and the total economic loss exceeded a billion dollars. Poor farm families spent days on their rooftops, some eating dead animals that floated by. When the water finally subsided, whole portions of many towns had "become heaps of splintered lumber, like the leavings of a tornado," according to historian John M. Barry. And the river's rich sedimentary muck lay stacked upon the land to a depth of several feet in some places.

It was the last, wild hurrah of the lower Mississippi. After the 1927 flood, the Corps of Engineers led efforts to tame the water for good by building stronger and taller levees, straightening the river's channel in places, and constructing several major floodways. By the 1930s the river was pretty much finished as a land-building force not only because of the new flood-control measures but because it had been locked into a course which now carried the water to the very edge of the continental shelf, dumping 300 million tons of sediments into oblivion each year.

Yet the consensus belief in coastal "equilibrium" continued to hold well into the 1960s. This despite growing eyewitness evidence of substantial subsidence and at least one scientific study in the 1950s confirming the erosion of the state's outer shoreline without quantifying land loss for the estuary as a whole. Meanwhile, oystermen continued to scream year after year about the growing intrusion of salt water until, in 1965, the U.S. Congress agreed to match state funds for the construction of four modest structures to divert fresh Mississippi water into surrounding marshes south of New Orleans. But the state of Louisiana failed to authorize its own funds, so the structures were not built.

Then, in 1968, the people of Texas helped Louisiana finally come to terms with its problem. In that year, Texas asked the Corps of Engineers to consider diverting almost a third of the Mississippi's flow from a point in Arkansas and channeling it seven hundred miles to the drought-plagued high plains of West Texas for drinking water and irrigation use. Unsure of the consequences of such an ambitious project, the Corps of Engineers turned to a young team of researchers at LSU led by a reputed genius named Sherwood "Woody" Gagliano. How, the Corps wanted to know, would such a large reduction in the Mississippi's discharge into the Gulf affect landforms along coastal Louisiana?

Gagliano was a New Orleans native who by the age of thirty-two had earned no fewer than three degrees from LSU, including a doctorate in geomorphology (the study of the configuration and evolution of landforms). As a first step, he and his team decided to determine the relative stability of *current* landforms along the coast. Gagliano had studied under Dr. Richard J. Russell, a world-renowned geomorphologist at LSU and prominent subscriber to the concept of coastal equilibrium. But Gagliano had always had his doubts, having witnessed firsthand since childhood erosion and subsidence wherever he went in Louisiana: the barrier islands, the marshes, the coastal beaches.

Now came the chance to test his lifelong observations. Without the aid of digitized mapping or satellite imagery—both were still several years away—Gagliano's study team went about plotting the ratio of water to land in several study areas across the coast. Using mechanical calculators, the team then painstakingly crunched the numbers, comparing the results against old aerial photographs and successive periods of topographical maps going back to the 1890s.

Gagliano was at his lab inside an old wooden World War II barracks on the LSU campus when the final results began to take shape. The state of Louisiana, the numbers revealed, was losing 16.5 square miles of land *every year.* Working feverishly, under deadline, Gagliano would drive home late at night, rubbing his eyes with fatigue, his head buzzing in disbelief, thinking this really can't be happening. But the numbers were real—16.5 square miles—several times what Gagliano had anticipated even as a worst-case scenario. Indeed, the data suggested the state had already lost hundreds of square miles of territory without anyone quite knowing it. Worse, the problem appeared to be growing geometrically. By the 1980s the state would be losing an area 1.5 times the size of Manhattan every year.

More mapping and radiocarbon dating of buried marsh peats eventually showed that the coast's annual, ancient accrual of new land had ended sometime in the 1880s. After that, net land loss took over. By 1913 the loss was around 7 square miles per year, but soon grew considerably faster in part due to the additional harm caused by oil and gas exploitation. Among many firsts, Gagliano identified and measured the erosion caused by the industry's many canals.

The overall findings were so unexpected and so shocking in scale that many Louisianans, including many state leaders and Corps of Engineers officials, were highly skeptical upon their release. Most of the oil companies rejected the data outright, clearly fearing they'd be blamed the most for the coast's destruction. (In fairness, almost all of the industry canals, dug as far back as the 1930s, were created before anyone fully understood the problem of erosion. And the marsh itself, until the early 1970s, was widely perceived as a kind of indestructible wasteland of little intrinsic value. It's where you went fishing and got mosquito bites.)

Despite the wave of public doubts, Gagliano and his team pressed on. Between 1970 and 1973 they produced a landmark series of twenty-five technical reports identifying all the fundamental dynamics of Louisiana land loss and offering a wide range of restoration strategies, including closing various navigation channels and building major diversions from the Mississippi River into the marshes. This body of work represented a fantastic explosion of geomorphologic understanding coupled with creative solutions that today still set the parameters of discussions of coastal decline and restoration.

Still, few people paid much attention until, in the late 1970s, three subsequent studies using newly available satellite imagery and computer mapping confirmed everything Gagliano and his team had reported. The new studies showed that land loss was actually even worse than Gagliano first determined, and had jumped to 39.4 square miles per year by 1980.

With these findings, the state government finally got involved in 1981, providing funds for the first time for modest "pilot projects" to help fight the problem. These included construction of the small river diversion that oystermen in Plaquemines Parish had been waiting for since its approval by Congress way back in 1965. If Gagliano was right, the thinking went, this structure, called the Caernarvon Freshwater Diversion Project, would do more than just help oystermen. It would eventually

create land by restoring and expanding nearby marshes. A rehabilitation experiment was now under way. Meanwhile, across
the state, the need for more public education on coastal issues
remained extremely urgent. One of the leading debates of the
time, for example, was whether the barrier islands were worth
saving at all.

Then, in the mid-1980s, a worldwide crash in oil and gas
prices threw thousands of South Louisianans out of work, sending many of them back to traditional family fishing businesses
they'd left behind years before. What these fishermen found
upon their return was a wetland landscape barely recognizable
to them. Huge areas had simply disappeared. Many landowners,
meanwhile, had begun throwing up fences across the marsh,
denying fishermen access to traditional navigation routes and
fishing grounds. The landowners, in a surreal situation, were
trying to protect their partially submerged wetland property
from a Louisiana law stipulating that whenever private land
turns to open water it automatically becomes property of the
state.

Several shrimpers went to court but failed in a bid to
remove these fences and regain access to the waterways, resulting in navigational inconvenience and a reduction in fishing
grounds that continues today. The whole situation served to
awaken coastal communities to the fact that something very,
very bad was happening. Both a way of life and the land upon
which it was based were approaching extinction.

Finally, in 1986, Rob Gorman, a social worker for the
Catholic church who had spent years advocating for shrimpers'
rights and wetlands preservation, helped move the cause forward in a huge way. He became a founding member and the first
chairman of the Coalition to Restore Coastal Louisiana. This
grassroots organization, made up of concerned churches, fisher-

men, wetland scientists, environmentalists, and businessmen, urgently compiled a landmark report called *Coastal Louisiana: Here Today, Gone Tomorrow?* The report, after all these years, fervently embraced almost all of Woody Gagliano's findings of the early seventies and most of his proposed solutions, including construction of an enormous and unprecedented river diversion for the sole purpose of reviving marsh and creating new land.

A burst of legislative and regulatory triumphs quickly followed the coalition's historic and widely circulated report. A federal bill was passed—the Breaux Act—to deal with coastal wetlands issues. The state created a wetlands trust fund. The Barataria-Terrebonne National Estuary Program was founded (Kerry St. Pé's group). And a federal-state task force went to work implementing restoration projects with annual funds of about $40 million. By the early 1990s "No Net Loss of Wetlands" became a mantra across the coast.

Interestingly, at about the same time, the Netherlands was coming to terms with its own centuries-long experiment with strict estuary control. Today, a full third of Holland is below sea level and still subsiding at an alarming rate, protected from the stormy North Sea only by a massive seawall. Plans adopted there in 1990 call for returning 10 percent of all reclaimed wetlands to a natural state, thus reducing soil subsidence, improving habitat for fish and wildlife, and creating natural areas for tourists to visit.

Back in Louisiana, meanwhile, optimism was high in the early 1990s that the hardest legislative work was now over and that a series of projects on the ground could start turning the tide on land loss. The projects included restoring wetlands near New Orleans with the help of mechanical pumps, building "riprap" rock walls along the eroding coast of Cameron Parish to the west, and "nourishing" a few select barrier island beaches with new sand.

But by 1995 the realization was dawning that $40 million per year doesn't go very far to resuscitate a severely ill patient twice the size of Delaware. While many of these initial projects were successful in saving hundreds of acres here and there, the coast as a whole was still hurtling toward complete ecological collapse. Onshore lighthouses were now out in the Gulf. Barrier islands were disappearing. Drinking water was turning salty. Net land loss, which had peaked in the 1980s at about 40 square miles per year, was still going strong at 25 square miles annually in the mid-nineties. The decrease in the rate of loss was due less to human restoration efforts than to the fact that there was increasingly less land left *to* subside. The coast had tipped toward a final vanishing act.

One thing $40 million per year couldn't buy was the one thing almost everyone agreed the state needed most: a massive river diversion bringing as much as a third of the Mississippi's flow down to the basins of Terrebonne Bay and Barataria Bay. This was doubly unfortunate because by 1995 something very interesting was happening in Breton Sound south of New Orleans. The oystermen who in the 1890s had first complained about levees creating saltwater intrusion and who had kept up the chorus against the ill effects of levees throughout the twentieth century, finally got their Caernarvon freshwater diversion built in 1991. Just four years later, color infrared aerial photos showed, once again, that Woody Gagliano and others were right: the diversion was preserving existing wetlands and creating new land. Hundreds of acres per year, in fact. Possibly thousands.

The time had finally come to take this evidence and make

one last push for survival. What was needed now was a plan big enough, bold enough, and with enough funding to match the scale of the problem. That plan had to include a major river diversion, the full and complete restoration of barrier islands, a set of comprehensive strategies for watershed management and repair, and the closing of damaging navigation channels.

By 1999 a diverse group of interested parties including, again, churches, scientists, environmentalists, and fishermen as well as numerous state and federal agencies with wetlands oversight produced exactly such a plan, this one designed to carry South Louisiana into the twenty-first century. Called *Coast 2050: Toward a Sustainable Coastal Louisiana,* this book-length blueprint offered scores of specific strategy recommendations. The cost of fulfilling the plan over the next fifty years would be the not-so-cheap sum of $14 billion. The cost of doing nothing, however, would be at least $100 billion in lost jobs, lost infrastructure, lost fishing, lost wildlife, and increased damage from hurricanes, according to the report.

The problem now was finding all that restoration money. Lobbied hard enough, the federal government might be persuaded to match state funds three to one. But entering the year 2000, the Louisiana state government was itself tragically broke. While the rest of America was enjoying an unprecedented economic boom and state governments everywhere were experiencing big budget surpluses, the situation in Louisiana couldn't have been worse. Poor fiscal management in the face of falling oil and gas revenues had left the state with chronic revenue shortfalls, forcing it to raise taxes and, among other measures, deny schoolteachers long-promised raises.

Nonetheless, observers agreed that in order to save the coast the state had to make the cause a top priority immediately, finding hundreds of millions of dollars even in a time of fiscal belt-tightening. Many speculated that only a major crisis—read: massive hurricane—could move the state to commit the required resources in time. But by then, ironically, there might be nothing left to save.

Meanwhile, restoration proponents like Kerry St. Pé and Mark Davis remained bitterly frustrated. On the national level, there was still an almost total lack of awareness of the problem. Even the nation's major environmental groups were conspicuously uninvolved for reasons open to speculation. Perhaps it was a built-in bias against big ecological projects in the "backward" Deep South. Or maybe it was the coast's lack of "charismatic megafauna," those large animals so popular with the public like manatees in South Florida, wolves in Yellowstone, grizzlies in Alaska. Louisiana shrimp and muskrats simply don't make sexy calendar covers at fund-raising time.

Whatever the reason, virtually no one outside Louisiana was paying any attention even now. The Everglades, deservedly, was getting almost $8 billion in federal and state money for restoration. The city of Boston, deservedly or not, was getting $14 billion to build an underground highway, the notorious "Big Dig." For almost the exact same price, coastal Louisiana— the birds, the beauty, the seafood, the culture, the source of energy, the buffer against hurricanes—could be saved.

Instead, as the twenty-first century dawned, it kept right on dying.

A gust of wind sends our tiny twin-propeller airplane into a sudden, nerve-racking drop. Turbulence has been increasing gradually all morning, and Bruce, our pilot, decides it's unsafe to fly east all the way to the Mississippi River. So we won't see the Caernarvon freshwater diversion Kerry wants to show me.

We won't see the marshes restored there by new sediments and nutrients, where oyster production has tripled, wetland vegetation has more than doubled, and new habitat for waterfowl expands dramatically every year.

But, it turns out, we don't need to fly all the way to Caernarvon to see the phenomenon of land-building. The miracle exists at another spot. We head west toward the mouth of the Atchafalaya River, the sole major "distributary" of the Mississippi. From a point one hundred miles north of here, the Atchafalaya branches off from the master stream and guides a portion of its flow to the shallow waters of Atchafalaya Bay just south of Morgan City. The results are impressive new wetlands.

"This," Kerry says, pointing out the window, "is what all the area around Leeville and Dulac and Golden Meadow could look like within a few short decades."

Below us is an Eden of natural beauty. Nourished by sediments, the marsh grass is thick and unbroken, stretching away for long distances with the delicate yet durable quality of a very fine carpet. There are no straight lines here, no canals, just the graceful curves of tiny bayous where a few dolphins show their dorsal fins below flocks of circling terns. This marsh is a work of art, completely self-maintaining, the most beautiful I've seen yet in Louisiana. And every year it gets bigger. Amid the nightmare of wetlands retreat all around, the Atchafalaya is crafting a small new delta here, a full three square miles of newborn land per year.

"That's all the proof we need that man-made diversions can do the same thing on a very large scale," Kerry says. "To save the rest of the coast we have to harness that force and put it right where we need it most."

As a sad counterpoint, we reach one of those places of

greatest need toward the end of our flight: Bayou Lafourche and the area around Leeville. From the air, the town looks like a thin snake of connected houses, docks, and boats swimming through a seemingly flooded area of submerged telephone poles and water lapping both sides of Route 1. Only fragmentary tracts of grass interrupt the water all around.

An exceptionally high number of oil and gas canals did most of the damage around Leeville. Today, it's almost impossible for companies to get a permit to dredge a canal or otherwise destroy wetlands intentionally. But the legacy of past deeds keeps right on giving. "Regulations against more dredging won't save us now," Kerry says. "We're beyond that point."

Before turning north and heading back to the airfield, we fly over one of the most isolated bayou communities in all of Louisiana. For centuries European settlers had pushed the state's largest tribes of Native Americans, including the Houma and Chitimacha, down from the state's interior and into the swamps and wetlands of the southern coast, farther and farther until there was nowhere left to go. As a result, the largest concentrations of Louisiana Indians today are at the very end of the some of the coast's most obscure bayous, the communities teetering at land's edge, where the Gulf meets Louisiana, bearing down hard.

One of those communities is the village of Isle de Jean Charles, now directly below us, where even mild storms flood the one connecting road and kids regularly have to reach their school bus atop the hulls of their fathers' crab boats. There's not a stitch of protective marsh remaining anywhere near that road or around much of the island itself. Just open water.

The village is completely exposed.

"God help those people when the next hurricane hits," Kerry says.

A feeling of numbness and sensory fatigue fills my body as we touch down at the Houma-Terrebonne Airport. I walk across the tarmac to Kerry's truck and open the passenger door. I get in. Then, moments later, like magic, we're driving through the streets of the city of Houma and it's as if the last hour simply hadn't happened. Everything seems so normal, so incongruously placid. We pass a tidy middle-class subdivision, a roadside vegetable stand, a Dairy Queen. We pass schoolchildren playing outside at recess. A traffic light turns red and Kerry stops the truck. Pedestrians pass before us, crossing the street, everything so orderly, so calm and routine.

And yet we were just up there. Up in the air. We just saw the shattered barrier islands and the receding wetlands with our own eyes. This town of Houma, where the drinking water is going salty, is hanging by a thread just like the rest of the coast. Yet here we are, at a red light, quietly waiting.

Kerry's truck happens to be facing north at the moment, away from the coast, and as we wait at the red light I suddenly experience a moment of extreme anxiety. Triggered by the images I've just processed aloft, I have a keen sense that something really, really huge is right behind us. I can *feel* it right behind us. And that something, in my mind, is a giant tidal wave. I'm suddenly sure that if I glance in the sideview mirror or turn around quickly and look back, I'll see the shimmering, curling, mammoth wall of liquid sweeping toward us, sweeping inland, as tall as a skyscraper. Or if I do nothing, just look straight ahead, the wave's enormous shadow, fast-moving and death-dark, will overtake the truck and the pedestrians before us, a prelude to the hammer blow just seconds away.

Even after I'm able to shake off this strange moment of insanity, returning to the safe reality of my passenger seat, I can't shake the image itself. It's too close to truth. I visualize the pedestrians right in front of me being swept away. There's a woman pushing a stroller. A pair of teenage lovers holding hands. A postal worker in uniform. They're so ordinary, these people, and yet seemingly tragic—tragically oblivious to what, in reality, is increasingly likely to happen here, the great wave of natural disaster and economic loss about to hit.

Despite thirty years of scientific documentation, despite public reports and repeated calls for change, despite firsthand evidence of land loss before the very eyes of almost every single coastal resident, nothing of sufficient scale is being done to save the region. Why is this woman pushing her baby? Why is this man delivering letters? Why are these lovers holding hands? Why aren't they rioting in the streets, demanding immediate steps to rescue the ecological base upon which their property, their livelihoods, rest?

"I know exactly what you mean," Kerry says when I describe the images and thoughts going through my head. "It's like these people are in a dream state, and no matter how much the rest of us yell and scream, we can't wake them up."

I tell Kerry what Father Pilola had said to me the day before, that many people feel the problem is just too big for them to solve. Despite articles in the newspaper and community meetings at the local churches, all showing that diversions and other measures are technically feasible, many locals still have the feeling that stopping the land from sinking is like a few people standing on a beach before a giant storm and trying to turn it away by yelling and waving their arms.

"And that's *so* wrong," says Kerry. "These people can make the change happen. They have the power. They just have to demand it. They have to demand their leaders take action. They have the power in a democratic system to make it happen."

The traffic light changes and we move on. We pass a gardener planting a tree outside a Catholic church, a merchant changing his marquee to announce a "*très bon* sale," a man selling crabs from the back of his truck, $9.99 a dozen.

"So why don't they do it?" I ask. "What's holding back the groundswell of demand for change? What's the problem?"

"What do I *really* think the problem is?" Kerry says.

"Yeah."

"The estuary itself," he says.

"Huh?"

"The estuary itself. Our biggest problem is the great productivity of this estuary itself. Even wounded, it's still amazingly productive. Lots of people are making a living in the oil field. Lots of people are still catching lots and lots of shrimp and crabs. A huge part of America's seafood still comes from here. The ducks are still coming down in the fall. So a lot of people, I think, have been hearing the dire predictions of a collapse of the system for thirty years now—*accurate* predictions—but here it is the year 2000 and all these people are still making a decent living out in the remaining marsh and so they start to think that maybe the predictions are a little off base, even though they themselves see the land turning to water all the time. It's all just more evidence of what a huge, huge treasure we have here. Even on its last leg, this coast is overflowing with riches.

"But it's not going to last," he continues. "Absolutely not. Biologists have been saying for a long time that in terms of the fishery, productivity will be high—will even *increase*—until right before a very rapid and total collapse. So right now, shrimpers are still catching shrimp. It's sometimes hard to get ten shrimpers to agree on what day of the week it is, much less get them together and get them politically organized—especially when they're *still catching shrimp*. It's a cruel situation. It works directly against us in what we need to do right now."

Kerry switches themes for a moment, stressing again that this is a national problem. This coast belongs to the whole country, he says, with economic and environmental impacts that will be felt nationally. So it would be a mistake for the rest of America to wait for a few fishing communities along the coast of Louisiana to rise up in time to save something that belongs to 280 million people.

"We Louisianans need to do more," Kerry says. "There's no question about it. And we're working on that part of the puzzle. But this is a war, like I said before. Imagine if some foreign enemy were taking away land from California and that state didn't have enough money to win or enough soldiers able to fight. The rest of us wouldn't sit back and say, 'Oh, that's California's problem.' No, we'd all pitch in. It's our *country*. That's what needs to happen here."

"And what if it *doesn't* happen?" I say.

We come to another traffic light. The sky is growing progressively darker and the wind is blowing hard, racing across a land that's as flat as the ocean itself for almost one hundred miles into the interior. In front of us, the traffic light is swaying in the wind, and I recall that the right hurricane, from the right direction, could send a surge of water all the way to the suburbs of Baton Rouge.

I roll up my window against the approaching rain.

"If it doesn't happen soon enough?" Kerry says, forcing himself to address the sort of final defeat he's been fighting all his career to prevent. "If it doesn't happen, then we need to start getting people out of here. It's that simple. We need to start evacuating people and relocating towns and abandoning this beautiful coast right now. Either we do what's necessary to save it—things we know we *can* do—or we spend billions of dollars leading a retreat away from here. It's one or the other. One or the other."

# Five

In mid-autumn in the Gulf of Mexico, when the first serious cold fronts drift down from the nation's midsection and push haltingly across Louisiana's subtropical coast, the temperature of the ocean water begins to drop considerably. Miles offshore, inside the minuscule brain of Louisiana's female brown shrimp— a.k.a. *Farfante penaeus aztecus*—this sudden Gulf cooling acts as an ancient trigger.

The female shrimp has already mated. She did so months earlier, back in the marsh, just after molting, when she was still sexually immature. She has carried the male sperm in a sac in her head all this time, and now, in the cooling weather of the open ocean, at a depth of at least thirty feet, she begins to spawn. From ovaries barely the size of peas, inside a body maybe six inches long, a half million eggs somehow emerge. The eggs enter the cool water and then drift, subsumed in the vast ocean environment, sprayed only with a protective coat of jelly as a parting maternal act, then left totally on their own.

By November the water off Louisiana's coast is a veritable soup of trillions and trillions of microscopic shrimp larvae squirming with new life. So many are there that if all the larvae of just three successive generations of *Farfante penaeus aztecus* were to survive to adulthood and reproduce, the resulting shrimp would be equal to the volume of the sun in less than two years. A few years more and every inch of the universe would be filled with shrimp, the mass of crustaceans expanding outward at the speed of light.

But of course most of the larvae don't grow to be adults. They'll be devoured by a fantastic array of predators, or they'll lose their way during the long migration now before them, a migration as epic and perilous as that of the Pacific salmon and the common eel.

Afloat in the Gulf current, the spherical shrimp eggs hatch into first-phase larvae less than a millimeter in size, having the look not of shrimp but of grotesque monsters worthy of battle with Odysseus. They have only one eye, their bodies opaque and pear-shaped, with triangular spines and whiplike appendages for swimming. A series of successive molts give the larvae the even stranger look of multi-limbed space aliens, with dozens of barbed digits protruding from bifurcating arms, a video-game villain from a galaxy far, far away.

But after two or three weeks, these odd changes stop and the final product emerges at last: tiny shrimp, just half an inch long, but with the familiar stalked eyes and armored tail and protruding antennae longer than the body itself. Now, in order to survive, these newly morphed creatures must somehow get themselves out of the big ocean and into the estuarine coastal marshes a long way away to the north.

For help, the infant crustaceans, roughly the length and width of grains of rice, turn to a spherical body 92 million miles away in outer space, a G2 dwarf star otherwise known as our sun. Twice a month this fiery body of hydrogen gas nearly a million miles in diameter joins forces with the earth's moon, a mere 238,000 miles away, to create a combined gravitational and centrifugal force of enormous power. This force generates ocean tides on earth—so-called spring tides—which are much greater than the tides occurring daily throughout the rest of the month. Every two weeks, when the moon shows itself to the earth either as a barely visible new moon or as a blazing full moon, the phenomenon is at work: the moon and the sun have fallen into a straight line relative to the earth, reinforcing each other's gravitational tug, pulling the earth's oceans into two bulging masses of liquid on opposite sides of the globe. These fantastic waves, these great heaping ridges of water, are brought into collision with the earth's landmasses twice a day as the planet rotates. This, in the simplest terms, is how tides happen, and spring tides are the bimonthly champions. So strong is the combined pull of the sun and moon during this period that even the earth's atmosphere bends outward and parts of the continents bulge ever so slightly.

For the trillions of minute shrimp struggling down there in the earth's Gulf of Mexico, this celestial force is plenty strong enough to bear them landward in a high incoming tide that squeezes between Louisiana's barrier islands and sweeps the shrimp up into the food-rich interior marshes. By March, thanks to the spring tides, all the autumn-spawned brown shrimp lucky enough to have survived the marathon journey—

perhaps one in a hundred—are now inside the estuary nursery grounds where they begin to feed ravenously.

Brown shrimp, as they grow up, are famously indiscriminate eaters. They are what biologists call "encounter feeders" and "opportunistic omnivores," meaning they'll eat pretty much whatever organic matter they stumble into: decaying plants, animals, algae, fecal pellets, amphipods. Sometimes each other.

This ability to ingest a wide range of food accounts for their rapid growth rate, especially beginning in April when the water temperature starts to rise toward 70 degrees Fahrenheit in the coastal marshes and the shrimp grow as much as an inch per week. If both temperature and water salinity remain favorable, the fast growth rate continues and combines with the initial fecundity of the spawning females to produce truly skyrocketing results. In collective size and numbers, the shrimp, in the spring, reach massive proportions. It's a shrimp explosion.

And that's when the slaughter starts.

Cajun fishermen like to say that when God created shrimp, he created food for just about everybody. Anything in the marsh that can swim, crawl, walk, or fly is, in the spring, most likely looking for shrimp. But it's the fish who go especially wild. Speckled trout mercilessly hunt down brown shrimp in the flooded marsh grass each night. Drumfish raid the marsh-bottom burrows the shrimp dig for protection by day. The clever southern flounder exerts less energy, simply lying motionless along muddy bottoms and ambushing all unsuspecting shrimp who tiptoe by. Each of these fish species can eat a full third of its body weight in shrimp every day.

But despite the assaults, the shrimp population remains miraculously huge, almost beyond comprehension. In early May, across vast stretches of the interior wetlands, the water is literally boiling with shrimp when the oldest of the autumn-spawned class reach a length of around four inches and begin the reverse migration back to the sea, their goal to live and reproduce out in the Gulf, completing the cycle.

For help, these maturing shrimp once again turn to their celestial accomplices. As the elliptical orbit of the moon brings it in sync with the mighty sun to form a straight line with the earth, a powerful spring tide occurs, bringing a heaping rise of water into the wetlands. For those shrimp now old enough to migrate, the subsequent outgoing tide acts as both a stimulus to get going and an aid in getting out. The water bears the shrimp out of the marshes and into the bays and, finally, past the barrier islands back to the Gulf.

But the most clever and efficient predator of all, the one who's been conspicuously missing from the hunt up to this point, is, in early May, waiting as the shrimp try to escape. With their Lafitte skiffs and lugger boats, their skim nets and depth finders and GPS's, Louisiana fishermen congregate in large numbers in the passes, between the barrier islands, waiting like the wily southern flounder in ambush. The ban on shrimping inside the barrier islands is still in effect most years when that first class of adult brown shrimp begins to head back out to the Gulf in early May. Unable to go into the wetlands to get the shrimp for another week or so, the fishermen have to let the shrimp come to them.

And like the crustaceans they seek, the boat captains keep an eye on the moon in early May. When it's full or new, and when the astronomically enhanced tide begins to rise, the boats accumulate in lines between the islands just like the shrimp accumulate in schools coming out. In a good year, so many shrimp are migrating, attracting so many boats, that you can literally see the thick line of vessels in satellite photographs, a great floating dragnet of human-made seacraft penciling in the outline of Louisiana's southern border between the islands.

And what actually happens when all those shrimp finally collide with all those boats is a bona fide spectacle. There, after sunset, with the high tide roaring out under the big tug of that mysterious moon, the drama and uncertainty and touch of real danger that have been the stuff of fishermen's lives since time immemorial are all played out in the ancient competition for Mother Ocean's bounty. Sicily, five thousand miles away, may have its centuries-old *mattanza*, its ritual spearing of tuna in labyrinths of netting set out in the Mediterranean Sea each spring. And Alaska has its great herring run along Sitka Sound, where lines of purse-seine boats jockey wildly for position above a darting school of millions.

But Louisiana need not look on in envy. For even at this late and increasingly sad date way down south near the mouth of the Mississippi River, the spring run of *Farfante penaeus aztecus* endures, the creatures bursting through the passes between the barrier islands, running for their lives, almost home, only to be met by fishermen who, like their fathers and grandfathers before them, do absolutely everything in their power to bring them up to the suffocating air of the dark and sultry Louisiana night.

By midafternoon the weather clears as I head south along Route 1, following Bayou Lafourche. Thick clouds, around since early morning, dissolve completely and the sky turns blue and there it is outside my window: a faint nail-paring moon low in the eastern sky. It's only the second day of the new moon, meaning a high spring tide is very much in effect during these first few days of May. The brown shrimp are out there, all around—

in the bays, the bayous, the marshes, the lakes—having already migrated in from the Gulf. And tonight many of them will try to escape, rendezvousing with trawlers in the passes, creating a timing that's just too good to pass up. So I resolve to drive farther south to the ocean's edge that afternoon and try to hitchhike aboard a trawler out into the Gulf. I want to see this lively old fishing tradition myself before, as may easily happen, it disappears forever in the next few years.

But first I have to make the long trek down the bayou where, I realize, I've become something of a veteran. The scenery, like an old friend, is familiar, the reunion a pleasant one against that dark flow of reflective water. Going no faster than thirty miles an hour for long stretches, I pass through languorous waterside Cajun towns strung together like beads on a string: Matthews, Lockport, Larose, Cut Off, Galliano, Golden Meadow. In the lush shade of a colossal live oak I stop at a wooden shack selling "snowballs," a South Louisiana specialty of crushed ice in a paper cup with creamy toppings like Praline Supreme, Bayou Brandy, and Cajun Red Hot.

Having cooled my palate in the rising afternoon heat, I press on, noticing that Adam's Fruit Market has added alligator meat and frogs' legs and pork cracklin' to its maze of hand-painted signs out front. I turn on the radio to 100.3 FM, the Cajun station out of Larose, and for the first time in my life hear major league baseball scores in French: *Les Chausettes Rouges de Boston, deux. Les Chausettes Blanches de Chicago, un.* The station then switches back to the usual mix of Cajun and country western fare.

In Cut Off, still hungry, I pull into Duet's bakery and am amazed to see hardtack for sale. It's a stiff, crackerlike bread baked very slowly and sold here in bags of four. I've never actually seen this culinary relic before, nor imagined it still existed, having only read about it in Civil War histories: "The regiment drew rations of hardtack and dried meat after the battle and slept on their arms. . . ." But there it is, real hardtack. Duet's cheerful baker, Gwen Theriot, tells me the giant round crackers were once very popular among bayou shrimpers because they kept forever at sea before the days when diesel engines allowed for more frequent trips back to shore for fresh food. Gwen adds that shrimpers traditionally carried hardtack in pillowcases hung from wheelhouse walls, but now only the old-timers, most of them long since retired, buy the stuff, dipping it in their coffee to soften it up while no doubt telling stories about how it *used* to be out there trawling. Subsequent research confirms that Duet's is one of the very last places in Louisiana, and surely all of America, still making hardtack. I decide to buy a bag for my fishing excursion that night, sentimentally betting the old-time nourishment will bring me good luck and keep me safe.

And safety, it turns out, is precisely what I'll need if I go forward with my shrimping plans.

"Do you know how to fight?" asks Tim Melancon as I pull up to his camp in Leeville an hour later. "You better know how to fight, cuz dat's a crazy scene out dere in dose passes dis time a year."

He's standing on his boat, still overhauling his engine, as I explain my strategy: I'll follow Route 1 another twenty miles southeast to where it dead-ends, literally runs out of land, on Grand Isle. There I'll look for a trawler heading out to the pass between Grand Isle and the neighboring island Grand Terre.

"De problem," Tim says, "is dat dere are lots and lots a boats who want to get between dose islands and dere's only so much space, and ever'body wants to be in de front. So people start cutting each udder off and ramming each udder and t'rowing t'ings, and fistfights break out. You gotta be bad to go out with dat bunch. You sure you wanna go?"

I tell him I think I'm sure. I add that the Louisiana Department of Wildlife and Fisheries guy who first told me about "shrimping the moons in May in the passes" never mentioned such hazards. Tim just shrugs and says, "Suit yourself." But *he* never trawls between those islands, he says. It's too chaotic and, he implies, somehow undignified. He does the more civilized thing of simply waiting for the inside season to open in a few days like most shrimpers.

My visit with Tim turns out to be short. He tells me that Phyllis is still up in Galliano with Tee Tim, still mad at him for throwing their son out of the house. She hasn't called or come by once, and Tim's not about to go up there, electing to remain all alone at the camp instead, stewing. It's a standoff and Tim still looks very sad about the whole thing—and very distracted by all the engine work—so I push on.

Beyond Leeville, Route 1 becomes nothing more than a straight and narrow causeway through tattered marsh, with occasional roadside camps on ten-foot stilts and endless telephone poles in the water. Sportfishermen—lots of them—cast their bait along narrow shoulders made of crushed shell, just inches above the encroaching water. I see men with open-face reels sitting atop coolers and old black women in lounge chairs, down from Houma and New Orleans, with cane poles and straw hats. Overall, it's a rather down-home, fun-loving, beer-drinking crowd, one that prompts occasional motels along the way to post signs in rooms saying: "Do *not* clean fish in your room. Do *not* bring boat batteries into your room. Beer only. No whiskey. *Merci.*"

At last, a low concrete bridge ushers Route 1 up and over Caminada Pass, and suddenly I'm driving along the western tip of Grand Isle, Louisiana's largest barrier island and the only one still inhabited. Too battered by storms to support upscale resorts, the island has the homespun feel of a vacation retreat befitting its local nickname: the Cajun Bahamas. Modest cottages and pink-painted low-rent motels cater to anglers and bird-watchers and the handful of sunbathers who don't mind the sight of dozens of offshore oil wells floating in the distant Gulf haze.

The beach, of course, is eroding like all the state's other barrier islands, and the marsh behind the island is all but gone. At least one insurance company has told property owners that after the next big hurricane, it will pay only for relocation off the island, nothing more. The endless string of beachside pleasure camps, meanwhile, passing by my open car window, seem to capture the crazy sand-castle fragility of the entire Louisiana coast. Like boats, each camp has a hand-painted name across its front, ranging from "Riptide," to "C'est la Vie," to "Driftwood," to, my personal favorite, "Double or Nothing."

But a brave sort of charm somehow endures on this island. Sun-bleached boardwalks rise up and over beautiful dunes and past sea oats to the surf. Oleander and hibiscus bloom seemingly everywhere in the soft, salty breezes. And a thick bayside forest of twisted oaks and chinaberry trees buffers a bird rookery nearly equal to Raccoon Island, with thousands of nesting pairs.

Tim had told me that most of the commercial fishermen congregate on the eastern tip of this narrow, eight-mile-long island, so that's where I head along Route 1, passing T-shirt shops and scattered bars with sandy parking lots. Up ahead, finally, I see the familiar forest of shrimp-boat booms and green netting and hovering seagulls scavenging for by-catch. Past aging wharves, I pull up to the first "shrimp shed" I see: a lively pavilion where shrimp are off-loaded from boats, then weighed and purchased. There in a gravel parking lot full of American-made pickups I ask a passing shrimper where I can find the shed proprietor.

"You mean Dean?" he says. He turns toward a tin-sided office hemmed in by hanging scales and huge vats of crushed ice for shipping shrimp as far away as Florida, and yells, "Dean! *Dean!* Somebody here to see ya!"

The man in his early forties who eventually emerges from the air-conditioned office in no way looks like a multimillionaire. Dean Blanchard is wearing a limp tank top and gym shorts and a scuffed-up pair of white rubber boots, the classic Cajun Reeboks. The ashes of a half-spent cigarette dangle from a tanned, boyish face several days past due for a shave. But, I soon learn, the man standing before me now, with his penchant for driving used cars and sleeping on his office floor, is positively Monsieur Chevrette, a.k.a. Mr. Shrimp, one of the biggest dockside buyers along the entire Louisiana coast. Brown shrimp, white shrimp, sea bobs, royal reds—you name it, whatever's in season, Dean Blanchard will buy your catch. His dockhands unload boats sometimes twenty-four hours a day, nonstop, along an extensive network of bayside wharves. Then they ship the shrimp in a fleet of five 18-wheel refrigeration trucks to processing plants in five states.

Dean Blanchard is also something of an outlaw, I soon learn, a notorious Cajun bad boy who, intentionally or not, has created for himself the almost folkloric image of a modern-day Jesse James, a guy who'll break the law when necessary to help the little guy, the shrimper. As a result, among countless coastal fishermen—certainly all the ones I talk to—he's held in decidedly high regard.

But today Dean is mostly just tired. After greetings, he tells me he's been putting in long days getting ready for the upcoming inland shrimp season. This on top of buying and shipping out all the shrimp now coming down through the passes. And on top of *this*, his grandmother just had a stroke and he's been busy checking in on her.

"Funny t'ing is," he says of his *grand-mère,* speaking to me in a low, smoke-cured Cajun voice, "after de stroke, she forgot all her English. She only speaks French now. Ain't dat strange? Dat's de only way we can speak to her now, in French."

I quickly explain to Dean why I've come, asking if he knows of a shrimper who'll let me tag along to the pass tonight. I'm happy to work as a deckhand, I add.

"You mean de battlefield?" Dean says. "You wanna go out to de battlefield tonight?"

His choice of words isn't exactly reassuring. "The *battle-field?*" I say. "Is it really like that out there? I mean, should an inexperienced hand like me not go?"

"Oh, I wouldn't worry too much," he says. "Sure, it can get hot in de pass, especially if de shrimp really start coming out. I've broken up fights here at de shed after everyone comes in— seventy-year-old men so mad dey try to whip twenty-year-old deckhands. But if you want to go and you're willin' to work, you'll be okay. I'll send you out wit' Knuckles—Knuckles Mayeux. He's a great trawler. Dey call him Knuckles cuz he was a good fistfighter as a kid, I t'ink. Anyway, he'll take good care of you."

I'm starting to feel a lot deeper in this thing than I wanted to be. But there's still plenty of time to back out. It's only 4 P.M. and none of the shrimpers will be heading out for another couple of hours. For now I decide to just hang around the shed and watch Dean Blanchard work.

A boat comes in loaded with shrimp and Dean shows me how the catch is brought to a dockside vat of salty water which separates the shrimp from the ice that's been keeping it fresh at sea. A simple conveyor belt made of meshlike chain then brings the shrimp up to a scale for weighing. The price paid by the shed depends on how many shrimp it takes to make a pound.

Size, in other words, matters very much. Just like at the grocery store fish stand, the big thirty-to-thirty-five-count shrimp are worth as much as 60 or 70 percent more per pound than the smaller seventy–eighties.

Thus, at that crucial moment when a shrimper brings in his catch after a long, hard day of dragging nets, the count is all that's on his mind. The count is everything. And there in the middle of this open-sided shed, amid all the scales and conveyor belts and forklifts buzzing about, amid the boom of boat horns and screeching seagulls and ten-pound hammers mending a boat hull somewhere, lies the object of everyone's attention: the "counting board." It's a wooden, tablelike platform about chest high where the verdict is carefully rendered. Two pounds of shrimp are weighed and dumped onto that board and then the shed proprietor or a dockhand begins counting.

When you're selling as much as 1,500 pounds of shrimp, getting a forty–fifty count versus a fifty–sixty can be a matter of several hundred dollars. It can be a big slice of the profit. Which is why a permanent pall of tension seems to hang over that simple wooden board. Walk past any Louisiana shrimp shed almost any time of day during high shrimp season and you'll likely hear the voice of some poor, sleep-deprived shrimper saying, "Come on! Whattaya mean seventy–eighties? What kinda count is dat? How'd you come up with dat number?"

But Dean Blanchard has a reputation for always giving his shrimpers a fair shake, ceding borderline counts to them and always paying as high or higher per pound as his competitors. Trawlers from as far away as Dulac and Lafitte regularly come here to sell.

But if he's good to his fishermen, Dean's decidedly less generous to the people he sells *to*. Another boat pulls up just as Dean gets a call on his portable phone. It's one of the processing

plants he does business with, where shrimp are prepared in fac-
torylike fashion for markets all across America: deheaded and
shipped fresh to stores or else peeled and dried or cooked and
canned.

Later Dean tells me, "De first t'ing I do every morning is I
phone about fifteen of my clients at de plants to get me a feel for
who wants de shrimp de most. Den I lie to one guy and tell 'im
de other guy's willin' to pay more, so I get de price up. Den we
load up de trucks and roll 'em out."

We go to Dean's office, a tiny place barely bigger than an
average-size toolshed. It's full of filing cabinets, cigarette smoke,
a rack of time cards for his employees, and an elaborate moon
chart.

Dean seems most proud of the eight-by-ten color photograph above his desk, the one of him in his inmate's uniform at
a federal penitentiary in Texarkana, Texas. In the shot he's got
his arm around his alluring blond wife, Jodie, who had come to
see him during visitation hours.

"Seventeen mont's I spent at dat joint," Dean says. "Seventeen mont's. All cuz I tried to help out a few starvin' fishermen."

Dean sits down at his desk, taking a break. He lights
another Belair cigarette, leans back, and, in the best tradition of
good southern storytelling, props his feet on his desk and com-
mences to make yarn.

"Did your daddy ever tell you never to lend money to a
friend?" he asks me. "It's de best way to lose your friend *and*
your money. But here's de catch: if a shrimper I been knowin' all
my life comes up to me and says he's about to have his electricity cut off and he ain't got no groceries for his kids, what am I
gonna do?

"Dat's what happened in 1994. We had a terrible, terrible

shrimp season dat year. De tide was low all season. No shrimp all year. So suddenly I got all dese starvin' shrimpers on my hands, beggin' me to help 'em make it t'rough de winter. So I give out maybe three hundred thousand dollars in loans, but den I cain't do dat no more. So I tell 'em, 'Y'all gotta go get some fish or somethin' for me to sell.' And de next t'ing I know dey're all bringin' in red snapper even dough de season for snapper don't open for anudder few weeks. But hey, dey need food for dere kids right now so I buy it up and put it all on a truck—nine thousand pounds—and de truck, it gets inspected at de factory in Texas, don't you know, de game wardens just waitin', and I'm busted. A federal offense. It was Friday de thirteenth. I'll never forget it. Friday de damn thirteenth.

"De feds, dey really tried hard to get me to tell who de fishermen were, who caught all dat red snapper, offering me deals and stuff if I told, but I didn't rat on one single man. I'm not a rat. I called all dose government lawyers a bunch of Communists instead. Dat really made 'em mad."

Dean paid a $60,000 fine and did his seventeen months, getting out just four months before I met him, on three years' supervised release.

Being away from the business all that time nearly killed him. "It was like a nail in my heart every day," he said. "I love de shrimp business. I love it. De past eighteen years, I worked probably thirteen or fourteen Christmas Days. I just cain't stay away. I like de excitement. What's de next boat gonna bring? I like de people *on* dose boats. And when de season's at its peak, I won't go home for days. I take showers on de boats dat come in. I sleep on my office floor. Dere's just too much going on to leave. And some days we'll really make out good. *Really* good. We'll gross maybe fifty or sixty thousand dollars. In a *day!*"

But no matter how hard he works, Dean never forgets that

it's the fishermen who actually bring in the shrimp. They've helped make him a very rich man from rather modest beginnings. Today he's worth $5 million or $6 million, with a total of five different shrimp sheds. Hence his strong belief in taking very good care of those fishermen, even if it means trafficking in red snapper out of season and then taking the fall, going to prison. Even if it means going all the way to Washington, D.C., to protest "TEDs."

"Protest what?" I say.

"TEDs," Dean replies. *"TEDs."*

In 1970, he explains, the U.S. Fish and Wildlife Service gave endangered-species status to the Gulf's Kemp's ridley turtle, a graceful olive-gray creature that's the smallest among the world's sea turtles. Twenty years later shrimpers all across the Atlantic and Gulf coasts were ordered to attach turtle excluder devices—TEDs—to their trawl nets. This grid of bars fitted into the neck of a trawl net prevents turtles—but not shrimp—from passing into the net, thus preventing the turtles' death as bycatch. But fishermen have always sworn that lots of shrimp are lost because of TEDs, despite government claims to the contrary. Even now, years after they were first imposed, nothing gets a Louisiana shrimper's dander up more than the simple mention of this contraption, as if the very letters T-E-D were a hateful slur spit in the face of every fisherman's mother.

"When de government first came up with dat ridiculous TED crap, we were furious," Dean tells me. "I mean furious. I been doin' dis work all my life and I had never even *seen* a Kemp's ridley turtle and neither had anyone else here. So how was it we were de ones killin' de turtle? It was de government killin' *us*, instead, lettin' all our shrimp t'rough dose TEDs.

"So a bunch of us from Grand Isle, we printed up a bunch of T-shirts and hats dat said 'Stop TEDs' and we all bought train tickets up to Washington [from New Orleans] to protest dis shit. And at first we had us a helluva good trip. Don't you know dat by de time we got to Atlanta, dat car of us coon asses had drunk up all de beer on dat train. All of it. Every drop. De train attendants, dey said dey had never seen dat happen before. Dey had to send someone out in Atlanta to quick buy some more beer and bring it back to de train for de rest of de way up to Washington.

"So we get to D.C., and all of us we go up dem Capitol steps and go inside with our 'Stop TEDs' hats and T-shirts to show everybody dat Louisiana fishermen aren't going to take it any-more—and what's de first t'ing dat happens? All dese Capitol security police wit' guns and badges, dey all surround us and put us up against de wall and yell, 'Don't move! Don't move! Stay right dere.' Dese idiots t'ink we're dere to fuck wit' Ted fuckin' Kennedy! Oh Lord. Ted Kennedy! 'Stop Ted!' Dat gov-ernment, I'm tellin' you. Dey can't get nothin' right."

Not surprisingly, this Cajun lobbying mission failed to repeal the laws mandating TEDs, leaving Dean mad enough to want to burn down all of Washington, D.C., an act he was thankfully talked out of. Before leaving, he *did* manage to set fire to the front steps of a D.C. whorehouse after a fellow Cajun was almost robbed—but that's another story.

Given his maverick record of spirited, take-charge actions, I ask Dean if he's ever gone to Washington or Baton Rouge and demanded government action to stanch the ruinous disappear-ance of land all around him down here on the coast. After all, few people have as much to lose as Dean Blanchard does from a total collapse of this ecosystem. Who cares about TEDs if there are no shrimp in the water to begin with? But Dean's answer is a rather casual no. He's never put much time or energy into lob-bying for coastal restoration, he says. He's never been to Wash-ington over the issue or had T-shirts printed up.

His response might have surprised me if not for my conversation with Kerry St. Pé that very same morning. Sure, Dean's got a lot to lose. But a turtle excluder device, that's something tangible. You can hold it in your hand. One year it didn't exist, the next it was imposed on everybody, an immediate and concrete threat. But land loss, that's a harder issue. It's *been* happening all of Dean Blanchard's life and he's *still* buying and selling lots of shrimp. He's still pretty satisfied with what the water gives to him. The problem, as Kerry would say, is the estuary itself. These still-bountiful wetlands have cruelly co-opted Dean's proven capacity to move and shake and assert his will to protect his interests and those of his fishermen.

"And frankly," Dean tells me, "I have a lot of trouble believing de government has de competence to undertake a project as huge as dis so-called 'savin' de coast' t'ing. I mean, who built all de levees on de Mississippi River to begin wit' and who authorized all de oil and gas canals across de marsh? De Army Corps of Engineers. Dat's who. And now dey're involved in *restoration?*"

He's right about the Corps's role in muzzling the river, and that the Corps is now, ironically, in the thick of the restoration efforts. Under the federal Breaux Act, the Corps helps administer the largest pot of money now available for coastal rehabilitation, roughly $40 million annually. And in recent years there's been lots of criticism of the Corps's bureaucratic slowness and penchant for turf warfare.

"Everybody and dere brother likes to trash de Corps of Engineers," Dean said. "But it's real. Dey're idiots. When I built dis shed a few years ago, it took me two *years* to get all de permits I needed from de damn government. One Corps of Engineers inspector came out here wit' a map and den pointed to one of my docks and told me de dock was nine hundred feet from where de regulations said it should be. I said 'What?' and leaned over and glanced at his map for a split second and realized de idiot had de map upside down. It was up . . . *fuckin'* . . . side down.

"And now dese same people, dey're going to save de coast? Dey're going to build diversions and fix up all de marshes dat *dey* destroyed to begin wit'?"

His questions are valid, but I tell him I think he might be oversimplifying things a bit. The Corps is only one of several federal and state agencies now involved in restoration. Plus there's the alliance of churches, fishermen, wetland scientists, and others who first began banging the recovery drum loudly in the 1980s with the founding of the Coalition to Restore Coastal Louisiana. Almost everyone now agrees that nongovernmental groups like this will continue to play a big role in bringing both urgency and commonsense policies to future restoration efforts.

Which is all very good news because, when pressed, Dean agrees emphatically that something pretty damn big has to be done pretty damn soon to save the coast—and he's even willing to pay a high personal price for it. He supports Woody Gagliano's idea of diverting a huge portion of the Mississippi River into the Terrebonne and Barataria basins, allowing the water to create two new subdeltas on either side of Bayou Lafourche. This despite the fact that in the near term the increase in fresh water in these basins will almost certainly depress the production of brown shrimp, which thrive in saltier interior water.

"But we'll take dat hit," Dean says. "We're not in dis t'ing for just a year or two. Dis is our life. We're in it for de long haul. If a diversion is what's necessary to save de marsh our shrimp depend on, den we're all for it. Bring on de Mississippi River. If it means our kids can do dis work after us, we'll bear our sacrifice."

But talking to Dean, I realize something troubling: Kerry St. Pé and all the other restoration activists have a real image problem on their hands as they try to prod the state and federal governments into massively expanded action. Among many of the fishermen whose support is critical, virtually any form of ambitious government action is seen as synonymous with the whole sorry history of state corruption and the Army Corps's incompetence; with turtle excluder devices and Dean Blanchard's prison term and with all the other rules and regulations perceived, rightly or wrongly, as silly and unjustly imposed on their historically isolated and fiercely self-reliant lifestyles.

"I just wish," Dean says with a sigh of vexation, "dere was a way to get de job done without all dose fools in de government gettin' involved. Dat's all."

Like the land itself, a huge amount of trust has been lost in these parts, washed away over the years, and now, somehow, that trust must be rebuilt as rapidly and as thoroughly as the fragile coastline itself.

Dean and I have been talking a long time when a knock comes at the office door. It's Dean's dock foreman, Tee George.

"Knuckles is here," Tee George says. "He just pulled up."

Dean stands up and motions for me to head for the door.

"Come on," he says. "Let's go meet de man who'll take you shrimpin' tonight."


"De battlefield? You want to go out to the battlefield? With *me*?"

There's that word again.

This time it's coming from the mouth of Knuckles Mayeux. He's standing at the stern of his trawler—an old wooden affair called *Kajun's Darlins*—and he's looking every bit the part I imagined for him: dark wraparound sunglasses on a thickly bearded face, broad shoulders and unruly hair parted down the middle, the slightly wild look of an aging Wolfman Jack. He's wearing a tight black T-shirt, the sort favored by bikers, and sure enough he's a Harley-Davidson enthusiast, has a '96 1200 Sportster back at the house, and now that T-shirt, adorned with a rather extravagant gold chain that hangs down to the middle of his chest, shows off an impressively muscular physique for a man in his late fifties. Knuckles, I soon learn, grew up the son of a bar owner in Chalmette, Louisiana, and ran with such a rough crowd and got into so much trouble that everyone called him "knucklehead" until finally it just became Knuckles for short.

And there next to Knuckles, at the rear of the boat, is a red-headed woman, also in sunglasses, his wife, Rose. She's a tough customer herself, a woman who quit work as a police officer handling German shepherds on K-9 patrol in some of New Orleans' toughest neighborhoods—quit all this to eventually help Knuckles run the shrimp boat.

And so here they are, this couple, complete strangers to me, with dossiers like these, asking if they are correct in under-standing that I want to go out with them to a place everyone keeps calling a battlefield, a place for real badasses. Maybe I should have thought harder about my decision. Maybe I should have asked them more questions about who they are and what's in store. But these people make it just too darn easy to tag along without another thought in the world.

"We'd *loooove* to have you come," says Rose. "Have you eaten? Come onboard."

"Let me get dat bag for you," says Knuckles.

In a region overflowing with friendly souls, Knuckles and Rose Mayeux turn out to be two of the friendliest and most polite I've met yet.

Knuckles gives me a hand climbing over and says, "Make yourself comfortable. Dere are Cokes in de fridge if you're t'irsty. Right now, I gotta hurry and get us out to de pass to get our spot."

And so we pull away and Dean's shed gets smaller and smaller and suddenly we're out in Barataria Bay, heading east aboard the *Kajun's Darlins* to where the bay meets the Gulf of Mexico between Grand Isle and Grand Terre. It's an unbelievably beautiful evening, almost sunset, with the birds and clouds and water all bathed in muted pastels, soft and surreal. A pair of dolphins appear from nowhere and begin escorting our boat out to sea, rising and diving just ahead of the hull, their gray bodies glistening in movements graceful and playful.

Then we see it, up ahead, another fine spectacle: the long line of fishing boats.

"Dat's de pass right dere," Knuckles says. He points to the east and I go up to the bow for a better look. In the slanting evening light I can see the tip of Grand Isle and, farther out, the golden-green terrain of Grand Terre. But the quarter-mile gap of water between these islands, known formally as Barataria Pass, is not visible. From this angle all I see are boats, dozens and dozens and dozens of boats.

"Somewhere out dere," Knuckles says, "we've got to squeeze into dat line of trawlers."

It's hard to deny the martial atmosphere of the scene: all those boats in formation, hulls pointed north, the whole fleet arranged in a V formation with its vertex pointed out toward the onrushing foe, toward the bay, and the sides slanting back in perfect defensive order toward the tips of the islands, guarding an area that must be held at all costs, protecting a rear that is the entire Gulf of Mexico.

The closer we get, the more dramatic it all looks. Every tenth boat or so has a Confederate flag fluttering in the wind high above the rigging, each vessel looking like the designated color-bearer for an entire regiment. Up and down the lines, nets are being lowered into the water, the booms clicking into place like guns being cocked, ready for the assault guaranteed to come just after sunset.

Maybe my imagination's working overtime—we're only talking shrimp, after all—but this remarkable line of vessels really does look, well, heroic somehow, everyone taking his place, preparing for a pitched battle. Two implacable forces are going to collide right here, tonight, right at this spot, and all that's missing, it seems, are the Rebel yells—with Cajun accents—and an opening salvo of cannon fire.

Knuckles steers us behind the lines, scouting for an opening. We pass the sterns of several boats with names like *Captain Scar* and *Cajun Storm*, where at least some of the deckhands match the advanced billing with their sleeveless T-shirts and smokeless tobacco, their Popeye arms and rippling tattoos, their bandannas wrapped pirate-style around their heads.

Brown shrimp tend to wait till nightfall to begin migrating, but a few boats have already netted a few pounds and some of the ruffian deckhands are picking shrimp without gloves, I notice, callously grabbing angry crabs and the spines of poisonous catfish with their bare hands, tossing them overboard.

"See those guys over there," Rose says, pointing to a distant boat. "They shrimped in a hurricane once. A hurricane came and they went out in the Gulf, figuring a lot of shrimp were going to be movin' around. So they dragged their nets in that storm, with hurricane waves and hurricane wind and whatnot. And they caught shrimp—lots of shrimp—and they made it back alive."

Knuckles finds us a spot in line next to a green Coast Guard buoy with a brown pelican perched on it, then goes to the back of the cabin to check on the engine. Above the roar of his 471 GM diesel, he yells to me, "De tide's going out pretty strong right now and we have to keep de engine almost wide open just to stay still. All dese boats, dey're all working hard, engines really open, just to stay in de line."

It's a spring tide, sure enough, a big one under that new moon, and these fishermen couldn't be happier. A symphony of diesels—Caterpillars, Detroits, Cumminses; V6s, V8s, V12s—fills the air while water churns off every stern, propellers spinning furiously, all the captains concentrating on keeping their position in the V formation, steering carefully like crack pilots in a Blue Angels air show, trying not to clip the wings (i.e., net frames) of the guy next to them.

More boats are arriving all the time and a second line forms behind ours. We're at the pass maybe fifteen minutes when the first accident nearly happens. Knuckles takes his eyes off the wheel for a moment, telling Rose he wants to change the engine oil soon, when she yells "Knuckles!" Our boat has drifted backward, out of position, and almost hits the boat behind us before Knuckles can increase the throttle and steer us back. "Don't worry," he says to me immediately afterward. "Accidents happen out here all the time. But I promise we won't sink."

Just last week, he says, a shrimper was nearly run over by an oil-company boat trying to get through the line. The shrimper lost his entire net frame on one side. Other times, boats struggling to stay in the line against the outgoing current will blow an engine and then drift back, powerless, smashing into the boats behind them. But most common in these tight quarters is the problem of boats running over each other's "tails"—the ends of their nets. Propellers chew up the green mesh, freeing captured shrimp and prompting retaliation sometimes in the form of the ramming or bumping of one boat into another or an aggrieved captain opening up with a water hose and spraying the offending boat crew. One fisherman out here, an ornery eighty-year-old named Levi, is famous for throwing shackles (small metal rings) at any boat that gets too close to his.

Yet despite the stress and occasional madness, most of the Cajun fishermen out here wouldn't think of forgoing the usual rituals of their favorite pasttime: eating great food. They cook up savory grub right here in Barataria Pass, in the wheelhouse, amid the chaos, or bring along dishes already prepared. As Knuckles lowers his nets to start the hunt that night, Rose pulls out a shallow pan from home full of jumbo shrimp sautéed in butter with celery, sweet peppers, onions, and lemon slices—and we dig in. The dish is swimming in a delectable soupy juice we sop up with pieces of French bread torn from long fresh loaves.

A little while later, just after sunset, Rose puts on gloves and a rubber apron and raises the nets by hydraulic pulley and dumps the contents onto the fiberglass "picking" table out back. There aren't many shrimp, maybe thirty pounds' worth, but they're pretty big. "Forty–fifties," Rose says. There will be more shrimp as the tide builds further and night descends in full, she says.

Rose hands me gloves and my own apron and we pick the shrimp, tossing overboard the by-catch of small fish, crabs, eels, and squid. Once overboard, the by-catch is quickly scooped up by hovering seagulls or devoured by the hundreds of dolphins now swimming all around this thickening band of boats.

Rose puts the thousand or so shrimp in a large plastic basket called a *champagne* and then ices them down. In February these same shrimp migrated in from the Gulf, perhaps entering through this very same pass. They were very small then; a half dozen could fit on your fingertip. Now, after feeding and growing in the remarkably rich wetlands north of here, in fragile marshes getting smaller each year, the shrimp are a good four or five inches long.

"I know it sounds kinda hokey," says Rose, pausing in her work to push back bangs of reddish hair from her striking gray-green eyes. "But as a mother, it's sometimes painful for me to catch these shrimp. They're trying with all their might to get back to the ocean and grow up and make their own babies, and then we catch 'em. Doesn't seem fair sometimes."

Rose has two kids of her own from a previous marriage, she tells me, while Knuckles, also previously married, has three. She and Knuckles grew up together in Chalmette, outside New Orleans, but didn't see each other for years and years until 1988, when, both recently divorced, they met by chance at Bubba John's restaurant in the old neighborhood. They fell madly in love and have stayed that way ever since. So far this trip I've heard Knuckles call Rose nothing but "babe." A few years ago, when she turned fifty, Rose got drunk and had a dolphin tattooed onto her right thigh. Then Knuckles had an eagle tattooed on his arm, and as the tattooist was starting his work, Knuckles told him to put "Rose" across the bottom. "I cried and cried when he did that," she says.

As she begins rinsing down the picking table with a water hose, Rose tells me she'd never shrimped before in her life until marrying Knuckles. She was working for the Port of New Orleans Police along the riverfront before they met. One night she arrested a man who had molested a fourteen-year-old girl, but a judge later let the man go scot free on condition he join the army and keep a clean nose. Rose was utterly outraged by the decision. "My own daughter was eleven years old at the time, and I decided I just wasn't going to put my life on the line anymore for a justice system like that."

So she quit and later became first mate on Knuckles' boat.

In all my journeys through the Louisiana bayou country, I've never heard of, much less met, a female who is owner and captain of her own trawler. But some wives like Rose work as almost-equal partners in this enduringly male-dominated profession. Most women prefer to stay behind, onshore, working as bank tellers or schoolteachers or entrepreneurs or simply doing the hard work of raising young children without a dad around much of the time. But some moms head for the water, too, bringing the kids. On board, most of the engine work and driving is left to the men, and most of the cooking to the women, but many of the remaining chores are split pretty much down the middle. Tim and Phyllis Melancon, when they're not feuding, are shrimp-boat partners like this.

Over the next hour, Rose and I lift and empty the shrimp nets twice more, again with modest results. After picking, I head to the wheelhouse to ask Knuckles if he's growing disappointed with the catch so far. He's seated on a swivel chair there in the dark cabin, hands on the wheel, his bearded face illuminated by the faint glow of instrument panels. "Shrimp," he reminds me, "travel in schools. So it's a crap shoot sometimes. One guy in de line, he might not catch shit, while de guy two boats down, he gets hit head-on wit' a huge mass of 'em, a whole school. T'ousands of pounds."

He points to a boat off in the distance. "See dat?"

Sure enough, the boat's back deck and picking table are brimming with mounds of glistening brown shrimp. Under fluorescent deck lights, three men—including the driver, who steers from a second boat wheel at the stern—are madly picking the shrimp and icing them down.

"So we might just get lucky too," Knuckles says. "It's still early."

At least one captain in this gaggle of boats is trying to eliminate the element of chance altogether. I had already noticed this boat behind the lines, zigzagging all around, going back and forth across the pass, even moving up into the V formation and weaving in and out between boats.

"Dat guy's named Notch," Knuckles tells me. "He's a character. See, his t'inkin' is, 'Well, if de shrimp are movin' in schools, den I'll move around all de time, weaving back and fort', and I'm bound to hit a school sooner or later.' Dat's one way of doin' it. He's sure got dem Caterpillars workin' hard."

With all the boats in such close quarters, Notch's technique seems rather dangerous to me, if not outright insane, but to my immense surprise Knuckles says that soon *all* the boats in the pass will be roaming around just like Notch.

"De tide's not going to keep going out all night," Knuckles says. "It's gonna slow up, den reverse itself. Den it's gonna try to pull all our boats into de bay. But we can't shrimp inside de bay. Season's not open yet. And wit' de tide goin' de udder way, goin' *in*, it's impossible to keep orderly lines, so it'll be every man for himself. A cluster fuck. Everybody pushin' and weavin' around. You ain't seen nothin' yet. No sir."

To be honest, I can't quite imagine what it is he's trying to describe. So, instead, I just stare out at the relative orderliness of the boats as they are now, still grouped in this massive wedge. Deep darkness has now settled in and suddenly I realize that, from one end of the pass to the other, everything looks, well, like Christmas. Red is a required color for boat running lights. As is green. So there's a wonderful visual festiveness to the strands of vessels, like strings on a Christmas tree, the lights twinkling brightly in the otherwise vast and lonely darkness of the pass.

But soon a new light appears in the pass, a huge spotlight coming from behind us, from the Gulf side. "Ah shit," Knuckles says. Just then all the radios of all the shrimp boats, including ours, crackle with a message from an oil-industry supply boat.

We hear the captain's voice. He's coming back from an offshore rig and he needs to get through the pass, which is completely clogged with trawlers, of course. The settled procedure is for the oil boat to shine a powerful spotlight at the point in the line where it wants to pass, and all the shrimp boats which find themselves illuminated must fall back or scoot to the side carefully, very carefully, without causing accidents, and let the vessel pass. Somehow, in a matter of minutes, this process is accomplished and the breach is closed.

Around 8 P.M. the tide reaches its peak and Knuckles has the engine wide open, giving all he's got just to stay in the line. Rose, meanwhile, lifts the nets, and finally we have a very nice haul, more than 100 pounds' worth, shrimp spilling across the deck, inundating the picking table: *Farfante penaeus aztecus.* They're snapping their meaty tails, looking oddly confused with those stalked eyes and limp, weirdly long antennae. I guide fistfuls of shrimp onto a hand shovel, then deposit them in the big plastic *champagnes* at my feet. I'm careful to avoid those serrated horns above the eyes, the *piquants,* which can stab right through rubber gloves.

Just a few hundred more feet and these shrimp would have been through the pass, out in the Gulf, past one of the biggest obstacles in their peril-filled lives. Now they're on ice, just one step shy of filé gumbo, one boiling pot short of the cocktail sauce.

For the next several hours, the tide gradually lessens, creating difficult choices for Knuckles. By 10 P.M., he's unhappy with his position in the line, complaining that he's not getting enough water through his nets. "Shrimpin'," he tells me, "is all about water. De more water goes through your nets, de more shrimp you're gonna catch."

To increase that volume, he decides to leave the front line and to move two or three boats to the rear and then several hundred feet to the right to the edge of a strange and powerful whirlpool.

As tides rise and fall, sweeping past and around landforms, the water doesn't move uniformly but behaves much like a river, with eddies and main currents. The boats in this pass tonight are arranged in the shape of an inverted V precisely because three different "rivers" come together here. One tidal current is coming from the west, from behind Grand Isle, flushing out water from Caminada Bay and beyond. The other two currents are coming from the northeast and northwest, straight down from the main body of Barataria Bay. The two flanks of fishing boats are meant to capture these three currents. Once past the boats, the three currents join together and, because of their angles of approach, collide and form a giant whirlpool, where water spins violently round and round before finally being squeezed forcefully through the pass. Knuckles calls this whirlpool the "rip" current, and now he wants to shrimp right on the edge of that current, dramatically increasing the amount of water passing through his nets.

But you have to be careful doing this, careful not to get so far out in the current that the fast-moving water overwhelms your trawler engine, carrying you against your will along its rotating current and then shooting you right out into the Gulf, past the islands, ending your night of shrimping. Complicating things further, the rip current itself is unstable. It shifts from side to side like the random movements of a child's spinning top on a kitchen floor. One minute you're on the edge of the whirlpool right where you want to be, then, without warning and without moving your boat, you're right in the middle of the swirling current and struggling to get out. Or, conversely, you're suddenly sitting uselessly in slow-moving water because the whirlpool has shifted away from you.

Knuckles successfully negotiates the edge of the rip for an hour or so and we catch more shrimp, but even this current slows after a while as the tide finally gives out completely. Sometime before midnight, the neat formation of stationary boats set in straight lines disintegrates completely and a period of utter anarchy erupts. Like Notch, a hundred or so shrimp boats all begin zigzagging across the narrow pass, back and forth between the islands, like a swarm of bees crowding the surface of a honeycombed nest. There's no precise rhyme or reason to each captain's direction. He's just trying to keep moving, trying to keep water flowing through his nets because water equals shrimp. The goal now is to mop up all the shrimp that didn't get out with the tide and are now stuck—and to seize those shrimp coming back *in,* the ones that got past the islands but then were too young or weak to resist the now reversing tide.

I'm not sure I would have believed the insanity of all these boats constantly and chaotically flirting with collision had I not seen it myself. From every direction boats are now coming toward us. We turn to avoid ramming one vessel broadside just as another boat turns to avoid running into us, and so on. It's more like a session of dodge cars now. Or a nonstop game of chicken, with endless challengers everywhere you turn, one after the other.

It's not enough, of course, to avoid hitting each other's hulls. There are the nets to contend with, those vulnerable booms extending like wings sixteen feet on either side, plus the tails drifting a good twenty feet behind the stern.

No sooner had we joined this orgy of roaming boats than Rose, on the back deck, shouts "Watch out!" She runs to the suspended rope connected to the starboard net and pulls down with all her might, bringing the net's tail closer to the stern. Only then do I understand why. A boat is bearing down on us so fast, heading straight for our starboard net, that there's no time even for Rose to activate the mechanical pulley. She has to pull the rope manually, giving it all she's got, removing the net from the offending boat's path and then hanging on as the reverse momentum of the heavy net pulls her up into the air. If she lets go quickly, the net could get caught in *our* propeller. So she has to hang on and let herself be carried precariously off the deck. The reckless boat passes without harm, but there's Rose, still dangling in the air, hanging on to the rope, her apron all aflutter, cussing a blue streak. She shimmies down. *"Asshole!"* she yells one last time as the intruding boat disappears into the confusion of traffic beyond.

"I *hate* this part of trawlin' here," she says to me. "Makes me nervous with all these boats goin' around like this. I can't swim, you know. I can dog-paddle for a minute, but then I sink." Yet neither she nor anyone else out here wears a life preserver. "It just gets in the way," she says.

Knuckles, meanwhile, up in the wheelhouse, is a study in total concentration. He's gripping the wheel with both hands, hunkered down in his little command central, assessing the great disarray of traffic before him. He dodges and turns away from some boats, then roars straight ahead toward others, challenging them to turn away from him. It's all too nerve-racking for me. At one point the mood borders on abject terror. I watch as five boats, ours included, approach a single point of collision from five different angles. The huge impending pileup seems almost choreographed. Seconds pass and no one shows any sign of backing down until, at the last moment, three of the boats turn sharply away while the two others, ours being one, go full steam ahead, damn the torpedoes, and somehow avoid collision, the booms passing within a few breathtaking feet of each other.

Rose, a while later, begins shouting from the port gunwale, "Knuckles! Knuckles! Look to your left! Your left!" A lugger is coming right at us with such abandon that the captain is clearly either suicidal or has fallen asleep. "Look, Knuckles!"

But Knuckles doesn't even glance at the boat. Instead, for the first and only time that night, he gets testy with Rose. "*I'm* watching de boats in front of me," he shouts. "Let dat guy watch de boats in front of *him.*"

Somehow, just in time, the other boat veers to the side. But the tension remains high, hanging in the air, clinging to our skin like the humidity, and finally I understand why on Knuckles' cabin wall, right next to the cans of mosquito repellent and the decorative anchor made of seashells, lies one of the biggest bottles of Pepto-Bismol I've ever seen.

Just when things can't get nuttier, they do: around 1 A.M. another oil boat shows up from the Gulf and needs to get through the pass. Already these shrimp boats can barely keep track of the moving objects around them, but here comes this huge supply boat, shining its spotlight right into the knotted heart of the trawlers, approaching in a perfectly straight line, at a steady speed, without hesitation, as if it were possible to walk straight through a raging barroom brawl without getting the slightest scratch. But that's exactly what happens.

Amid all the drama, of course, everyone keeps right on catching shrimp. Each vessel passing by us has a brightly lit stern where deckhands like Rose and myself busily lift nets and pick shrimp and shovel ice. Tens of thousands of pounds of Louisiana brown shrimp will be plucked from this pass tonight, much of it bound for grocery stores all across America where buyers will have no idea what strange rituals and acts of derring-do first went into getting those shrimp onto their dining room tables.

"Shit! Shit! Shit!" Rose yells suddenly, running again to the rope connected to the starboard net. Another boat is about to clip our tail. She pulls down with all her might, saves the net from disaster, gets pulled several feet off the deck again, then shimmies down. Incredibly, it's the same boat that almost destroyed our net an hour ago, and Rose is livid. She grabs the water hose next to the picking table, opens it to full blast, and yells to Knuckles: "Follow that boat! The asshole did it again!"

"What?" Knuckles yells back from the wheel. "What?"

"That boat!" she says. "Pull up beside it. I wanna spray that guy."

There's a pause, then Knuckles says, "Ah babe, come on. Let it go. Let it go, babe."

The episode reveals just how tired everyone's getting. It's almost 2 A.M. and the catch has dropped off dramatically. At least half the trawlers in the pass have already left for home. Finally Knuckles says, "I surrender," and begins turning our own trawler back toward Grand Isle. It's quittin' time.

On the back deck, in five different *champagnes,* lie over 300 pounds of shrimp. Not a great night, but not a bust. We just never got lucky, never hit a big school. Later, at Dean's shed, we'll learn that some boats did close to 2,000 pounds.

And miraculously, despite all the near misses and occasional heated words out on the "battlefield," there were no accidents on the water or fistfights back at the shed. On the contrary, one shrimper's engine failed and before he could be washed helplessly out into the Gulf, several nearby boats rushed to his aid, dropping everything, towing him to the safety of the bay. Now, as Knuckles and Rose and I head in, hosing off the decks and putting away gear and raising the nets of the *Kajun's Darlins*, we see that same crippled boat being towed by another trawler all the way back to its home in Lafitte, Louisiana, three hours away.

After the cleanup, the ride back to the shed is a pleasant one. I sit in the wheelhouse next to Knuckles, glad to be off my feet, my body suffused with that sweet fatigue that comes from physical labor that's both strenuous and rewarding. Knuckles leans back in his captain's chair and steers casually with only one hand now, rubbing his neck with the other. He's in good spirits as he talks to Rose, who's sitting in the cabin doorway, legs crossed, smoking a Virginia Slims.

It's dark in the wheelhouse except for the orange tip of that cigarette and the almost eerie green glow of Knuckles' GPS system. With the help of several satellites in outer space, the GPS, on a TV-like screen, shows our boat pulling away from the pass. Our vessel is indicated by a green X while the water is colored black and the islands and surrounding marsh are a solid fluorescent green.

Behind us, the engine hums rhythmically, running at reduced throttle, and the gentle waves of our wake shimmer with the faintest hue of silver from the starscape above.

Knuckles and Rose will make around $450 from tonight's catch thanks to momentarily high shrimp prices. But a large amount of that sum will be eaten up by expenses. Together, this shrimping couple pockets between $20,000 and $30,000 a year in profit. It's not enough to make them rich, but they work for themselves and own their own boat and have a house on Grand Isle just two blocks from the beach. They catch king mackerel in the summer for fun and take long motorcycle trips in the winter on their Harley, often down to the beaches south of Corpus Christi, Texas. They are deeply proud of what they do for a living. The tattoo on Knuckles' arm, the one you can see if he lifts his sleeve, may bear Rose's name, but the gold chain around his neck, resting across the middle of his chest for all the world to see all the time, supports a gold boat wheel with an intricately rendered 24-karat Louisiana shrimp right in the middle of it.

These people feed us. And sharing their world for one night has been a reassuring lesson in the universe's old rhythms and pleasing cycles. Despite the amazing dragnet of boats, despite our own *champagnes* iced down and ready for market, great hordes of shrimp did escape into the Gulf of Mexico that night, many destined to reproduce in the autumn, renewing the cycle of life. Come early next May, no matter where I happen to be, Knuckles and Rose Mayeux will be right back here, back in Barataria Pass, dodging and picking and battling the "rip," catching shrimp in celestial conspiracy with the sun and the moon. That thought is pleasing to me. And for a moment a feeling of deep and satisfying peace settles over me. All seems right with the world. Right with Louisiana.

But the moment doesn't last. For when I look up a short time later and glance toward the front of the wheelhouse, I see an accident coming. Out of nowhere land appears before our boat and I watch, astonished, as the vessel plows headlong into the shore. It happens so fast that I have only a split second to brace for impact. It's the worst sort of collision. Knuckles fails to slow down even slightly, so we hit with maximum force. But even as we skid violently across tens of feet of land, the windshield doesn't shatter and I'm not thrown forward. There's no sound of splintering hull beams or exploding fuel tanks. That's because the collision happens only on the GPS screen.

Knuckles and Rose are discussing some important matter,

one that holds their attention completely, as my eyes first wander up to that GPS. On the screen, this is what I see: our boat, our little X on that avenue of black water, is heading toward a place it shouldn't be going. We're heading right for a narrow strip of land, an island of solid fluorescent green on the screen, definitely terra firma. We get closer and closer . . . yet Knuckles doesn't maneuver out of the way. He's not even watching, in fact he's still talking to Rose.

"Knuckles," I say softly, unsure of what's happening since outside our windshield everything is dark and I can't see any land at all. But the GPS shows us getting closer and closer to that implacable mass north of Grand Isle. Then it happens: we hit. The screen shows us hitting. And for several seconds we're plowing through green, through a spread of solid ground.

"Knuckles," I say again.

He finally turns to me. "Yes?"

"Your GPS isn't working."

On the screen the boat's just finished passing through the thin strip of green.

"Why?" Knuckles says. "What happened?"

"I swear I just saw your boat go through land up there."

"Land?"

"Yeah."

"Oh, *dat,*" he says. "Dat happens all de time. Dat map on de screen—I bought dat computer map in 1993. But de GPS position of our boat, de X on de screen, is coming from satellites right now, in real time."

It suddenly makes sense now. In the seven years since he bought this map, so much land has disappeared that his boat sometimes appears to be going through solid ground when it's actually going through open water.

"Not sometimes," Knuckles says. "A *lot* of times." He points to a huge area of green on the map northwest of Barataria Pass, a solid area that must be a good square mile in size, with blunt tongues of territory thrusting down toward Grand Isle.

"Dis was all marsh in 1993," Knuckles says. "See here? At low tide you could walk across dis area. Now tons of it is gone. Just water. I really gotta get me an updated map, for sure."

There in the dark of the wheelhouse, with dolphins outside again escorting us through the water and scattered trawlers following us in, Knuckles begins calling up onto the GPS screen a series of computerized maps covering most of coastal Louisiana, from the islands of Plaquemines Parish to the spartina grass of Vermilion Bay and everything in between.

"Okay, see dis right here?" he says. "See all dis along Bayou Blue? Dat's all gone now." He calls up another map. "And dat marsh behind Caillou Island? It's not dere anymore." Another map. "And dis and dis and dis—all water. Totally gone."

All since 1993. Seven life cycles of the brown shrimp.

Most horrendous is the region around Old Lady Lake, about halfway between Bayou Lafourche and Bayou Petit Caillou. Knuckles calls up the '93 map of Old Lady Lake, showing the lake surrounded by a huge swath of land, thousands of acres, so much land that the solid green on the screen causes the dark wheelhouse to glow with a ghostly green hue. It's 2 A.M. and I feel like I'm dreaming as Knuckles reaches up and moves his finger slowly across that wide expanse of green on the screen, moving in a straight line.

"We used to had to zig and zag t'rough canals and bayous here," he says. "Now it's a straight shot. Takes about t'irty or forty minutes. De whole time, de GPS says we're going t'rough land. But you look all around your boat and all you see is water. For t'irty or forty minutes."

Seven life cycles.

At least one industry is guaranteed to keep busy as lower Louisiana keeps disappearing. Any map down here older than two years is a bona fide relic. You've got to buy a new one. And every year those GPS maps sold to fishermen have less on them than the year before. The blackness of the water keeps getting bigger. The green keeps getting smaller. The trend says there aren't too many life cycles left in this old fishing region. The maps will eventually grow blank, fading completely to black.

And the old migration will end.

# Six

So important have rivers been in the long march of human civilization that the earliest known permanent settlements of *Homo sapiens* are found along their banks, reaching back ten thousand years to the ancient community of Jericho on the Jordan River. After 4000 B.C., more sophisticated cultures began to rise along the Tigris-Euphrates and Nile Valleys in the Middle East, the Indus and Ganges Valleys in South Asia, and the Huang Ho and Yangtze Valleys in China. So dependent were these cultures on river functions that anthropologists call them "hydraulic" civilizations, where rivers provided water for drinking, irrigation, transport, crop fertilization, and rapid communication.

On down the ages, human beings have never stopped bending rivers to the service of human needs. These coursing ribbons have provided routes of exploration for conquerors, traders, and settlers. Rivers have milled our flour, sawed our wood, floated our logs. They've served as natural borders between states and bloody battle lines between warring armies. A thirteenth-century Mongol khan once killed his enemies using a river, luring twelve thousand troops into a valley and then destroying a dam and drowning them all. Less violently, cultures the world over have used rivers to bury their dead, lowering the bodies intact, weighted by stones, or burning them, the ashes scattered.

Today rivers give us hydroelectric power and a means to cool industrial hot-water discharges. They take our garbage, our feces, our urine, our PCBs, and other chemical wastes and runoff. Smaller branches, reengineered by human hands, serve as safety-valve spillways for flood-prone larger streams. Rivers give us wild stocks of fish and bankside space for aquaculture. They give us watery real estate around the world for entire communities living the buoyant life, atop houseboats. Rivers offer us recreation, soothing our minds aboard quiet canoes or wading through trout streams or tour-boating past castles along the Rhine—and they feed our souls through holy purification. Millions of Hindus erase their sins each year in the sacred Ganges, whose water is believed to be the goddess Ganga herself come to earth, the celebrated "giver of life."

But in this ancient riparian dance between people and water, there's one thing rivers have never been asked to do. Never in recorded history has a river been harnessed on a massive scale to do what it does naturally, to simply deposit its vast sediment load in its delta region, but to do so in a targeted way, guided by human beings, to the benefit of both people and nature. Never, in other words, has a river been specifically asked to create huge tracts of land.

But that, of course, is precisely what many Louisianans now

have in mind for the lower Mississippi River. With a life-or-death urgency as great as any irrigation project in the Ming dynasty period or crop-fertilization requirements of the great pharaohs, Louisiana needs the Mississippi River to manufacture land—islands, wetlands, stable shorelines—so that an entire culture and economic way of life can survive. And it needs this to happen right away.

In part this can be accomplished in numerous small ways. Modest quantities of river water can be captured by various pumping stations, siphons, and weirs along the Mississippi, the water then directed by pipeline or canal to patches of failing wetlands or to the outer edges of hurricane levees, creating thin aprons of buffering marsh grass. And out in the Gulf, dredge barges can harvest soils deposited by the river long ago along the ocean floor, relocating them to the beaches and dunes of barrier islands.

But these methods are mere child's play, their combined effect of little consequence compared to the massive man-made river Woody Gagliano would like to build, the so-called Third Delta Conveyance Channel. This hulking waterway, carrying up to 200,000 cubic feet per second (cfs) of water, would be a workhorse of land-building the likes of which the world simply never stopped to dream up before.

Indeed, it's hard to imagine taking an elevator six hundred feet to the top of the Gateway Arch in St. Louis, Missouri, or climbing the steps to the highest row of seats at Busch Stadium, then looking down at the river, the mighty Mississippi far below, seeing those half-mile-long bridges under which float 1,000-ton barges—seeing this great, wide, flowing work of God—and trying to imagine human beings creating a river that big, an artificial river with an average flow equal to that at St. Louis: 200,000 cfs. Not only a river that big, but one which, halfway along its man-made course, would split in two per the wishes of its masters, creating two smaller rivers each *larger* than the lower Missouri River, and each finally creating deltas of its own along the Louisiana coast with a combined size and area of influence equal to one-fifth the Nile Delta.

And all this work, all this land-building, accomplished by a quantity of water equaling barely a third of the flow of the lower Mississippi River, diverted from the master stream just below Donaldsonville, sixty miles upstream from New Orleans. The remaining Mississippi water would roll right on past the Big Easy to the sea, the usual course.

How truly massive this river must be, so close to its mouth, to have this much water to spare, this much power to lend. If nothing else, my time in the bayous has made me conscious—acutely so—of just how great the Mississippi's influence is everywhere you turn, all across lower Louisiana, its presence felt even hundreds of miles from its actual course. It's a river which, one way or another, is always calling the shots. Always.

Which is why you can never quite get it out of your mind.

That's certainly the case the night Knuckles and Rose and I come back from shrimping in Barataria Pass. Perhaps it's the gentle rocking of Knuckles' boat as I sleep that makes me dream of water that night. Or maybe it's being tied to a dock on an island, Grand Isle, itself created by the Mississippi River, that makes me dream not just of water but of a mighty river. What-ever the reason, when we return to shore at three in the morn-ing and Knuckles and Rose offer me the wheelhouse bunk while they head off to their island home, a feeling of total exhaustion overtakes me, producing a deep sleep which in turn creates the fantastic image in my mind.

There I am, in my dream, in the middle of the ocean, tread-ing water all alone, totally by myself, without a boat or a piece of land anywhere in sight under a marvelously blue and cloudless sky. Except it's not the ocean I'm in. It's a river, one that stretches away forever, in every direction, past every horizon, covering the whole earth. There are no waves striking me, no wind, and no sound except the voice of this giant stream, a million soft gurgling voices that carry me gently along, briskly along, a cork in infinite water, down this watery path that covers the whole of the earth under that blue, blue sky and bright pleasing sun.

I don't know why I have this dream except that perhaps I know it's time I finally went to the Mississippi River myself, to see it up close, in person, and try to better visualize just how the proposed diversion of water from its flow—historic and huge—might actually work. Of course the man-made river Woody Gagliano has in mind, the Third Delta Conveyance Channel, wouldn't be quite as big as the river in my dream, but the engineering challenges would be very large indeed. You can't create a St. Louis-league river without taking great care, and you can't do it all in one day no matter how much the engineering process resembles playing God.

But if the state of Louisiana ever gets the money it needs to fully implement the Coast 2050 plan—that last-ditch master plan for coastal survival—this is how the diversion might work:

First, according to plans developed by Gagliano and codesigner J. L. van Beek, a massive concrete and steel "control structure" would be built along the western bank of the Mississippi just below the Sunshine Bridge, south of Donaldsonville. Equipped with a row of 400-ton steel gates seventy-five feet tall, this structure would control the flow of water leaving the river and entering the diversion channel. The control structure would be located on the outside edge of a big bend of the Mississippi and would draw water from near the bottom of the river's flow, maximizing the amount of sediment captured as the current pools up around the curve.

Next, a ninety-five-mile-long channel would be dredged between the control structure and the target marshes to the south, traversing mostly wetland terrain free of population centers. This dredged pathway would guide the emerging river but would itself be incongruously small, just fifteen feet deep and barely two hundred feet wide, nothing close to the size needed to float all those barges past Busch Stadium. But this smallness is an engineering trick. In nature, rivers that flow out of larger rivers—i.e., distributaries—develop gradually, gaining in size as the force of their current scours out their riverbeds, gradually making room for more volume from the master stream. The Third Delta Conveyance Channel would do the same thing. The initially small guidance ditch would allow the new river to do most of the construction work itself, literally enlarging itself by mimicking natural river development and growth.

Initial flow out of the control structure would be right around 20,000 cfs, but would grow to 200,000 cfs over a fifty-year period as the new river crafts its own earthen bed, scouring away millions of tons of river-bottom sediment. This not only saves human beings the trouble of digging out the whole bed themselves but conveniently contributes to the final goal: delivering soil to the badly needed target deltas downstream. Even the soil dredged for the initial guidance ditch would be stacked up right next to the young river, creating a "sacrificial levee" which would gradually be eroded away as the river grows, that soil delivered to the deltas too. All told, the amount of earth displaced by human hands and the river itself would equal twenty times that dug to create the Erie Canal.

But for all this clever use of nature's personality traits, lots of math and science would be hovering offstage, writing most of the script. In Gagliano and van Beek's illustrated manual detailing the basic design of this grand diversion, they state, for example, that an optimal initial flow of 20,000 cfs has been

> worked out using a combination of HEC-RAS model runs and application of the hydraulic relationship between velocity, channel dimensions, and gradient, as expressed in Manning's equation ($v = 1.49[R2/3s1/2]/n$) in which $v$ is the average flow velocity in ft/s, $R$ equals the hydraulic radius of the flow area, $s$ is the gradient, and $n$ equals a roughness coefficient.

A bit more than just turning on the tap and letting the water run, in other words.

There's also the challenge of pipelines. Dozens of oil and gas pipelines lie in the path of the proposed channel, some active, some abandoned, many unmapped, creating the potential for messy spills if any are discovered unexpectedly by the teeth of a backhoe. The pipelines would have to be restructured to run underneath the channel bottom or suspended bridgelike above the current, contributing enormously to the channel's estimated $2 billion construction cost.

But with the pipelines gone and the guidance ditch complete, new land would start to take form from the very first day water entered the channel and advanced seaward. As the powerful flow emptied into the open water of Terrebonne and Barrataria Bays, the current would lose velocity and the sediment load would begin to fall to the bay floor, forming bars and shoals. These emerging landforms would act as natural barriers that further slow the river's flow, encouraging the current to branch off and fan out, widening the sediment distribution. The seeds of wetland grasses, carried down by the river current or deposited by birds, would quickly colonize the emerging bars. The new grass would then act as an additional trap to sediments, accelerating a building process that would eventually result in fan-shaped "subdelta lobes" stretching over a vast area.

But using a man-made river to induce these natural processes would also bring nature's eventual headaches. The channel, like any delta-building river, would gradually become clogged and stymied by its own land-building success, its flow impeded and its route to the sea eventually no longer the shortest available. The river would then want to jump track, perhaps wildly and dangerously. As a result, Louisianans four or five centuries from now would face the odd necessity of carefully diverting the *diversion*.

In another twist, this conveyance channel would do more than just create land. It would reduce and perhaps one day help eliminate the infamous "dead zone" presently at the mouth of the Mississippi River. Each year, nitrogen-rich fertilizers and animal manure from all across America's farm belt wash into the Mississippi and flow out the river's mouth, creating a New Jersey-size area in the Gulf prone to massive and recurring algae blooms. These blooms deplete the water of dissolved oxygen, making life impossible for most marine species and so leaving an eerie and grotesque zone of nothingness now famous worldwide.

Diverting a third of the Mississippi's flow into the Third Delta Conveyance Channel would not only reduce the nitrogen load feeding the Gulf algae, it would actually fertilize the coastal grasses so desperately in need of stimulation. As part of their natural filtration capacity, wetland grasses can safely absorb the water's excess nitrogen and phosphorus—and thrive as a result. Indeed, LSU researchers have shown that Louisiana's coastal grasses are two to three times more productive when exposed to the Mississippi's "fertilized" flow. The diversion would thus help solve two enormous problems at once.

But what, exactly, would the Louisiana coast look like if this mammoth channel were actually built? Gagliano and van Beek provide answers by analyzing the geologic record of the Mississippi's past land-building and by studying the current land-creation rate of the Atchafalaya River (to the west) and its own man-made distributary: the Wax Lake Outlet. Using these analyses, the projections are quite encouraging. In just fifty years the state of Louisiana, with the help of the Third Delta Conveyance Channel, would have two new subdeltas fanning out along its coast, situated on either side of the Golden Meadow–Leeville area. Each subdelta would be at least seventy-five square miles in size and made up mostly of marsh grass but with scattered small islands and natural levees along the channel so large you could build a highway on top of them as well as houses. These subdeltas, which would then double in size during the *next* fifty years, would also nourish and maintain hundreds of square miles of already existing marsh, preventing their loss to subsidence.

Here's the bottom line: If the Third Delta Conveyance Channel were built today, combined with strategies to maximize present land-building from the Atchafalaya, combined with the construction of a dozen much smaller sediment diversions (similar to Caernarvon) scattered all along the Mississippi below Donaldsonville—if all of this were done very soon, the state of Louisiana's net land loss would come to an end sometime around the middle of this century. Then, after a 150-year hiatus, a reversal would occur. The old miracle would return. The disaster would finally end.

Louisiana would start to grow again.

I pull away from Dean Blanchard's shed around 11 A.M., waving goodbye to Knuckles and Rose. They're mending a net aboard

the *Kajun's Darlins,* having just sold last night's catch and pock-
eted a check. They've invited me out for a second night of
shrimping, of course, but I just can't bear the pain. I, too, have a
history of back ailments, and leaning over the picking table last
night, tossing fish overboard while shoveling up shrimp, has
left my cranky spine a total wreck. I wake that morning in the
wheelhouse bunk, staring up at the slightly rocking ceiling, my
teeth clenched tight.

In the car, I just try to put up with it. I use a pillow for lum-
bar support as I head slowly back up Bayou Lafourche, leaving
Grand Isle behind atop two-lane Route 1. Weeks earlier I had
contacted a noted geomorphologist at the University of New
Orleans who agreed to accompany me to the banks of the Mississippi River south of the city. The purpose: to inspect the
Caernarvon freshwater diversion there, the one created to help
rejuvenate oyster beds but which has started building land as
well. Unable to see the Caernarvon structure from the air with
Kerry St. Pé due to bad weather, I now want to get an eye-level
view with a trained specialist, hoping to learn as much as possible about how this small phenomenon of land-building works.

But the Caernarvon journey isn't scheduled for several days
hence, leaving me with time to kill and no concrete plans. The
week before, Tim Melancon had invited me to "camp out" at his
place for as long as I wanted in light of the sadly reduced occu-
pancy there. I was, he said, welcome to Tee Tim's room.

So an hour later I pull up to Leeville and see Tim outside his
camp. The first thing he says to me isn't hello. It isn't "How are
you?" Instead he yells: "Can you drive a truck wit' a boat trailer
hitched to it?"

Tim's not alone. He's standing next to his twenty-eight-
year-old second cousin and best friend Emory Melancon, otherwise known as "Big E." At six foot five, 300 pounds, Big E is a

giant of a man. He wears size 14 Cajun Reeboks, has massive shoulders, a titanic head, and almost no neck. People call him the "human crane," which is precisely why Tim has asked him over and why Tim is now asking me if I can handle a boat trailer.

Big E's hand swallows mine in a handshake. *"Comment ça va?"* he says. "How's it going?"

Tim suddenly throws me the truck keys before even confirming my driving skills and the two cousins take off down the bayou in Tim's crab boat, heading for a boat ramp on the other side of Leeville where I meet them, backing the trailer into the water. Moments later, having hauled the boat back to the camp, I watch in amazement as Big E—by himself—lifts a damaged Mercury 40 outboard engine from the stern and carries it to a storage spot under the camp. He then lifts another, functioning outboard, again by himself, and drops it onto the boat stern.

"De human fuckin' crane!" Tim says with obvious pride at his cousin's miraculous strength. Big E goes inside for a much deserved glass of water, and Tim says to me, "Dat boy's as dumb as a post, but he'll give ya de heart right out of his chest if ya need it."

Big E comes back and I learn he's the dock foreman at a shrimp shed in Leeville. He's been particularly close to Tim and Phyllis ever since the tragic death of his mother to a drunk driver a year earlier. Every day, for hours, Tim and Big E form an inseparable odd couple, one man of enormous size, the other quite small, their ages separated by seventeen years. But you can't keep them apart. When Tim wanders a few feet away looking for some tools, Big E turns to me and rolls his eyes toward Tim and whispers, "He's as dumb as a post, but you'd look a long time for a better partner."

In a way, this friendship was sealed in blood three years ago, and Big E has the big pink scar on his right leg to prove it. The two men were relaxing at the Gray Goose bar in Delcambre, Louisiana, having just finished a day catching white shrimp in Vermilion Bay, when the bar owner announced loudly that he had a seven-foot alligator in a pen out back and would give a hundred dollars to any pair of men who thought they were tough enough to wrestle it onto its back for a pin.

"You got a deal," says Big E, slapping his giant hands against the beery bar counter.

So everybody in the bar goes around back and Tim and Big E jump in the muddy pen and the first thing Tim does is take off his shirt and put it over the gator's head, which instantly confuses the beast and makes it grow still. But then comes the hard part. Big E straddles the gator's back, keeping a close watch on that powerful tail. "De tail's whatta hurt you," he tells me. "It'll break bot' your ankles in one swipe."

So he pulls and tugs and struggles to turn the beast over while Tim, bare-chested, struggles equally to keep his shirt over the gator's eyes. Both men are getting covered in mud from head to toe when the gator suddenly scores a point, digging one of its back claws into Big E's right calf. The pain pisses off Big E so much he explodes with a final burst of strength and flips the 200-pound reptile over, exposing its white belly to the dozens of bargoers gathered round. "When you see dat white belly, it's all over," Big E tells me. "We fuckin' did it. We showed dem fuckers who was really from de swamp."

Muddy and exhausted, Tim still shirtless, Big E still bleeding, the two went back up to the bar for a final drink and to collect their hundred dollars.

They've been best friends ever since.

Back on the bayou that afternoon, having swapped the outboard motors, both Tim and Big E want to show me the new wharf they've just built right below the camp. Amazingly, they constructed the wharf entirely from driftwood. They scavenged various pilings and dock planks scattered along the coastal beaches and marshes after big storms. Then they rammed the pilings into place beside Tim's camp by crudely raising and lowering one of the booms of his shrimp boat, using the boom like a giant hammer. "Coon-ass engineering," Tim calls it.

This fully recycled wharf now supports two large troughs intended for watering cattle but converted by Tim to live wells for crabs ready for market.

"See dis PVC pipe right here?" Tim asks me, pointing to a circumferential ring of piping inside each round tank delivering oxygenated water to the crabs. "When I bought dat pipe, me, it wasn't curved in a circle like dis at all. Dose pieces of pipe, dey was all straight as boards. De people I bought it from asked me what I was going to use it for. I said I was going to bend it into a big circle for my crab tanks. Dose guys, dey said straight PVC pipe couldn't be bent dat way. It was too strong. I needed more expensive curved pipe. But I told dem dey didn't know Big E."

Sure enough, back at the camp, Big E took those straight pieces of pipe in his mighty arms and huffed and puffed and bent them just the way Tim wanted them, forming giant circles of piping. Another triumph of Cajun ingenuity in a pinch.

For me, just hearing all this talk of hard work and gator wrestling makes my ailing back wince. I'm standing in all sorts of strange positions, and Tim notices, asking me what's wrong. I explain about the shrimping last night, then tell him I've been to Western doctors, massage therapists, osteopaths, a Reiki specialist, and several "crackabones" (chiropractors). I've taken herbs and muscle relaxants, and had acupuncture needles stuck in me. But nothing has helped. When my back goes out, it just goes out.

"Have you tried a *traiteur*?" Tim asks.

He's got a look of genuine concern on his face as I tell him, no, I haven't tried a *traiteur*. But I know what one is, having read about these old-school "doctors" of South Louisiana tradition. Before the penetration of modern health care here, bayou people suffering from everything from heat stroke to liver cancer would turn to men and women with the "gift" of healing, so-called *traiteurs*, literally "treaters." Using an often effective mix of herbal remedies, prayer, and folk superstitions, *traiteurs* were once found in every bayou community, no matter how small. Now they've almost disappeared completely, though enough Louisianans still hew to the old ways, especially after Western medicine fails, to keep a handful of *traiteurs* in practice across the bayous, their ranks composed of men and women, blacks and whites, Cajuns and Indians.

"When I was seven years old," Tim tells me by way of endorsement, "I had dese five big ugly warts on my left hand, and my mama she said dey needed to come off. So we went up de baya to a *traiteur* in Golden Meadow and he took a piece of string and he tied five knots in dat string, one for every wart. Den he told me to go back to my house and t'row dat string over my shoulder into de bayou and *not* look back. So dat's what I done, and two mont's later, all my warts was gone. I swear to God right here, dey was gone."

If a *traiteur* could do the same for my ailing back, I thought, I was all for it, and I made a mental note to track one down before the end of this bayou journey.

Right now, the sun was sinking and a flock of glossy ibis were flying overhead, back to their nests in the distant sunlit grass, carrying food for their young. It's time for us to eat, too. Tim's pleasant, gray-haired, sixty-eight-year-old mother Neva has put together quite a supper of *ragoût de patate* (potato stew), more jambalaya, and speckled trout caught from right off the bayou dock and marinated in a special mustard sauce.

We dine in the kitchen of Neva's tin-roofed house immediately next to Tim's camp. The kitchen is tiny and the whole house can't be more than five hundred square feet. But everything's relative, and I'm starting to see the world like the bayou fishing families I spend time with. When half your life is spent out on trawlers and other fishing vessels, cooking and sleeping inside ten-by-fifteen foot cabins, the tiniest shoreside camp starts to look quite comfy and roomy. Who could need more space than this?

While Big E tears into a towering mound of jambalaya, I look over his shoulder at the framed family photos on the kitchen wall. These include Neva's four grandsons: Tee Shannon, Tee Ted, Tee Terral, and Tee Tim. The first three boys, like many Cajuns, have the middle names of Catholic saints: Michael, Anthony, and Anthony respectively. There's also a photo of Phyllis on the wall, taken six years ago when she was thirty-seven, dressed in her graduation gown and mortarboard, GED proudly rolled up in her hands. It's a sad reminder of her absence, this photo.

"Pass de Tabasco sauce," Big E says, taking the fire-orange bottle from Tim. To his food Big E applies an ample quantity of this piquant condiment native to South Louisiana, made from mashed capsicum peppers fermented for three years in oak barrels.

"I heard dey was gonna start repaintin' de Leeville Bridge," Tim volunteers, reaching for the hot sauce himself.

"What? When?" says Neva.

"It's about time," says Big E.

"In a few months. Dat's what I heard," Tim says.

"You t'ink dey'll go wit' gray again?" Big E asks.

"I don't know. Why do dey always paint bridges gray, anyway? Up and down de bayou, gray, gray, gray. Would it kill dem to try somet'ing different? What's wrong wit' green or blue? Would dat kill dem?"

Everyone at the table shrugs. Then there's some spirited disagreement as to when the Leeville Bridge was last painted and just how long it took. The eventual consensus is about twenty years and about three months, respectively.

The dinner talk goes on like this for most of the evening, decidedly prosaic, never straying from local and family matters, yet full of a certain small-town drama and passion.

"Oh my, I almost forgot!" Neva says, turning to Tim. "Patsy Ann called last night and you need to go up de baya and get your boat clutch out from under dat big oak tree she's got. Dey're gonna cut down dat old tree tomorrow."

"What? Why? Why dey cuttin' down de tree?"

"I don't know. But you better hurry up dere tomorrow."

For years Tim had stored a shrimp boat clutch—three feet long and three feet wide and 500 pounds in weight—under the biggest branch of that tree, on the property of Neva's cousin Patsy Ann in Golden Meadow. This way, if Tim ever needed to replace his current clutch, he'd be able to hoist the superheavy backup onto his pickup bed using chains thrown up and over the branch, and then drive it to the water.

But there was a feud of some kind going on between this upriver cousin and the Melancons of Leeville, and the tree-cutting threat was an apparent tit-for-tat matter.

Big E was fuming, his forehead perspiring from more than just the hot sauce.

"You just can't call people up one day and say, 'Come get your clutch real quick dis right-now second.' Dat's just no way to handle a clutch situation."

"Me, I never heard of such a t'ing," Tim says. "Scarin' a poor old tree like dat. I oughta charge dose people for de crabs I'm a gonna lose by comin' up dere tomorrow."

Throughout the meal at Neva's, various other members of

the Melancon extended family drop by. Tim's nephew Tee Terral
will be running Tim's crab traps during the shrimp season, and
he comes by to make sure Big E has hooked up the new outboard. Athanas, Phyllis's father, hollers through the door that
he's borrowing wire for making minnow traps. Ronnie, Tim's
distant cousin from Galliano, stops by to borrow a cooler for
an evening of sportfishing down the bayou. And Edwin, Tim's
uncle, comes by and grabs a plate because, well, he just smelled
the good food.

Indeed, during the next few days I spend with Tim, he's
rarely detached from the company of family members, even
with his wife and son gone. So close together do most Bayou
clans live even now, their lives intertwined in a daily way like
most Americans seventy-five and one hundred years ago in a
million long-gone rural settings, that some bayou priests today
will not marry a couple until multiple witnesses have testified
that the man and woman are, in fact, no more closely related
than third cousins.

That night, as all the relatives pass through the house, each
dutifully chimes in on the boat clutch controversy and the
painting of the Leeville Bridge, and everybody asks about the
little boy born to Tim's second cousin Nikia across the street.

And yes, there's a TV in Neva's house—a big color TV and
it's on throughout the supper. But unlike the relatively solitary
life of nuclear families across the rest of America, where it's just
mom and dad and the kids and long-distance calls to grandma
and cousins, the TV doesn't stand much of a chance among the
Melancons. Who could possibly follow the inane banter of *Who
Wants to Be a Millionaire* with so many kinfolk noisily coming and
going and doing all that talking, talking, talking?

————

Later that week, after a long day in the marsh with Tim checking crab traps in the morning and minnow traps in the evening, then another great meal at Neva's with Big E, we all go up to Tim's camp where I rest my back for a while.

And that's when it happens. The phone rings.

Tim picks it up. It's Phyllis on the other end. Big E can't believe it. He whispers to me that those two haven't talked in three months. But soon it becomes clear why Phyllis has called. She and Tim start arguing over unpaid bills—and Big E and I decide to give them privacy, heading outside onto the camp's back deck.

"He'll be back," Big E says, taking a seat on a wooden bench as channel mullet jump audibly in the bayou, splashing through the sticky night air.

"Who'll be back?"

"Tee Tim," he says. "All dat business about him takin' off cuz he don't want to work on de water no more is a bunch of crap. He's just *bon à rien* [lazy]. He'll be back."

The latest news is that Tee Tim is eyeing shipbuilding jobs as far away as Maine and Hawaii after his May 19 graduation. He might as well have been planning to go to the moon. But Big E doesn't buy it.

"Dis life down here," he says, "it's in Tee Tim's blood. He just don't realize it yet. He don't realize he can go wherever he wants but he'll never be happy unless he lives down de baya. What good's a job payin' a million dollars if you ain't happy?"

While most Americans would take the million dollars no matter what, bayou folks like Big E would instead *pay* a million dollars just to keep their lives exactly the way they are. Or so they say, and increasingly I take them at their word. But it'll take much more money than that to keep things the same down here. What cruel irony that this rare pocket of American contentment, free of the fever of never-ending acquisition, is at the mercy of such uncooperative geological phenomena rapidly at work underfoot.

"But why should Tee Tim come back here?" I ask Big E, playing devil's advocate. "Why should he crab and shrimp when, in his lifetime, there probably won't be any more crabs and shrimp to catch?"

Big E was born in 1972, around the same time Woody Gagliano was making his historic breakthrough in understanding the man-altered dynamics of the Louisiana coast. Yet nothing of significance had been done to slow the rate of land loss in all those years. Now Big E's a grown man, pushing thirty.

"Think of how much marsh you've seen disappear just in your lifetime," I say. "Why should Tee Tim come back here?"

"Because he belongs here," he says, mustering no greater explanation.

"Well," I say, "maybe if they build that big river diversion they're talking about, bringing Mississippi water down here to start creating new land . . ."

"Dat's never going to happen," says Big E.

"Why not?"

"Too much corruption," he says.

This time I insist on elaboration.

"T'ink about it," he says. "A few years ago, people said gambling casinos along de Mississippi and de coast were going to save de Louisiana economy. It was supposedly just what de state needed to survive. But instead it was just one big corruption where all de politicians got rich and [ex-governor Edwin] Edwards is now gonna go to jail for all de kickbacks he took, and de people who actually work for a living in dis state don't get shit. Now everybody's talkin' about bringing de Mississippi River itself down here and it's supposed to save our economy again, stop de erosion. But can you imagine all de corruption dat's gonna come wit' a project dat big? Dis is Louisiana, man. *Lou-ees-zi-an-a.* Don't you know our history? Even if dey *do* get some money to make somethin' happen, none of it will really get down de baya. And even if dey *do* manage to build dis damn thing, dis big fake river, who knows if it's gonna work?"

He stands suddenly. "You seen de *carré* yet?" he asks me. "De Christmas tree *carré*? Have you seen it?"

I shake my head. "Only from a distance."

"Come on," he says.

We cross Route 1 on foot and follow the edge of the marsh for a few moments. Even before reaching our destination, I can smell it: that wonderful, overpowering fragrance of spruce. Here in the middle of this giant salt marsh, in the month of May, with oyster beds scattered in the distance and shrimp boats steaming out to sea in the salty air, it smells like Christmas. We reach the source of the scent: hundreds of old and browning Christmas trees stacked in wall-like fashion in the open water, forming straight and porous barriers designed to protect the shore from wave action and foster marsh growth within the compounds.

"But dis," Big E says, "is like putting a Band-Aid on an artery dat's burst. It just don't work. Not one blade of grass has come up here. Not one. So if dey can't get dese *carrés* to do what dey're supposed to do, how are dey gonna bring dat big river down here and create land like dey say dey can?"

"But if you don't think a diversion will ever work," I say, "what's the point? Why should Tee Tim come back here? Where's the future in it for him? Or you?"

"Maybe dere *is* no future for us," Big E says. "Probably dere's not. But where are we gonna go? Dis is where we belong. Right here. We'll stay till de land's all gone and den maybe dat'll be de end of us too."

Back at the camp, Tim's got more immediate problems on his mind. He's just hung up with Phyllis, and he keeps telling Big E and me how it's been three months—three months!—and maybe he shouldn't have thrown Tee Tim out of the house in the first place. "I tried to do what I t'ought was right, and instead I just made ever't'ing worse," he says over and over again.

I sleep in the camp's conspicuously vacant bedroom that night, under a rack of three hunting rifles belonging to Tee Tim, including one with the stock cut in half by a father long ago so a little boy could rest it against his shoulder to fire at tin cans. Outside the room's sole window I can make out the family shrimp boat tied to the new wharf. It is, in more ways than one, Tim senior's entire universe floating out there, named after his only child, his only son, the large green letters painted across the white wooden hull: *Tee Tim*.


Not far from Tim's camp, past a jumble of old wharves and a sinking dirt parking lot that floods at high tide, stands a shrimp shed owned by a Vietnamese family. Many times, from a distance, I've seen this family and the Vietnamese fishermen who tie up to sell their catch there. But I haven't had a chance to meet these people. Nor, for that matter, have I seen anyone with a non-Vietnamese face on the property. Like most of the thousands of Vietnamese fishing people living up and down the bayous of South Louisiana, this group next door seems to inhabit a parallel universe.

You can hear the men talking on the wharves in their rapid-fire tonal language, no doubt discussing how the weather and tides will affect fishing that day. Busily the men buy and sell shrimp and crabs, then ice them down to be trucked off to market. They take breaks on the wharves, squatting Asian-style, resting on their haunches, smoking cigarettes or having meals together, eating from communal plates brought out by women often dressed in conical straw hats and black pantaloons. Such scenes are not uncommon across much of the coast, often played out within full view of busy Cajun shrimp sheds right next door. But the two worlds, again, are in separate orbits, side by side with amazingly little contact between them.

The Vietnamese have their own Buddhist temple near Houma and their own Catholic church in Larose. They have their own entire neighborhood outside of New Orleans and live together in smaller pockets of frame houses and mobile homes along the backcountry bayous. They have their own seafood sheds, their own boat-building yards, their own net-repair shops. Even at the Blessing of the Fleet ceremonies in the spring, so important to the rest of the bayou community, you never see a Vietnamese face. Not one. But neither do you see Cajuns lighting fireworks in January, giving gifts of money in red envelopes and drinking rice liquor per the Vietnamese tradition for the Tet lunar new year.

I've only glimpsed this Vietnamese universe from afar, waving to the passing shrimp boats with names like *Captain Tran* and *Captain Huy* and *Sea Dragon,* many steered by veterans of the old South Vietnamese army. From the wheelhouse comes a friendly smile on an Asian face and sometimes a whiff of food trailing behind, lemongrass soup, maybe, with shrimp and vegetables, what the Vietnamese call "Mekong gumbo" down here. But it's just a whiff. And just a wave. And then the moment's gone. Or I'm standing in line at the Piggly Wiggly watching two Vietnamese boys buying cilantro and fish sauce, both stone silent until they say, in English, "How much does dis cost?" and "T'ank you," their speech imbued with a distinctly Cajun accent.

This separation of worlds inevitably breeds misunderstandings and the occasional bad joke. Perplexed by all the strange Vietnamese foods, one Cajun tells another, "Did you ever notice how dere were no more stray dogs along de roads after dose people showed up?"

And with Vietnamese children excelling in most bayou schools, there's the joke about the Cajun who telephones the police:

"Officer, some Vietnamese people robbed my home while I was gone."

"How do you know they were Vietnamese?"

"Because dey stole de TV and de stereo and dey did my son's homework."

I'm growing impatient with these secondhand portraits, however, and so I resolve to cross the cultural divide myself for a closer look. I walk from Tim's camp one morning over to the Vietnamese shed next door, locating the boss's office. A diminutive Vietnamese man named Victor, the owner here for several years, holds a portable phone to his ear with one hand and a new, fine-bristle toothbrush with the other, meticulously cleaning dust from every square inch of a completely disassembled fax machine.

"You want sell swimp?" he asks me, pausing briefly from his double duties.

I shake my head.

"Cwab?"

"No."

"One minute," he says, and goes back to his phone call and fax cleaning.

I wait longer than one minute amid the incomprehensible sea of Vietnamese voices all around. Dockhands with arms bulging from shoveling ice—cigarettes dangling from their mouths—unload a boat called *Serpent King* as hanging scales do their job and money changes hands. But Victor stays on the phone and I finally grow weary of waiting.

"Any luck?" Tim asks when I return.

"They all seem too busy to talk right now," I said. "I'll try later."

"Shit yeah, dey're too busy," Tim says, lapsing into his occasional and unappealing fondness for racial slurs. "Dere's not a Cajun anywhere can work as hard as a damn gook. No sir. Dose gooks, dey didn't come here to fuckin' play around."

That unfortunate appellation—gook—was popular among American soldiers during the Vietnam War, of course, signifying as well as anything the great cultural gulf and distrust that contributed so mightily to the fall of Saigon in 1975. Soon after the war, Louisianans began to see the first of many Vietnamese refugee families settling down along the state's coast, followed by a second wave in the late 1970s with the so-called "boat people" exodus. For those South Vietnamese wishing to flee Communist rule, the options were very few. Who had the best chance to leave? People with boats. Who had boats? Fishermen.

Many of those who survived the treachery of both pirates and the open sea ended up in makeshift refugee camps in countries like Thailand and Indonesia, many eating rationed rice from wooden bowls they carved themselves for lack of supplies. With help from the U.S. government and several American religious charities, tens of thousands made it to the West Coast of America with the promise of asylum. Among the many Vietnamese who were fishermen, word spread: You can go to Alaska, where the fishing is very good but the freezing climate is the perfect opposite of the Mekong Delta. Or you can go to South Louisiana: hot, steamy, flat, bountiful Louisiana, with marsh and prawns and a climate good for growing lemongrass and banana trees, a veritable Mekong itself. To boot, most of the Americans down there are Catholic, like many Vietnamese, and lots of them speak French, the old colonial language of Vietnam still spoken by large numbers of the elders.

So Vietnamese families came to the bayous and many promptly followed a similar trail to success. First they rented tiny trailers and other small homes along the water while pooling money among families for that first small crab boat and set of traps. Next, again with pooled money, came the first shrimp boat, maybe a little twenty-five-footer. Then, a few years later, a bigger trawler, fifty or sixty feet long, where a pair of families could not only work but *live* much of the year. Then came bigger trawlers still, eighty-footers and up, with double 1,000-horsepower engines for the big, lucrative, year-round hauls out in the Gulf of Mexico.

It wasn't long before a majority of the biggest shrimp boats out in the Gulf belonged to Vietnamese captains while other Vietnamese were going in the opposite direction, abandoning shrimp boats completely and setting up their own sheds or ascending to that highest stratum of fishing-industry aristocracy: catching tuna and swordfish on electronics-laden "longline" boats hundreds of miles out in the Gulf. With a thousand or so hand-size number 8 hooks, each baited with a pound of squid on trawl lines typically forty *miles* long and monitored by radar, these boats sometimes haul in 5,000 pounds of swordfish or yellowfin tuna on a single two-week trip, netting up to $30,000 in profit.

Of course the Cajuns have watched all this happen, have seen the great prosperity enjoyed by these newly arrived immigrants, but don't feel particularly welcoming toward the Vietnamese. Those people keep to themselves so completely, Cajuns complain, not even coming to the boat-blessing festivities while catching huge quantities of seafood once belonging to native

Louisianans alone. After more than two decades, few Cajuns can count even one friend among the Vietnamese. "They never came here with the intention of assimilating," one Cajun told me later. "They came here with the intention of flat-out taking over."

How much of this is true and how much is just good old-fashioned jealousy talking is hard to know. What's certain is that much of the story is not fully appreciated by native Louisianans. For while many Vietnamese now captain big boats and own fully equipped seafood sheds, their homes along the bayous still tend to be modest, with some families living in the same cramped mobile homes they first rented and then purchased twenty years ago. That's because every month the great majority of Louisiana's Vietnamese wire money back to Truc Giang and Vung Tau and Ap Long Ha and hundreds of other small towns and villages spread across southern Vietnam. This vast Louisiana estuary, supporting a billion-dollar seafood industry that puts nourishment on millions of American plates, also feeds and clothes entire families and communities eleven thousand miles away in Southeast Asia.

But who *are* the Vietnamese here? Who are the ones actually shipping all those dollars? I still don't know, having yet to cross the divide into the elusive Little Vietnam of the bayous. So again I try, walking down to a second shrimp shed, this one owned by a Vietnamese family on the other side of Leeville, slightly up the bayou. But again the shed owner, when I arrive, is chatting away in his native tongue on a marathon telephone call inside a small office. I wait outside next to a poster offering ten dollars for mako shark jaws to be shipped back to Vietnam for traditional medicinal use.

My feeling of déjà vu intensifies as the office call goes on and on. I give up and wander out onto the wharf, stopping at the first trawler I see. It's a steel-hulled hundred-footer called *Cap-*

*tain Doan,* easily one of the biggest shrimp boats I've seen but also one of the most beat-up and rust-covered and the only one so extensively adorned with laundry lines strung between masts and booms. It's midafternoon, a slow time at the shed, and no one's in sight. I yell hello across the boat deck but get no answer. I decide it's okay to board the vessel to holler a little closer, into the open wheelhouse door. Peering inside the cabin, I see a traditional Vietnamese Buddhist shrine mounted against a back wall, supporting a sculpted Buddha head and delicate lacquer vases full of unlit sticks of sandalwood incense. I yell hello again and this time hear a voice behind me.

"They all sleep now," says a Vietnamese shed hand, standing on the wharf. "They come back late last night with big catch." Then he disappears. That's all he says.

So it was a good trip last night. A big catch. The shrimp were giving nicely out in the Gulf.

But there's little reason to feel good as I turn and wander back to Tim's camp. It's too bad for these Vietnamese fishermen that 95 percent of all of Louisiana's coastal fish and shellfish are critically dependent on the state's vanishing wetlands. Many of these Asian immigrants have been in Louisiana almost as long as Big E has been alive. They've seen the same losses he's seen over those years.

So while twenty-five years of being neighbors hasn't brought the Cajuns and Vietnamese newcomers much closer together, there's one thing these two peoples have very much in common. This exceptionally rich region, for the Vietnamese, was supposed to be a promised land, too. It was supposed to be a final stopping point after years of struggle. Now, having arrived two hundred years apart, having both fled savage wars in old colonial lands, the Cajuns and Vietnamese appear destined to pack up their bags, once and for all, and leave together.

# Seven

I depart Leeville several days later on a morning so warm and muggy my car door feels hot to the touch at 6 A.M. I'm headed for New Orleans and the banks of the Mississippi and the chance, at long last, to better imagine how this fantastic stream—*le fleuve,* as the Cajuns simply call it—might actually save Louisiana.

Near the town of Raceland I say goodbye to the languid current of Bayou Lafourche, and an hour later I'm stuck in rush-hour traffic on Interstate 10 near New Orleans. One lane is closed for construction. Another is blocked by an accident. So there I sit with thousands of other cars, going nowhere in the 8 A.M. heat and thickening soup of tailpipe emissions. After the wide-open expanse of the bayou backcountry, after the endless miles of grasses and waterways, I've never felt so restless and ridiculous locked up inside my car.

An obnoxious driver honks behind me, letting me know I'm slow by a nanosecond to edge forward six inches with the car in front of me. No wonder so many bayou people think it's madness in the extreme to go to New Orleans for any reason whatsoever. The phenomenon of traffic, this act of being controlled and restrained, of being stuck in a nonstop landscape of concrete, is to the bayou mind-set and esprit the moral equivalent of burning in hell.

Yet in one respect New Orleans *is* like the backcountry coast: both places are sinking for the same reason. In fact, looking out from my car window at those distant skyscrapers and the Superdome and the elevated highways of downtown, it's hard to believe that much of this city lies not only below sea level but *below* the Mississippi River itself. The river winds through the city's core like an elevated aqueduct held aloft and held back by terrific levees amid the lowering city blocks all around. Indeed, no fewer than 129 miles of river levees and hurricane levees keep everyone dry and protected with the added help of twenty-two powerful pumping stations which evacuate every drop of rainfall from this giant bowl of a town. But as New Orleans sinks, so do those great levees, requiring that their tops be raised with more earth every few decades, creating surreal infrastructure headaches as overpasses leading into the city must periodically be torn down and rebuilt higher and higher, up and over the growing walls of dirt.

The levees won't work forever, of course, if the wetlands south and east of the city continue to disappear. Soon there simply won't be anything left to impede hurricanes from smashing right into the walled city. Which is precisely why Dr. Denise Reed, huddled in her office north of downtown, on the campus of the University of New Orleans, is so important to this city, whether its 1.2 million citizens realize it or not.

Denise is a marsh geomorphologist, one who studies the processes by which marshes are created and destroyed. For obvious reasons, South Louisiana is probably *the* place on earth to be for someone of her ilk. The social importance of the work, not to mention the feast of scientific challenges, is immense. She's in great demand.

"I'll be with you in just a minute," she says in a pleasant British accent as I enter her office near the south shore of Lake Pontchartrain. A tall, freckled, frenetic woman who never seems to stop moving in her white blouse and casual jeans, Denise drinks two cups of coffee over the next thirty minutes while giving orders to a swirl of graduate-student researchers.

Finally seated at her desk, she tells me she moved here from England in 1986 and, after a couple of years of "just trying to figure out how people talked," eventually plunged headlong into coastal restoration efforts as both a scientist and an advocate. Today she's involved in special projects all across the coast, from monitoring the impacts of offshore dredging to evaluating marsh rehabilitation programs. For several years she was a member of the planning management team of the Coast 2050 campaign.

"I'll be honest," she says, swallowing the last of her coffee. "I'm cynical about what we've accomplished so far. But I'm optimistic about what we can accomplish in the future. We just have to hurry. *Really* hurry."

As if to underscore the point, she abruptly grabs her purse and keys and says, "Come on. Let's go to Caernarvon," and we rush out the door. Passing the magnolias and oaks of this serene southern campus, we reach her car and I'm somewhat surprised. It's a BMW. A flashy silver 323i.

"The newly *redesigned* 323i," she says with pride before confessing, "I'm not a tree hugger. I believe in reasonable environmental stewardship. But I'm not a radical, all-out tree hugger."

So in the sporty BMW we head out of town, passing streets reflecting New Orleans' natural surroundings as well as its French and southern heritage, with names like Robert E. Lee Boulevard and Paris Avenue and Heron Street. We follow the shore of Lake Pontchartrain, just a few miles north of the lovely wrought-iron balconies of the French Quarter and the wild excesses of Bourbon Street, where midget men with signboards hustle tourists into topless bars and poor black kids on sidewalks dance for coins with bottle caps glued to their shoe soles.

As she drives, Denise tells me her interest in coastal marshes began in childhood. "England's a small island," she says. "The ocean's never very far away. So my family always went to the seaside on holiday." She pauses and laughs. "Or as you Yanks say, 'We'd go to the beach for vacation.' "

It seems appropriate, given our destination, that Denise announces early on that she's a "stream-of-consciousness kind of person." And sure enough, as we talk, her prodigious mind begins to move like a mighty river at flood stage, racing along in one direction only to jump its banks without warning, pouring into new areas.

"Coastal restoration is much more complex than is generally understood," she says, putting on sunglasses in the now blazing Louisiana sun. "No one likes to admit it, but there are real gaps in our knowledge of how the coast works. Like we still don't understand really clearly the relative response of marsh plants to the relative importance of salinity-versus-flooding stress. What levels of salinity can different marshes tolerate? And what about sea-level rise from global climate change? How high will it be? And with major river diversions, how much will the brown shrimp, which likes saltier water, be hurt by the fresh water in the near term? Will they disappear from parts of the coast completely? We don't know. We haven't done this before. So we have to be honest with fishermen and everyone else and tell them we know we can do good things with the Mississippi River but we can't predict all the consequences."

The sprawl of outer suburbia now looms into view, with fast-food pits and cell phone towers headlining the visual blight as Denise continues: "But despite gaps in our understanding, we have to move forward or we'll lose everything. We have to approach restoration with a strategy of 'adaptive management.' You start with a good conceptual model, then you adjust the operational regime as you learn along the way."

Her mind now streams away from science and toward one of her biggest frustrations: the continuing lack of national media coverage of the problem. Last month a team of *Time* magazine reporters traveled down the entire Mississippi on a boat, collecting stories. By the time they got to New Orleans, though, they really just wanted to party and have a good time like most visitors to the city, she says.

"So unfortunately I met this one reporter in the party context. I'm not sure how serious he is about writing about our plight."

Another problem is the state's current governor, Republican Mike Foster.

"We so desperately need his support and leadership on this issue," Denise emphasizes. "But the words 'coastal restoration' never come out of his mouth. He's too busy promising salary raises to the state's teachers and then reneging. I'm not sure how much integrity the man has left."

Just then, as if to mock the bitter impatience of conservationists across the state, we pass a sprawling 140-acre monument to human fantasy and entertainment on the eastern edge of the city. Inside the towering gates of Jazzland, New Orleans' brand-new "amusement park for the twenty-first century," two high-tech roller coasters called Mega Zeph and Zydeco Scream whip passengers around curves at speeds approaching seventy miles per hour. Elsewhere, the outsize mechanical arms of the Krazy Krewe, using hydraulic compression and thousands of kilowatts of electricity, carry groups of people aloft and then turn them upside down, their hair dangling from upside-down heads. Next comes the Bayou Blaster, an immense slingshot rocketing passengers two hundred feet into the air, strapped onto chairs. Afterward, for anyone with stomach left, vendors sell cotton candy and red beans and rice, side by side, this being New Orleans. The cost of this newly minted amusement park: $110 million. Measured another way, it's roughly the same amount of money spent on all coastal restoration projects in Louisiana over the past three years.

"Clearly we've got priority issues," Denise deadpans as we pass the park.

We gradually enter more rural country, moving through a perfectly flat landscape of pecan groves and small vegetable farms along two-lane Louisiana Route 46, heading due south. Near the small community of Docville we enter an enchanted, quarter-mile-long tunnel of ancient oaks arranged in straight lines on either side of the road. The trees are real grandfathers, planted generations ago, their towering, tangled boughs forming a verdant canopy from which deep pools of shade gather to shelter travelers from the late morning sun.

We're edging into "deep delta" country now, that last great finger of land straddling the banks of the Mississippi River and stretching from New Orleans eighty miles southeast to the river's mouth at the Gulf. The river itself is just to our right now, a few hundred yards away. The road parallels its course. Yet oddly, we can't see a single drop of water. The prodigious flow is completely obscured to us. That's because, in the distance, the land rises a good twenty feet to block our view. It rises sharply, at an angle too abrupt and too uniform to be natural. What we're seeing is the back side of a fantastically long levee, its crown and rear slope covered with just-cut grass like the lawn of a well-kept backyard. The levee goes on and on and on, making it impossible to see the mother stream, immediately behind, even though we're close enough to splash a stone in its current. Only the startling appearance now and again of particularly tall river vessels, their upper decks gliding above the levee top as if floating through air—radar panels spinning, river pilots peering through binoculars, all above perfectly dry land—only this reminds me of what's over that berm.

To our left, meanwhile, much farther away, lies another levee, this one protecting against hurricanes approaching from the east. In my passenger seat, I glance furtively at these encircling walls, fighting off a mild case of claustrophobia even as we pass through this expansive stretch of open farm country.

Just west of Poydras, Louisiana, my anticipation grows. The place of magic—Caernarvon—is just around the corner. We're almost there. But as we finally pull up to this famed diversion site, credited with creating so much new land just a few miles from here, the moment turns quickly to anticlimax. I'm not sure what I expected, but there's just not much to look at here. Denise steers the BMW to a small crushed-shell parking lot and we get out and climb the tall grassy levee to a rectangular concrete structure embedded right in the earthen dike. It's only eighty feet long and fifteen feet wide, this structure, enclosed by a cyclone fence with strands of barbed wire on top. Behind the fence are a few floodlights on poles and a minimal number of spare mechanical gadgets, including five large turnwheels for manually adjusting water intake.

And that's it. There's no technician on duty here. No attendant of any kind. Just a big red sign that says "Danger: Stay Clear of Structure." The place operates completely on its own, using gravity to channel river water into five concrete culverts which promptly travel underground—below the levee, below the two-lane rural road, below a railroad track paralleling the road—and emerge at a wide canal on the other side, a thousand feet away. The canal then quietly transports the river water to distant marshes.

A passing driver would never have guessed that this underwhelming edifice—this structure so simple it looks more like a small refueling dock for riverboats or an electrical relay station of some kind—holds within its concrete design the hopes and prayers, the very future, of most of coastal Louisiana.

Yet not everything here is so understated. What boggles the mind is the river itself. As Denise and I climb those last few feet to the top of the levee, pulling ourselves onto the crown, the river explodes into view like a powerful stage performer too long behind the curtain, eager to show off its innate gifts of poetry and power, its grace of motion and dramatic flow. Before us, more than half a mile wide and two hundred feet deep, carrying water from the Rockies and the Alleghenies and all points in between at a rate of around 600,000 cubic feet per second, is the Mississippi.

For a while I just sit there and drink in the marvelous stream, sublime in its immensity, its color a complex pale brown touched by green. That earthy hue explains in part the river's enormous size. There's land in that flow, lots of it, 160 million tons per year, waiting to be squeezed out. Indeed, so thick are the suspended sediments from Montana farms and New York State suburbs that one's hand quickly disappears when placed less than a foot below the river's surface. On this very day, at this very spot, several hundred thousand *tons* of earth will flow by, headed for the Gulf of Mexico and the abyss of the continental shelf.

I continue to watch the display, gazing at foaming eddies the size of city blocks and the queer swirls and roiling ripples of competing currents within the current, rising and clashing powerfully at the river's center. A human being might last a few minutes out there before being sucked down into a chaos of pummeling, neck-jarring, death-dealing ropes of water.

But here on the bank, with scattered willows and cottonwoods offering shade and giant pillows of Gulf clouds overhead, all is calm. Caernarvon sits on a long and indolent bend of the river, a curve so large that a seagoing cargo ship, just now coming into view upstream, looks like a tiny, tiny ant as it begins the turn. It's a mile and a half away, that vessel. "When God created the world," a bayou priest once told me, grinning, "he accidentally made the Mississippi more powerful than he intended, then found his mistake too powerful to correct."

Denise reminds me that Caernarvon is a "freshwater" diversion, officially built not to create land but to help nearby oyster farmers whose beds were being clobbered downstream by the ever-advancing Gulf. But oysters are also disturbed by excessive sediments in the water. So ironically Caernarvon is designed to deliver water that's as sediment-free as possible. That's why the structure draws from the river's surface and from the inner edge of a bend. That's also why the captured water is carried by canal to a "sediment trap," a three-square-mile impoundment lake about a mile from here. There the water pools up, stagnating temporarily, allowing most of the sediments to fall to the lake bottom before the water gradually flows on out to the target oyster beds farther south.

Yet even with this sediment trap, even with both hands tied behind its back, the Caernarvon water is miraculously creating land downstream. The Louisiana Department of Natural Resources reports that since 1991, when the $26 million structure came on line, not only have thousands of new acres of wetlands emerged, but populations of waterfowl, alligators, muskrats, and fish have grown dramatically in the same area. Before Caernarvon, this same area was losing one thousand acres of marsh per year.

Of course the much more massive Third Delta Conveyance Channel proposed by Woody Gagliano and others would be a *sediment* diversion, with features built in to maximize, not impede, the flow of nutrients and sedimentation across a wide stretch of coastline. The Mississippi River, in other words, would be totally set free to do its work, its powerful hands completely unbound.

Denise and I decide to rest by the river's edge for a while. We descend the levee's inner slope to a large driftwood log tossed up on the bank just a few feet from the water. There we sit, partially shaded by an overhanging willow, gazing out at the luxuriant and massive sheet of water coasting by, muse to Twain and Audubon and numberless other writers, poets, and artists. We chuckle at a juvenile egret way out in the current's center, all alone, happily riding its own driftwood log down the river.

There inside the levee, with nothing between us and the river, Denise's thoughts again start to flow rapidly, gathering momentum like the great current at our feet.

"When you ask a giant river to do unnatural things," she says, gesturing to the water and then to the levee behind us, "when you ask it to stay inside impenetrable dikes all the way to the Gulf, then you get unnatural results: the entire estuary system starts to collapse and disappear. But when you ask the river to simply do what it does naturally, you get different results entirely.

"For years," she continues, "Louisiana has dominated this force of nature totally, and for years the strategy has worked pretty well. With levees and canals and pumps, people were able to live all along the coast without fear of floods while catching lots of seafood and extracting lots of oil. The only problem, as we all now know, is that the arrangement isn't sustainable. If you manage the coast to death, that's what it does, it dies.

"So the question we faced in putting together the Coast 2050 plan was deciding what the ultimate goal was. If the goal was simply to sustain fisheries productivity, we could turn the whole damn coast into a giant shrimp farm and get that. If the goal was just maintaining hurricane protection, we could build a bloody huge system of bigger and bigger levees and get that.

"But there's another way," she says. "By asking the river to create land where we need land to be created, we're not asking it to do anything it doesn't do naturally. And so we get all the *multiple* benefits which come *naturally* from the newly created land: hurricane protection for homes and industry, plus habitat for wildlife, including birds and fisheries."

Listening to Denise just now, I suddenly understand why this diversion structure is so simple and basic in its function. It takes an enormous amount of energy to control the Mississippi River, to shackle it so thoroughly that a mammoth portion of the state, ecologically connected, vanishes as a result. It takes the mountain of a levee right behind us and all the levees we've seen that morning driving down. But to simply let the river loose, to let it go, takes much less energy. A few miles from here, at this very moment, this man-made diversion is creating soft, grass-crowned soil without a single soul present to manage the operation or otherwise oversee this concrete diversion structure so unobtrusive I doubt many of the locals even remember it's here. Had I not come with Denise I might never have found the place.

"Come on," I say, standing up from our driftwood bench just then, momentarily interrupting her. "Let's go to the other side and see where the water flows out."

We climb up and over the levee, and just like that the gigantic river vanishes behind us. With the blink of an eye, as if it had all been a mirage, it's gone, concealed by the dike. We cross the road and then the train track and then there it is again: the water of the Mississippi River flowing outside the Mississippi. Diverted. The five concrete culverts, side by side, are busily disgorging 2,000 cubic feet of water per second into the canal.

Standing there beside the emerging water, I suddenly detect a curious noise, almost a vibration, hovering in the air. It's definitely not the splash of fish jumping a few feet away or the swish of willow branches in a rare midday breeze. It's something else. Something louder. Deeper. It's coming from inside the tunnels. I squat nearer to the water, trying to better hear the sound as Denise keeps talking.

"Never have human beings done this before," she says, pointing to the lush brown current hastening off to make real estate. "You can create land one of two ways, basically. There's the Dutch model where you hold *back* the water, seizing land from the sea with the help of levees and then turning the captured land into fields for agriculture. Or you can create land by just letting the water go. After all these years we're finally talking about the latter option, about creating land—with water— for natural resources purposes; creating new and restored *natural* features and systems. It's never been done but it's the only way to sustain the full range of human activities along this coast. At last we can stop clobbering nature and finally let nature *help* us."

I press closer to the outer edge of the nearest culvert, leaning down farther, cocking my head toward the structure. The noise still seems far away, deep inside the tunnels. It's a rumbling sound, muffled but powerful. It's the sound of water, I realize, falling and churning and flowing out.

And it is, unmistakably, a roar.

# Eight

Lawrence "King Coon" Billiot, one of the last French-speaking Native American *traiteurs* in the United States, is on his way to "smoke a baby" when I pull up to his corrugated-tin shack along a wide and languorous bayou. I've followed a gravel road to this place hoping Lawrence can help my ailing back, but he's got that baby foremost on his mind.

"He's been *beaucoup* spittin' up," he says of the child he plans to cure. "He's got congestion. But I'll smoke him, dat angel, and he'll be fine. I've smoked all de babies in my family."

Lawrence, fifty-two, is shirtless and barefoot in a pair of dirty black jeans. His home exudes evidence of stark poverty and self-styled shamanism, with pet goats and mongrel dogs dozing in the shade, handmade quilts tacked up for bedroom doors, and a big dream catcher on a wall next to kitschy New Age paintings of Indian maidens running with wolves.

I sidestep a junked car and rusting StairMaster out front, shaking Lawrence's big beefy hand. Like most members of Louisiana's United Houma Nation, he's of conspicuously mixed ancestry, with enough Cajun blood to give him pale eyes and rounded cheekbones. Add to this his almost completely bald pate and obese 275-pound body and you wouldn't pick him out of a crowd as an Indian healer of local renown, one fiercely loyal to Native American practices, especially the sacred and curative power of smoke.

Lawrence's tools also include prayer, herbal remedies, fortune-telling, and direct touch. Though he sees dozens of patients each month, he doesn't charge for his services, which largely explains the poverty. There's no phone here, and what electricity reaches his house is regularly cut off due to the sparse paycheck from his part-time job delivering the local newspaper, a paper that's unintelligible to him because he can't read or write.

"Can you read?" he asks soon after I arrive, posing a question I can't recall being asked in my entire adult life.

"Yes," I say.

"Good." He pulls down a note taped to his plywood front door and hands it to me. It's written on a ragged piece of brown grocery-bag paper. "People are always leaving dese on my door 'cause dey need my help. Will you read dis one?"

Out loud, I convey the message: "Cher Lawrence. Miss Boudreaux in Lockport just came home from the hospital. Doctor says they can't do nothing for her cancer. Please pray for her. Merci. P. Guidry."

"Ain't dat a shame," he says in a voice that's deep and husky, yet almost feminine, spiked with a Cajun accent. He rubs his bald head, then scratches his double chin, which hasn't seen a razor in days. "I gotta put dis one under a candle."

I follow Lawrence inside, past the tattered furniture he's collected from other people's roadside trash, past his pet cockatiel named Suzy Q, and into his dark and cavelike bedroom where one wall is lined with dozens of red votive candles as part of an elaborate home altar. He buys the candles at the Family Dollar in Larose, he says. Half of them have short handwritten notes stuck under their cylindrical glass holders. Lawrence puts Miss Guidry's message below a candle dedicated to the Blessed Virgin Mary, then mumbles a short prayer in French I can't understand.

"I t'ink she'll be better," he says afterward, switching back to English. We return to his tiny living room and I explain again why I've come, saying nothing seems to help my ailing back.

"You shoulda come to me a long time ago," he says. "Turn around."

There under the low corkboard ceiling, I do as I'm told, facing away from him. Lawrence puts on a T-shirt and suddenly I feel his ample belly against my back as he puts me in a firm full nelson. His hands then take hold of either side of my head. Too late to stop him, I realize he's going to adjust my neck, snapping it from side to side, a technique that creeps me out and terrifies me even when performed by a trained chiropractor. But this guy—I don't know anything about him save the wholly unconventional exhibits my eyes have taken in since my arrival. Before I can scream in horror, Lawrence has finished the procedure, changing my emotion from one of fear to concealed amusement. His version of a neck adjustment is pure pretense. He moves my head only very slightly to the left and then the right, applying almost no force at all, an imitation of the real thing that's completely ineffectual. My neck doesn't come close to making that sick cracking sound I dread so much.

Having finished this, he laces his fingers across my abdomen and gives me a solid squeeze—just a big hug, really—his belly pressing even more snugly against my back. Behind my left ear, meanwhile, I hear more praying in Cajun French. The words have the sound of a chant, whispered and unintelligible.

He releases me and makes the sign of the cross. "Your back will be fine now," he says, smiling. "Just leave all your back pain here wit' me. It's mine now."

"So that's it?" I say. "We're done?" The whole thing has taken maybe three minutes.

"That's it," he says. "And please don't t'ank me. De treatment works better if you don't t'ank me."

But the "adjustment" has done nothing for me, I'm sure. As for the prayer, I don't know. I ask Lawrence to translate the prayer, but he refuses, saying it would be a flagrant violation of the treater's code. He can reveal his prayers only to an avowed apprentice, and then only if the apprentice is younger than he is, he says.

He also refuses adamantly when I offer to pay for his service. I'd learned from others, though, that it's acceptable to discreetly leave a "gift" without the treater's knowledge. So I drop a twenty-dollar bill on Lawrence's scavenged living room coffee table. The table sits next to the room's only electrical outlet, from which a tangle of multi-pronged extenders spread juice to six different flimsy wires like a caricatured danger scene in a fire-safety manual.

I bend over and touch my back, confirming that it still feels lousy. Then I ask Lawrence: "What do you mean, exactly, when you say you're going to 'smoke a baby'?"

"Oh dat," he says. "I just bathe dat baby in smoke and he feels better. It's one of our oldest curin' ways."

I ask more questions before he happily invites me to come

see the ceremony myself. But first he needs to gather some herbs from along the bayou, he says.

Outside, still barefoot, Lawrence grabs a rusty shovel and leads me to the bayou bank a few yards away, thick with cane-brake and young willows. One tree shades a wooden rowboat Lawrence uses to explore the back bayous for a delicate blue lily used to ward off certain black-magic curses. He also uses the scarred-up vessel to catch fish and crabs, especially when the last penny of grocery money runs out. "I know how to survive," he says. "I'm de son of an Indian. Wit' dis boat I survive."

Officially the water here is not a bayou but Louisiana's portion of the Gulf Intracoastal Waterway, an east-west navigation channel that intersects Bayou Lafourche just east of here in Larose. A slow-moving tugboat putters past just now, the captain waving while the boat creates slow and lazy waves that roll across the dark mirror of liquid, lapping below the canebrake, sending a spotted sandpiper into flight.

"See dis here," Lawrence says, calling me over to a small plot where he cultivates herbs. He digs up a small root. "Dis here is ginger. Good for a woman who's just lost a baby. It helps a bad sex life, too.

"And dis," he continues, "is mint. Good for baby colic." He picks some of the leaves to take to the parents of the baby he's going to treat. "And dis," he says, "is mamou root. Good for chest colds and coughs."

"And see dat over dere?" He points across the gravel road to the string of tar-paper houses and appallingly run-down trailers where several other Indian families live with Lawrence in this isolated waterside ghetto, thoroughly removed from the main traffic of Route 1 and the string of Cajun towns along Bayou Lafourche, just a half mile away. "See dat Spanish moss in dose oaks? Dat's good for hemorrhoids. You boil de moss super hot, den add a little Vicks rub to de water, den you sit your butt over dat pot and let de steam fix ever't'ing."

So begins my daylong tutelage, informal though it is, in the backwoods medicine of South Louisiana, immersing myself in the often wise and still appreciated tradition of *les traiteurs*. The discipline survives today in the narrowing margins of a modern land, combining the scientifically established efficacy of certain plants (the active properties in mamou root, for example, are found in many over-the-counter cough medicines) with elements of old wives' tales and faith healing and a liberal overlay of Catholic ritual.

For the rest of the day Lawrence becomes a sort of walking, free-association encyclopedia of folk remedies, happy, in the company of an eager listener, to share all the knowledge not barred from disclosure by his ilk's secretive code of conduct. Often with no segue whatsoever, having just glimpsed a certain plant in the distance or had a relevant thought pop into his head, he blurts out a cure. Alligator grease for asthma. Boiled peach leaves for toothaches. Citronella for colds. Whatever curative herbs he can't find in his garden, he says, or growing wild along the bayous, he buys at the Wal-Mart on Highway 3235, driving there in his windowless '88 Mustang with the broken driver's seat.

But Lawrence's powers transcend mere plants and prayer. Or so he claims. We're walking through the tall grass along the channel bank, looking for more herbs, when he suddenly says, "Hear dat?" He stops abruptly and cocks his head. His face becomes creased with sudden concern.

"What?" I say. "I don't hear anything."

"Sssshhh!" He puts his finger to his lips and whispers. "Dat ol' snake over dere. Dere's a big rattlesnake by dat tree just in front of us. I can't see 'im, but I feel him dere."

I like snakes as much as the next guy, which is to say not one little bit. So I inventory the area around my feet, then step closer to Lawrence for what I hope is better protection, feeling chills run up my legs.

Lawrence, meanwhile, has begun making the most extraordinary snake sounds with his mouth, first a long hiss, then the terrifying sound of a rattling tail, then another long hiss. It sounds so real I can't believe it's coming from him, but it is.

Then he's quiet, his body rigid and motionless, almost as if he's in a trance. Still staring in the direction of the alleged snake, he says, "*Sonne la cloche. Sonne la cloche.*" Sound the bell. Sound the bell.

Then, suddenly, I have to duck out of the way as he turns to one side and spits seven times over his shoulder. After that he's quiet again. For a long time.

I'm afraid to ask any questions, afraid I'll upset whatever strange, inscrutable curse he's putting on that snake. More seconds pass and I'm dying to ask Lawrence where the damn snake is when he says "Hibiscus."

"What?" I whisper.

"Hibiscus," he says again, loudly this time, cheerfully turning to me. He's clearly coming out of whatever hypnosis he's been in, real or affected. "Hibiscus petals are good for pinkeye. You just rub de petals against de eye. And for heat stroke you wrap banana leaves around a person's head and let dem sit dere a while."

Incredibly, he's gone back to his free-association ramble of remedies.

"What about the snake?" I ask. "What happened to the snake?"

"Oh dat ol' snake is long gone. I made him run away. I have de power to do dat, you know. I can make snakes *come* to me too, but you don't want to see dat."

For the first time I start to think maybe Lawrence is flat-out insane, especially when he points to his eyes just then. "See," he says. "My eyes are different colors. That's how you know I have de power."

I hadn't noticed before, but sure enough, one eye is light gray and the other a pale green.

"Snake colors," Lawrence says. "And look at my arms."

He shows me the skin on the inside of his right arm, below the elbow. It's a strange, mottled mix of various olive and brown hues which, well . . .

"Just like the skin of a water moccasin," he says. Then he clenches his fist and somehow gets the skin on his arm to ripple and undulate in a way that has me picturing a slithering snake. I swallow hard, not sure what to make of this, but increasingly convinced that Lawrence is at least partly crazy.

Maybe he can read minds too, because he promptly says, "You can believe me or not. But dis is a sign of my power to heal. It's a good power. People can laugh all dey want at me, doesn't matter. I'm a treater. I'm real. If someone doesn't believe in me, den maybe he's lost somet'ing dat can save his own child's life."

He starts walking again along the waterside path, passing the spot where the alleged snake had been. He's obviously utterly unconcerned with my reaction to things, just wanting to get on with the tour of remedies, his bald head perspiring now in the late morning humidity.

"Dis here plant is called horsetail," he says, pointing to a bunch of knee-high green stalks. "*La prèle* in French. Good for de prostate. You boil it and drink it *without* sugar. And for nose-bleeds, I have a special prayer dat stops dose real good."

"But how did you learn all this?" I say, following behind, swatting a cloud of gnats in the thickening maze of grass and trees. "How did you become a treater?"

He stops to pick some of the horsetails, then looks at me with those different-colored eyes. "When I was a kid," he says, "I was always finding and playing wit' snakes along de baya. But dose snakes, dey never bit me even one time. I played by myself most of de time 'cause I was a fat kid and most of de udder children made fun of me and didn't want to play wit' me. So I stayed home wit' de adults a lot. I had seven uncles who were all treaters. De gift runs in our family. So I learned from dem a lot—bot' Indian and Cajun cures. By age twelve, I had already learned enough. I became a treater at twelve. I been doin' it ever since den."

I help Lawrence pick some more horsetails, still unsure what percent of him is authentic healer and what percent eccentric fake. But he's clearly a man of considerable kindness, totally committed to his lifelong "assignment" to care for the sick. "I love people," he tells me more than once. "I love *all* people. Dat's why I do it."

And as for all that other stuff, in the end, he doesn't have to convince me with words that he possesses certain inexplicable, extranormal powers. I'm too skeptical for words anyway.

He just proves it right before my eyes.

"Come on," he says, gathering the last of the herbs. "Let's go. I gotta go smoke dat baby."

Somehow Lawrence squeezes his outsize body into the driver's seat of his old convertible Mustang, the top pulled down. But there's a problem. The back of the driver's seat is broken, unable to stay upright. Lawrence fixes this by tying one end of a short piece of rope to the top of the seat, then pulling the other end toward the sideview mirror, keeping the rope taut until he simply shuts the door on it. It's not pretty, but the technique holds the chair upright, and Lawrence guides his big bare feet to the gas pedal and clutch, turning the key.

I keep glancing at the absurd rope arrangement, pulling my seat-belt strap extra tight, knowing that if that thin rope breaks or the door opens for any reason while Lawrence is driving, he'll be on his back in a split second, all 275 pounds of him, looking up at the sky while the car careens wildly into a swamp or kisses a telephone pole.

Engine wheezing and sputtering, Lawrence coaxes the car forward, and soon the gravel road leading away from his place gives way to pavement. We begin passing suburban-style Cajun houses and newer-model mobile homes with well-kept lawns and satellite dishes and kiddie pools and bass boats parked in carports and neat rows of okra growing in backyard gardens. The distance, spanned in just a few minutes, seems almost unbelievably extreme from the small Indian slum we just left behind, hidden back there along the water.

Lawrence skirts the west bank of Bayou Lafourche before heading west on Route 24 where a lush stretch of dark forest closes in, enveloping both sides of the narrow road with oaks and dwarf palmettos and thick woody vines. With the convertible top down, the overhanging branches, speckled with moss, seem to swallow us up completely with their beauty. The wind of our forward motion is a godsend on this day of soaring heat, blowing through our clothes as Lawrence begins merrily singing one of his favorite French songs—"La Belle de la Louisiane." (Refrain: She's pretty, she's delicate, but she's no good.)

We stop only once, to pick up an old rocking chair someone has thrown out along the road. Lawrence ties the chair to the rear of the car using the discarded plastic straps that bind the bundles of newspapers he delivers. Then he gets back in, again slamming the door on the rope that holds up his seat.

Before starting the engine, though, he turns to me and says, "Liver cancer." He then counts on his fingers. "First, you get some red country eggs. Not de white ones from de store, but red ones. Second, you remove de yokes. T'ird, you make some lemonade from fresh lemons. Fourt', you mix de egg whites into de lemonade and drink it all up. Dat's how you cure several kinds of liver cancer."

Having got that off his chest, Lawrence steers us back onto the road. We're headed for the village of Pointe-aux-Chenes, he tells me, a Houma settlement thirty miles away. Like many Houma communities scattered along the Louisiana coast, this one lies at the very end of the earth, at the extreme tip of a finger of land that juts out into a demiwilderness of wetlands, where people live almost as if on a raft, the seclusion a way of life.

Before making a series of southward turns which will lead us closer to this end-of-the-road place, Lawrence steers the car past Grand Bois park, a clearing in the forest along Route 24 where he says members of the Houma Nation and other Louisiana tribes gather twice a year.

"We have powwows here," he says. "Dancing and costumes and big meals and stories. Sometimes t'ousands of people come." His multicolored eyes shine with sudden pride.

The Indians gather here in a public park because there is no reservation land upon which to meet, Lawrence says. Despite constituting Louisiana's largest Indian tribe with fifteen thousand members (up from a decimated band of only sixty countable members in 1803), the Houma have never received formal recognition from the federal government. Hence there's no reservation homeland set aside for them; there's no casino or visitors' center or an indigenous crafts store for the fine palmetto baskets and Spanish-moss dolls many Houma artisans still make.

Several factors account for the lack of federal recognition. Unlike more warlike tribes out west, the Houma never waged a sustained war against white settlers and so never entered into formal treaties with them. And the tribe's extreme watery isolation over the past century and a half, with the population tucked into scattered pockets, presents a less than coherent portrait to government officials looking in.

Compounding the situation, the Houma have lost their native language, adopting Louisiana French many years back and taking French surnames while embracing a great many Cajun folkways (as Cajuns have embraced many of theirs). The Indians' racial purity has been diluted as well, in part due to white trappers drawn to the pelt-rich Houma wetlands who then took Indian wives there. By 1931 a special investigator from the U.S. Bureau of Indian Affairs pronounced the Houma too mixed to be considered Indian. This has led some subsequent writers and anthropologists to refer to them as "racial orphans" and "so-called Indians."

Mixed or not, most of the fifteen thousand Louisianans who today call themselves Houma passionately embrace their Indian identity, fighting in court and elsewhere to promote their tribal rights and cultural ways, and formally uniting as a nation—with a constitution and elected leadership—in 1979. Over the years the tribe has left an indelible mark on Louisiana, with the parish seat of Terrebonne Parish named after them and the capital Baton Rouge named after an old Houma territorial marker featuring a red stick.

The history of the Houma tribe certainly parallels that of many other Native Americans, characterized by brutal discrimination and forced exodus. Having originally occupied rich agricultural lands along the Mississippi River to the north, the Indians were systematically pushed farther and farther south

with each new wave of arriving white settlers. Finally the
Houma entered the watery remove of the coastal marshes and
swamps, with no one left to push them farther and nowhere left
to go besides. "One more step and we're out in the Gulf," the
Indians like to say today.

In Lawrence's car we retrace part of that old southward
migration, heading farther and farther into the deepest bayou
country. Just west of the settlement of Grand Bois, Lawrence
turns left on to Route 55 and we proceed due south along Bayou
Terrebonne. A few miles later he turns again, this time to the
southeast, and the road eventually parallels an even smaller
bayou with the same name as the village we're seeking: Pointe-
aux-Chenes. There are far fewer houses along this two-lane
road and almost no traffic heading in either direction. At one
point the oaks grow so dense and close to the road that curtains
of moss actually touch Lawrence's car, brushing up against the
windshield and forcing him to slow down as we both duck from
side to side to avoid the ticklish caress. To the west, the trees
eventually thin, giving way to open marsh. I see the hoary eyes
of a generously proportioned alligator protruding just above the
water, his body submerged, waiting patiently for a nearby night
heron or egret to mistake his long snout for a fine log upon
which to rest.

We eventually come to a narrow, one-lane bridge leading up
and over Bayou Pointe-aux-Chenes. We cross it and continue
farther south still until soon there it is, in the distance: the
"point of oaks," a copse of enormous, magical trees like none
I've seen before in Louisiana. They form an arboreal island,
sheltering a simple collection of Indian homes just now coming
into focus amid a sea of marsh grass all around. From here,
there's no more Louisiana. There's nowhere left to go. To leave,
you have to backtrack completely, retracing your steps.

The history of the Houma people is more than just one of being pushed back physically, of course. It's a history of being pushed back socially and economically, a fact that's very much on display as we pull into the village. For years classified as racially inferior, their status equivalent to that of southern blacks, most of the Indians were effectively barred from schools altogether until missionaries took an interest in the 1930s. Full access to quality, integrated public schools didn't come until the 1960s.

Along with the usual hardships imposed by ignorance, the Houma paid dearly in the 1920s when rising prices for muskrat pelts attracted "lease hounds" and "land frauds" to their previously uncoveted wetlands. Elders unwittingly signed away huge tracts by putting X's on documents they couldn't read. Similar land merchants arrived with the discovery of oil and gas in the 1930s. The Indians could only watch as outsiders got rich all around them while they, the Houma, now had to pay fees to hunt and trap on land previously their own, deepening their poverty.

Even the Cajuns, themselves victims of past prejudice and deep poverty, have traditionally considered themselves a half step up the social ladder, looking down on the Houma as lazy and untrustworthy and as unacceptable mates for their children, calling the Indians "Sabines," a derogatory Cajun term. These sentiments, among some Cajuns, still exist.

As a result of these many unhappy factors, illiteracy is still high among adults like Lawrence, and in villages like Pointe-aux-Chenes, phones, roads, and electricity are things many people grew up without. Yet the physical and social isolation has also served to preserve, as if in amber, many of the oldest bayou ways, from the work of *traiteurs* to the bloody sport of cockfighting to fishermen cast-netting from flat-bottom pirogues.

Here in Pointe-aux-Chenes, Indian children still grow up learning French (virtually unheard of among Cajuns) and people over seventy-five often speak no English whatsoever, needing an interpreter to visit the doctor or vote in elections or talk to "Anglo-Americans" visiting from the outside.

But it's the flags that get my attention most of all as Lawrence and I pull into the village. There along the dozing bayou water, atop an old fishing boat named *Geronimo* and under shade-giving oaks so mammoth they give the impression of dusk at midday, hangs an American flag like none other I've ever seen. Emblazoned across the familiar stars and bars is a proud and defiant-looking Indian warrior on horseback, his posture erect, shoulders thrown back, a single feather rising up from his shoulder-length black hair.

A second U.S. flag, this one ornamented on both sides with the chiseled face of a chief in full ceremonial headdress, hangs on the wall of a dockside shed. Several pounds of shrimp lay spread below the flag, drying atop boards the old-fashioned way in a narrow patch of sunlight while Zydeco music flows from a nearby radio. The French lyrics drift up to ubiquitous beards of Spanish moss swaying in a velvety Gulf breeze.

I have trouble imagining just what message these flags are meant to convey, and I quickly give up trying. For whoever these people are—French, southern, Indian, American—they are clearly citizens first and foremost of the deepest bayou country, defined by life on that outermost realm. Slowly we pass a string of frame houses and dirty pickup trucks fronting the glassy bayou. The homes are more basic than most Cajun camps I've seen. Many are on stilts made from railroad ties and with walls composed of nothing sturdier than half-inch-thick plywood. The front porches bear couches and rifle racks, with front doors flung open to interior walls crowded with trophy alligator heads and the twelve-point antlers of white-tailed bucks. Dark-haired children swim in the murky bayou alongside schools of two-pound channel mullet jumping all around and roosters crowing in every direction and cattle roaming free on nearby marsh islands.

One of my goals in returning to Louisiana had been to find a place just like this, a community so removed from the rest of the state that it doesn't show up on most maps; where children ride to school atop fishing boats when the tide gets too high; where you can stand in the middle of the village and peek through the oaks to the east and to the west and see only grass crowding the horizon; where the spoken language of the closest human settlement to the south is Spanish—because it's in Mexico.

It had been my goal, in short, to get lost in a place considered physically remote and culturally apart even by South Louisiana standards, where the term "bayou life" might be experienced in its deepest possible form while there was still enough coastal wetlands remaining to give expression to such a life.

And finally, somewhat by accident, in the presence of an Indian healer come to cure a sick baby, it's happened. I've arrived at just such a place.

A pit bull named Pork Chop, tied to a post by a chain leash, starts barking his head off as we pull up to the gray-painted shack of Margaret Verdin, Lawrence's sister-in-law.

"*Arrêt*, Pork Chop!" Margaret yells, sidestepping several baby chicks and a tin bucket full of fresh oysters on her porch. "It's just Lawrence. *Mon Dieu!*"

I double-check the thickness of that chain before stepping out into a yard of disintegrating boat hulls, twisted scrap metal, used tires, two rusting outboard motors, piles of rotting shrimp nets, and several old tanks of spent butane—a tort lawyer's dream. In the back there's a five-foot-long alligator restrained inside a cage, looking alert and incalculably displeased.

Margaret, in her forties, greets Lawrence with a serious look.

"*Est où l'enfant?*" Lawrence asks.

"*Il vient,*" she says.

Sure enough, moments later seventeen-year-old Jacqueline Guidry, Margaret's daughter-in-law, comes out holding two-month-old Tee Mel wrapped in a light blanket. Brown-skinned and oh so beautiful, the baby's napping right now.

"But he hasn't been sleeping so peaceful lately," Jacqueline says in English. "And de way he breathes, it's been kinda raspy-like."

Jacqueline is dressed in faded jeans and a halter top that shows her belly button. Her bare feet pad softly across the wood-plank porch.

"He been spittin' up enough to catch your attention any?" Lawrence asks.

"Spittin' up a lot," says Jacqueline. "Keepin' me washin' all kind of towels."

"And where's de fadder?" Lawrence asks, switching to English himself now because he doesn't want me to miss a single detail of what's about to happen, he says. "You know I can't do dis without de fadder here."

Mel Verdin, twenty, is hanging new shrimp nets on a boat just up the bayou, we're told; a messenger leaves to fetch him.

While we wait, Lawrence tells me what's already obvious: almost no one in this village of several hundred people has a "real job." Everyone lives pretty much off the land, working as trappers, alligator hunters, fin fishermen, shrimpers, crabbers, and oystermen. Several of the families here still use Lawrence's services, a fact he conveys with great satisfaction before killing time with a few more remedy recitations pulled down from his vast mental hard drive. These include a cure for warts where you bury a freshly cut potato under a rain gutter.

"And see dat willow over dere?" Lawrence says, pointing toward the bayou. "A man who's goin' bald can take some of dose leaves and boil 'em up real good. Den you take one Budweiser and mix it in and wash your hair in de liquid once a week or whenever you feel unsecure about your hair."

Mel Verdin, the father of the baby, walks up. He's shirtless, with the tattoo of an Indian brave on his right arm and an alligator-tooth necklace dangling across his chest. In a tribe where physical appearance runs the gamut from rich reddish skin and high cheekbones to blue eyes and freckles, Mel is somewhere in between, looking more Spanish or Italian than anything.

We all shake hands and Lawrence announces, "I need scissors and a big ashtray."

Mel reaches up to a porch shelf cluttered with flyswatters and Winchester shotgun shells and pulls down a big glass ashtray. Margaret brings scissors from inside the house and Lawrence gets ready to cut.

"First Jacqueline," he says.

She steps forward and he snips off a two-inch lock of her longish, thick hair, placing the hair in the ashtray. He takes an equal amount from Mel. "Now baby Tee Mel," Lawrence says, snipping a couple of hairs from the child's soft, fuzzy head, placing the strands in the ashtray.

"Now de clothing," Lawrence says. Jacqueline brings out one of her old blouses and one of Tee Mel's baby T-shirts. Lawrence cuts into each, taking away several cloth patches about the size of business cards.

"And Big Mel?" Lawrence says.

"Just cut from de jeans I'm wearing," Mel says.

Lawrence leans over, chooses from one of several holes already in the man's jeans, and cuts away a square, adding it to the others in the ashtray. He then places a small wad of tissue paper underneath the pile of hair and cloth, and pulls a butane lighter from his pocket.

"Come closer," he says to me, placing the ashtray on the porch floor, about to set it ablaze. I move forward a step. "No, *closer*," he says. "Real close. I want you to see dis real good. I'm gonna light all dis hair and clothes, and de smoke's gonna be full of de whole family spirit—and dat's what's gonna cure de baby. Dis is our tradition. Our ancestors didn't do not'ing wit'out smoke—feasts, pipe smoking, illnesses, bonfires. All dat."

He lights the hair and clothes, and the smoke begins rising up from the porch floor. He then takes Tee Mel from Jacqueline's arms. With his large right hand he supports the sleeping baby's head, putting his other hand on the boy's bottom.

"What I'm goin' to do," he says, looking around at Jacqueline, Mel, and me, "is move de baby t'rough de smoke t'ree times. On de first or second time, he's gonna wake up. On de t'ird time I bring him t'rough de smoke, he's gonna gasp. It'll just be a little gaspin' sound as he takes in a little smoke. You'll see him do it. Den he'll be cured of all his congestion."

Lawrence looks directly at me next. "Watch de baby's face, now," he says. "Watch de face real close."

I can't get much closer as Lawrence starts the ceremony. There's no praying this time. No appeal to the God of the Catholic church. Just Lawrence, the baby, the smoke, and the palpable presence of something else, a living thread of tradition wrapped around this moment and stretching back to a rich Indian past.

Lawrence guides the baby through the thickening plume of smoke rising from the floor. Then he pulls him back, out of the smoke, and the baby suddenly wakes up. He doesn't cry. He just opens his eyes and stares sleepily straight ahead. Lawrence pauses a moment, then guides the baby through a second time. On the third pass I'm close enough for the smoke to get in my eyes, but my vision's still perfectly fine as that baby's little mouth opens at precisely the same moment my ears record a faint but distinct sucking sound—a gasp.

I break into a big grin when this happens.

I look up from the baby's face to see Lawrence now cradling him in his arms. The ceremony's over, and a big smile stretches across the healer's face too. "You are such a precious little baby," he says. "So, so precious."

Jacqueline and Mel, likewise, are all grins. I wonder if it's more than just the relief of happy parents. I wonder if, like me, they felt another thing, something hard to describe, a vague but appreciable sense of well-being that came over me while I stood in that circle of witnesses, watching Lawrence and Tee Mel move through those faint curtains of smoke. It was like being given something very special you didn't ask for.

As for Tee Mel himself, it might be just a coincidence or it might be the simple fact that four adults are now looking down at him, all beaming, but just then the baby offers a big smile of his own. Jacqueline practically screams: "He smiled! He smiled! He's never smiled before. Dat's his first smile!"

"*C'est fini,*" Lawrence says, handing the baby back to the mother. "It's done. He's all better now. Let me know if I can be of any more help."

Lawrence's last act is to gather the resulting ashes and carry them over to the bayou, scattering them atop the water. He does this so no one can walk on top of the ashes, an act which would undo the cure, he says.

Margaret brings out a round of cold Cokes when Lawrence

returns, and Mel senior deepens our sense of welcome by giving us an extended tour of the place. He shows us his other two pit bulls, Smoky and Sonya, then takes us to a pen out back where he keeps a goat named Fred so big that Mel can actually ride him like a small horse. I'm curious about the huge gator tooth on Mel's necklace and he says it came from a twelve-footer shot right here along the bayou because it was a threat to swimming children.

Sipping my soda, enjoying the nuances of this one-of-a-kind place, I nonetheless begin to experience a feeling of letdown, sensing all the earlier excitement start to slip away. What Lawrence did with that baby, the way he foretold all that would happen, was amazing. But as the minutes pass, I find myself mentally stepping back from the scene and reexamining matters through a lens of skepticism. What, really, did Lawrence do back there, I wonder. Could he have pinched the baby somehow to get it to wake up? Could he have done something else to get it to gasp? Was it just the inhaled smoke? Somewhat repulsed by my ability to think so negatively, I nonetheless wonder if Lawrence isn't just a damn good magician. Besides, no matter what we think we just saw, who knows if the baby is truly better. How will his congestion be later tonight? Tomorrow?

Mel leads us next to the cage holding the five-foot alligator. Shockingly, he opens the door and, with lightning speed, wraps his hands around the gator's closed mouth and pulls the reptile out, whereupon he begins treating the beast like a plaything. He swings the gator around by its tail. He flips it on its back and brings it right side up, then props its mouth open with a ten-inch stick. The reptile's not that big, Mel complains, saying he's tackled bigger. This one might take off a man's hand, but certainly not a leg, he says.

Mel eventually grows tired of the performance and muscles

the gator back into its cage. The reptile is truly incensed now, slamming its tail against the cage and whipping its head around to glower at all of us looking on. It couldn't be more agitated.

"I need to calm dis creature down," Lawrence says.

He walks toward the cage.

"What do you mean?" I ask.

"Like dis," he says.

Lawrence calmly kneels next to the trapped animal and begins slowly rubbing his hands together, almost as if he's grinding some invisible substance between his palms. He stares at the gator all the while, shifting his gaze to meet the reptile's moving head until the animal stops moving and, remarkably, he and Lawrence seem to lock eyes. That's when Lawrence, still rubbing his hands together, begins imitating the guttural grunt-ing sound gators make. The animal doesn't respond with its own deep and primitive grunts. It just lowers its head slowly, lowers it closer and closer to the ground, the rest of its body now totally motionless. Then even the head stops moving.

"Dere," Lawrence says. "He's asleep."

"You're sure?" I say. "Really?"

Lawrence nods, standing up again. The gator's eyes have closed. Having been in a total state of rage just moments before, its head and tail whipping all around in protest of the abusive semitorture Mel just put it through, the gator is now conked out, perfectly still.

"Is that something a lot of people know how to do?" I ask Lawrence.

"No," he says. "It's kinda not so common."

I turn to Mel, the shirtless backwoodsman, the man with the tattoos and pit bulls and a gator necklace. "You ever seen this before?" I ask.

"Never," he says.

I ask Wayne Bellow, a neighbor who's just walked up. He echoes Mel's response. "Never."

Lawrence doesn't brag about the feat or congratulate himself in any way. Indeed, he quickly turns his attention to another matter. A young Indian girl has just walked up with a small puppy whose leg got caught under a rocking chair. She hands the puppy to Lawrence, hoping the visiting *traiteur* can help, and Lawrence begins massaging the leg and saying a prayer.

I, meanwhile, can't stop looking at that gator, still sound asleep. I later ask virtually every Louisiana backwoodsman I meet if he's ever seen anybody put an alligator to sleep this way. They all say no. I stop asking when I meet a stormy old Cajun from Lafitte so versed in the ways of reptiles he tells me he can snatch a water moccasin right off the water, grabbing it by its tail with his bare hand and then snapping the body like a whip so hard the snake's head just pops right off.

"So," I say, "can you make an alligator go to sleep?"

"Never heard of such a t'ing," the man says.

Lawrence has just finished treating the puppy. He hands it back to the girl. "I t'ink it'll be fine now," he says.

Then, standing there in the middle of that cluttered dirt yard, surrounded by a sleeping alligator and a now sleeping baby boy and a convalescing dog and all the rest of us just standing there next to the bayou looking at him with expressions of near-total awe, Lawrence says, "I t'ink ever'body's gonna be just fine. Just fine."

He puts his hands in his pockets and adds, "So I t'ink I can go home now."

# Nine

On a Monday in mid-May, at sunrise, the stampede began. All along the Louisiana coast, people rushed to their boats, tossing off dock ropes. After months of impatient waiting, of tuning engines and caulking decks and painting hulls, the moment had finally come: the "inside" season for brown shrimp was open.

That immense area inside the barrier islands—all the bays, the lakes, the ponds, the bayous, the inlets, the canals . . . any place with enough water to hide a shrimp or two—was now fair game for the next fifty days. And only fifty days.

For a visitor watching this mad dash to the water for the first time, gazing out at all those vessels shoving off from wooden wharves and concrete boat ramps, the comparison comes quickly and certainly to mind: This is Dunkirk. With great urgency, with a sense that the whole world depended on success right now, virtually everything that could float was pressed into service.

Leading the charge, of course, were the commercial shrimpers with their luggers and double riggers and Lafitte skiffs, their trawl nets and skim nets and flashy electronic gadgets nudging them toward the best hauls. But for the first two weeks or so, these vessels find themselves surrounded by a gnatlike swarm of crossover fishermen and outright hobbyists piloting whatever vessel will drag a net.

From the edge of Barataria Bay one evening I watch as two teenagers down from Baton Rouge pull a tattered, secondhand net behind their daddy's twelve-foot bass boat, emptying the respectable contents by hand every half hour, then tossing the net back out. Next to them glides a fifteen-foot crab boat turned temporary trawler, with makeshift net frames awkwardly welded to the gunwales. Farther out still, weaving recklessly between commercial rigs, is an honest-to-God catamaran, its sail puffed out by a steady breeze, trawl nets tied to the fiberglass pontoons.

Closer to shore, two boys pass by in a small flatboat, each holding a scoop net in the water—just scoop nets, like they're after goldfish—but they're catching shrimp. On the shore itself a spry grandmother operates a big square net attached to her dock by a hinged metal frame. The net is called a *paupière*—"eyelid" in French—because it goes down in the water, then back up, like a blinking eye.

At this time of year, many people with "land" jobs—car mechanics, insurance salesmen, oil-company welders, grocery store clerks—knock off at 5 P.M. and race to whatever boats they own, shrimping all night before returning to the garage or grocery store or office in the morning, sleepy and cranky but a little bit richer. And many coastal schools still look the other way in mid-May when the children of professional shrimpers turn up missing, felled by a creative range of illnesses whose cure, apparently, involves only one thing: long days working on their daddies' trawlers.

"Brown shrimp are like fruit on the vine or vegetables in the field," explained Dean Blanchard one afternoon at his shrimp shed on Grand Isle. "When they're ripe and ready for harvest, you gotta bring 'em in right then. Everybody's gotta help. Drop everything and go get the shrimp. Now!"

As it happens, this mad grab for *Farfante penaeus aztecus* in the latter half of May works to my advantage after I wander off the map and into the village of Pointe-aux-Chenes with Lawrence, the minor miracle worker, as my guide. As our afternoon visit that day winds down, I realize I'm nowhere near ready to leave this striking community of Indian fishing people. I also figure there's someone here bound to need a deckhand to help bring in the shrimp, allowing me to hang around a while longer.

Sure enough, Lawrence's distant cousin John Verdin Jr.—a young goateed shrimper who's returned home to weld shut a hole on his boat hull—tells me he knows a guy down the bayou who needs a hand. At this, I grab my backpack from Lawrence's car (I'd brought it along just in case) and shake the *traiteur*'s hand one last time before watching the old convertible Mustang roll away below those beautiful old oaks, heading north toward the rest of the world, seemingly so far away.

It turns out the shrimper who needs help lives *way* down the bayou, in a camp accessible only by boat, and John can't take me there until tomorrow. He offers me a room in his waterside mobile home for the night, then goes back to welding his boat as I roam Pointe-aux-Chenes on foot for a while.

An evening breeze caresses the shirts and sheets of front-yard clotheslines as I follow the bayou south by the fading light of a pumpkin-orange sunset. I come to the village center, featuring only a rope swing hanging from a mammoth tree and, next to it, a tin-roofed community pavilion adorned with milky-white statues of long-haired Indian women and warriors. I pass Houma men in camo baseball caps, gathered in small groups along the docks, leaning against their boats, speaking French and English and drinking cans of Budweiser. The season for "brownies" is already well under way and the men are resting up after several hard days out. They toss their empty Bud cans onto the narrow road, an act of callous littering that turns out to be nothing of the sort. A few passing pickup trucks soon flatten the cans exactly as desired by the barefoot children who eventually come behind collecting the cans for recycling money.

There are lots of collapsed wharves here and horribly rotten boat sheds, the product of past hurricanes and nagging poverty and, for some, outright sloth. But this remains one of the most beautiful bayous I've seen, narrow and dark, a soul-stirring ribbon below all those gnarled and delicate boughs and the streaking colors of exotic birds. I walk along the bank feeling like I'm moving through a painting.

With stilts for legs, the village houses stand back from the bayou. Their ample porches face the water, cluttered with outdoor lamps and chairs and, some, with electric freezers plugged in and humming right along with the evening cicadas. In the deepening darkness I watch the lights of those iceboxes blink on as men and women come outside and lift the tops and rummage through troves of deer meat and gator meat and ducks and shrimp and rabbits. Grocery bills are kept decidedly low around here.

I fall asleep that pitch-black night to bursts of ghostly white light coming in through the windows of John Verdin's mobile home. He's out there welding his boat, carrying on till nearly dawn. The boat is seaworthy the next morning but John's another story, his eyes frightfully bloodshot on an exhausted Indian face, his T-shirt full of holes from errant sparks. But fifty days is fifty days. Time to catch shrimp.

Once we're on the water, heading south, Pointe-aux-Chenes's island of oaks starts to fade behind us, swallowed whole by the universe of Louisiana grass. The salt marsh goes on and on and on, washed pink in the morning light as scattered shrimp boats come in and go out along interconnecting bayous and canals. John stands behind his boat wheel, yawning and stretching his arms. He points to the southeast, gesturing toward a tiny speck of something, a gray-and-white smudge, that interrupts the ruler-flat grassy horizon.

"Dat right dere," he says, "is de camp. Dat's de camp of Papoose Plaisance."

Trapped between the infinity of open sky and flat earth, the edifice looks wildly out of sync with the world. It remains just a speck—of roofing and boards and pilings—getting no bigger even as we get closer. The tin roof shimmers like a dull and distant coin, discarded atop that mat of never-ending grass, lost underneath billowy Gulf clouds that dwarf everything below. Those clouds could surely make raindrops bigger than this insignificant box of wood and tin that's dared to put itself in a world arranged completely to nature's scale, not man's.

The sight of the camp in this wide-open country thrills me. Never have I seen a place exude such loneliness and vulnerability and beauty. If Pointe-aux-Chenes is the end of the world, then here, impossibly, is a step beyond that.

This is no "pleasure camp" we're headed to, John tells me, gripping the boat wheel as the structure, leaning conspicuously to one side, finally draws closer. It isn't one of those weekend sissy hideouts the sportfishermen down from North Louisiana put together with their factory-outlet carpet and overstuffed chairs and wet bars and stereos run by diesel generators. This, rather, is an increasingly rare and old-fashioned arrangement: a working camp, for a working man, on nature's front line, with a cistern for water and a bucket-flush toilet and no electricity and a washboard for cleaning clothes.

If bayou life in its oldest, purest form was what I was after, hoping to take in the last echoes of fading traditions before they go silent forever, then here, clearly, was a promising little spot indeed.

"I got a deckhand for ya!" John yells out, turning off his boat engine as we reach our destination at last. The place is called Camp Chaoui—Camp Raccoon. And sure enough, twenty-seven-year-old Papoose Plaisance, proud member of the United Houma Nation, is using a hammer and nails to repair tears made by raccoons in the camp's screened-in front porch. The muddy prints of raccoon feet darken the old and weathered wharf, which creaks and shakes as John's boat bumps against it.

I grab my backpack and move toward the gunwale, waiting for Papoose to respond. He stops working and walks over to the boat, eyeing my REI-issue backpack, my North Face sleeping bag, looking confused.

"Are you lost or somet'in'?" he says. "You need help? How'd you get lost way down here?"

Yes, I'm lost, I want to say. But I tell Papoose I'm simply a traveler, making my way through the region, looking for work in exchange for room and board—and maybe a little beer—no more.

"You ever worked on a shrimp boat?" he asks.

When I say yes, he doesn't hesitate. He reaches for my back-pack. "Go ahead and get off dat boat," he says. "Yeah, I got food and beer. No problem. Sure do."

Papoose pulls my gear onto the wharf using his thick, mus-cular arms and broad shoulders stuffed inside a tight T-shirt, itself stuffed inside cutoff jeans. The smile on his face, tinged by a look of grateful surprise, draws out a pair of sun-rendered crow's-feet around his eyes, making him look several years older than his age. He has those telltale cheekbones, too, high and pronounced, but he's the first self-described Indian I've ever met with blue eyes.

As John pulls away, disappearing into the distance with his noisy outboard motor, Papoose tells me we won't be shrimping till sunset, though there's lots of work to be done around the camp before then. I'm only half listening, however, because an amazing quietude has settled over this place now that we're all alone, a near-total silence that confirms our remoteness. It's a silence broken only by the pleasing rhythmic lapping of water against the wharf and the low, lonely moan of wind whistling through the nets hanging from Papoose's docked Lafitte skiff. That same wind brings a faint hiss to the air, giving voice to the spartina grass bending and swaying gently on either side of this wide bayou. The camp, resting on the bayou's edge, is pleas-antly bathed in the sound of talking grass.

A fish breaks the surface of the water nearby, and I turn my head.

"Redfish," Papoose says, having glimpsed only the swell, not the fish itself. Like many bayou dwellers, he can tell the type of fish underneath simply by the swell it makes on the surface. "Dat redfish, he's gonna raise de water in a straight line right off de bank. But a puppy drum, he makes a straight line, den a sharp turn. And a garfish, he's gonna make a lot of splashin'. Dat's how you know it's a garfish. All de splashin'.'"

And what I had taken for a sloppy paint job atop this aging dock is nothing of the sort. So prolific is the bird life in this outer marsh that the boards are fairly covered with the leavings, everything stained a grayish white. Already, on the way out, I've seen black ducks, blue herons, marsh hens, and a lovely black skimmer scooping minnows from the water's surface. The skimmer has an orange beak whose lower half, rare in the world of birds, is much longer than the top. A striking sight.

Papoose points to the east to a couple of distant duck blinds he's built for the fall hunting season. As soon as the teals come down in September and the "greenheads" (mallards) in November, he poles out to those wooden blinds in a flat-bottom pirogue, following a shallow ditch called a *traînasse* that cuts a watery trail through the marsh.

Another gust of gentle wind sweeps over us just then, raising a million whispers from the grass. The hiss and *ssssshhhhh* fill my ears right in sync with the cool air on my face as I tell Papoose, with almost goofy enthusiasm, that I'd be happy to stay here for as long as he'll have me. Luckily, he seems not to mind when I mention that my back could be a problem, perhaps limiting me to just a couple of nights working on his boat, hauling and picking shrimp. "Dat's okay," he says. "Just follow me."

We stash my gear in the twenty-by-thirty foot camp, which consists of a room for cooking (on a butane stove) and relaxing on a simple couch and rocking chairs. Off to the side are two small bedrooms and, out back, a 1,200-gallon cistern on pilings with rainwater for showering.

For part of the morning Papoose and I work repairing the porch screen, then head across the bayou to put a new cable on his *paupière*, his stationary "eyelid" net. It rests on a dock by itself, bringing in extra shrimp at night while he's out trawling in the Lafitte skiff.

As we work, Papoose tells me that, like my friend Papoose Ledet on Bayou Lafourche, he got his nickname from his small size as a baby. He was still a relatively small guy, he adds, when, like many Houma, he dropped out of high school at the age of fifteen. He immediately went to work as a professional alligator hunter, and he's been earning his living off the water ever since, crabbing, trapping, hunting, and shrimping. For Houma young people today, formal education, effectively denied to the tribe until just a generation ago, still lacks the appeal of making money straight from the water the ancestral way, a life open even now to anyone mature enough to handle a boat wheel or kill a ten-foot alligator without damaging the hide.

But other distinctive features of this life come through as Papoose talks: he's never had health insurance one day in his life, never read a book, never been in an airplane or traveled far beyond Louisiana's borders. And he's never owned a credit card.

"I don't believe in debt," he says outright. "If I want something, I save up and pay cash. Seems dere'd be a lot less confusion in de world if everybody did dat."

One insurance policy he *does* have, like so many South Louisianans I meet, is burial insurance, a controversial type of coverage often criticized for exploiting the poor, who regularly pay many times more money for the insurance than what the burial eventually costs. But Papoose keeps devotedly current with his payments out of fear his relatives will be stuck paying for the expensive sarcophagus needed for aboveground burial in this low-lying land.

Papoose has a house and a wife, Joanna, up in the town of Grand Bois, thirty-five miles away, not far from where the

Houma hold their big powwows each year with drum competitions and Indian fried bread and dancers in beaded moccasins and buckskin clothing. But that thirty-five-mile trip is a nuisance, especially at 3 A.M. after a hard night of shrimping, so Papoose lives out here at the camp off and on during the year, including the entire brown shrimp season. Joanna served as his deckhand before giving birth to their first child, a son, Briar, ten months ago. Hence the appreciative grin on Papoose's face when, like a bolt from the blue, I landed on his wharf, ready to work.

Papoose says he prefers the primitive conditions of the camp. He loves the quiet, the lack of distractions, the immediacy of concentrating only on work and on simply feeding himself in a landscape that seems to swallow you up whole. It's a freedom and way of life which was once pretty much the norm among Louisiana's coastal fishing people. A hundred years ago, both Cajuns and Houmas lived year-round and in great numbers in far-flung camps like this, close to the shrimp and oysters and crabs and muskrats. But the arrival of boat motors in the 1920s and 1930s changed everything, allowing droves of coastal people to move to towns—with their greater amenities—while traveling back and forth to the fishing and trapping grounds with the relative ease of today.

Now working camps like Papoose's are almost gone, widely scattered and limping along as in the final days of an endangered species. From Papoose's place, a couple of abandoned camps are visible in the far distance, huddled in the grass below that mammoth sky, with horribly rusted roofs set atop salt-eaten boards that crumble, pop loose from nails, then disappear, forever, in the outgoing tide.

———

About an hour before sunset, we take off to catch shrimp. I can't be sure of the exact time because I don't wear a watch and neither does Papoose. There's no clock inside the camp, either, since measuring the march of hours is utterly unimportant here. In the sun-shot dreaminess of late afternoon, as roseate spoonbills and brown pelicans begin the flight back to roosts, Papoose simply picks a moment that feels right and we begin getting the boat ready. Many times he loses complete track of what day of the week it is out here, he says, and catches up only when someone mentions it while he's selling his shrimp back onshore, back in the land where time hovers like an oppressive humidity, getting into everything, impossible to escape, clinging to people's lives.

Papoose's skiff is a twenty-seven-footer with a 165 Volvo diesel. The engine is situated right behind the boat wheel, protruding above the deck inside a protective casing that allows no place to stand while one drives the boat. So Papoose has to sit right on top of the engine cover, legs folded Indian-style, as he steers the boat down the bayou and into the sunset.

"Take de wheel for a minute," he says after a short distance. "I gotta lower de nets."

I cross my legs atop the vibrating engine cover and grip the wheel.

"Follow de *fil du courant*," he tells me, "and stay away from de *batture*."

Papoose speaks good English, but he was raised on French and he isn't always aware when French words creep into his English. So I repeatedly have to scramble, pressing him for translations. The *fil du courant*, as I suspected, is the bayou's main current, recognizable by the glassy-smooth "thread" that cleaves through the bayou's otherwise rippling water. Most of the shrimp will be here, Papoose says, in the water's main flow.

*Batture,* meanwhile, is the shallow underwater bank of mud that extends sometimes twenty feet out from the bayou's grassy edge. Getting skim nets stuck in that booby trap of muck is a royal nuisance to be avoided at all costs.

As the sun sets in our wake, silhouetting the nets and the gaggle of laughing gulls gathering behind us, we make a couple of unspectacular hauls. But thirty minutes later, as nightfall descends in full, it happens: the nets feel like stone weights as we pull them in and Papoose lets go a loud, whooping yell.

"What have we *here*?" he says.

We untie the bulging "tails" of the nets and—voilà!—the shrimp crash down onto the picking table like pouring rain. They gush over the edges and onto the deck. Shrimp everywhere.

Papoose and I rapidly scoop the overflow back onto the table. "We just might have somet'ing going tonight," he says. "Just might."

I've never seen a haul like this. There must be 75 pounds in this one go alone, creating a sprawling field of armored tails, a weird forest of whiplike, wandering antennae.

But now the shrimp must be "picked" clean of the by-catch. This leads to another wave of panic as I ask Papoose where I can find his picking gloves. "Uh, hmm, we don't use gloves on dis boat," he says. "I don't have any."

I try to act casual about the news while inwardly I groan with horror at the sight of all those furious crabs and poison-finned catfish, not to mention the million spiky *piquants* of the shrimp themselves. Like it or not, I'll be picking with bare hands tonight, an aspect of this backcountry, hard-core experience I hadn't quite counted on. Within minutes, yowling like a demon, I'm lifting my hand with a baby crab attached to one finger. The death-grip hold of the claw is broken only by the snap of my wrist as I painfully fling the crab into the bayou. It's all downhill from there, my hands eventually growing numb, so poked and pinched and scraped and punctured that a few more insults with each new catch just don't seem to matter.

I barely have that first big batch picked clean and iced down when it's time to raise the nets again. It's another beautiful haul, another shrimp explosion. Out of necessity, Papoose comes back to help me at the picking table, leaving the boat without a pilot for a few minutes at a time, racing back as needed to adjust the wheel and stay clear of the *batture*. It's important to work fast now. We're hitting great schools of shrimp, what every captain dreams of, and the faster we can pull them in and ice them down, the faster we can bring in more.

Another set of full-to-bursting nets comes on board and I empty them. I swing the nets back out into the water next, careful not to let the outgoing ropes wrap around my ankles, pulling me into the bayou with them. More picking follows . . . and more and more and more, and my arms grow leaden and tired from tossing so many squid and jellyfish overboard, so many croakers and eel and crabs and catfish.

For our own bellies, Papoose puts an "eatin' bucket" on the picking table, into which go the biggest crabs and lots of jumbo shrimp to be boiled or fried the next day and served with mounds of white rice from a ten-pound bag stashed back at the camp.

We must have 500 pounds of shrimp when, around 10 P.M., a south wind picks up and the catch begins to taper off. The wind intensifies steadily and soon we're catching almost nothing at all.

"De wind's holding back de tide," Papoose says. "It's not letting de water out."

The shrimp can't get out either, of course, held hostage by

the blocked flow. So for the first time in hours, everything starts to slow down on the boat. I take an extended break, looking up to suddenly notice an amazing starscape painted across the night sky, powerfully bright and detailed out here so far from the interfering light of human homes and towns. In the middle of those stars lies a luminous three-quarter moon, so crisply defined and close you could almost hang your hat on it.

"How long do you think we'll have to wait?" I ask Papoose.

He looks back from the boat wheel. "Could be a while," he says. "Shrimpin', lots of times, is like any udder kind of fishin': de key is bein' patient. We just gotta be strong and wait it out until dat wind dies down. Den de logjam of water, he's gonna bust loose and all dem shrimp are gonna come right to us."

He tells me that sometimes, with a strong enough wind coming up from the south and a strong enough tide going out, you get a split tide, the water moving in both directions at the same time, the top few feet coming in, the bottom few feet flowing out. In Cajun, this odd phenomenon is often called *une marée folle,* a crazy tide.

We've been shrimping back and forth right in front of the camp all this time, moving up and down the bayou but never venturing more than half a mile in either direction. There's no need to burn diesel searching elsewhere, after all. The camp is right here, right where the shrimp are.

So every twenty minutes or so we pass the small structure and its connecting wharf. At this time of night even this camp looks abandoned and a bit forlorn, its interior all dark and lonely, its exterior a ghostly glow of silver from the dim shine of moonlight. Hours from now I'll stumble into a back bedroom of that camp, guided by a flashlight and candles, while Papoose carries up buckets of water, scooped from the bayou, for use in the crude bathroom.

But such camp conditions, Papoose tells me, are nothing compared to the hard life of his Indian ancestors. As we wait for the wind to die down under that astonishing assembly of stars, Papoose tells me the story of his great-grandmother. She lived not far from this very spot, on a spit of land, in a camp whose roof was made of palmetto fronds, the chimney of mud and Spanish moss. It was a time when many coastal Indians still used blowguns to hunt small game.

Tragically, just seven months after giving birth to her seventh child, Papoose's great-grandmother watched her husband draw his last breath atop a mattress of Spanish moss, felled by the influenza epidemic of 1918. Helped by the children, she lifted the body onto a wooden sled pulled by a horse—an old Houma technique—and dragged him to a burial ground. There, with a simple shovel and a baby at her breast, she buried him herself, wondering all the while how she would ever trap enough muskrats and catch enough shrimp with the family cast net to feed all those children. Only when the last child had fallen asleep that night, when they couldn't see or hear her momentarily lose her outward pose of strength, did she allow herself to weep, sobbing for hours, swept away by a fear and sorrow with no boundaries.


Maybe it's 1 A.M.—who knows?—when the wind finally dies down and the backed-up tide comes roaring out like an uncaged lion. Our nets are down, the bow pointed toward shore, when we get slammed. Swarms of shrimp, one after the other, come rolling out like shock waves heading toward the Gulf of Mexico. We haul in the nets, unloosen the barrage onto the picking table, return the nets, then pick furiously, Papoose and I, side by side.

We repeat the steps again and again, no longer concerned about those shrimp that spill off the table and onto the deck, covering everything. There's no time to scoop up all the overflow. Shrimp heads crunch beneath our shoes as we tote heavy baskets of cleaned brownies toward the bow, dumping them into a twenty-square-foot hold, adding ice. Soon we begin running out of storage space. The hold fills up entirely and Papoose starts pouring shrimp into rows of thirty-five-gallon coolers.

On and on, wave after wave, the shrimp keep coming. There in the deepest, darkest part of the night, in this isolated patch of Louisiana marsh, it all becomes a blur to me—of pricked fingers and bulging nets and buckets of ice and endless sea creatures, some to keep, some to throw back, while the engine drones on and sweat trickles down my back and salt water stings my beat-up hands. At one point Papoose turns on a bright spotlight near the boat wheel and shines it out on the dark water just ahead of us and we can see the shrimp jumping out of the water, roiling the surface, weird stalked eyes streaking through the air.

Eventually, in a haze of exhaustion, I hear Papoose tell me the coolers are all full. We're almost out of ice, too, he says. We don't know it yet, but there's half a ton of shrimp on the boat right now, more than 1,000 pounds. As a last resort, we start filling *champagnes* (baskets) with the shrimp still coming in. But we don't get very far because, at long last, the tide goes slack and our nets aren't bringing in enough to bother with. The shrimp have stopped giving. It's time to hit the camp. Time to sleep.

I remember jumping off the boat, onto the wharf, and feeling very strange. The whole world is rocking as I stagger up to the camp. The screen door is rocking as I grab the knob and pass through. My bed is rocking as I light a candle, cast off my fishy-wet clothes, and lie down. All my senses are still back on that boat, back on the water, as I drift toward a fitful sleep, seeing nothing but fields of endless shrimp before me and angry mobs of crabs pinching all my fingers.

The wind nudges me awake the next morning. Up from the Gulf it comes again, under puffy clouds and a sky as soft and blue as a baby's knit cap. The wind blows gently across the grass and across the bayou and into my open camp window, blowing against my tired body, chilling me. I reach for a second bedsheet and try to fall back to sleep. But I can't. The sound won't let me. In the tranquil quiet of this unhurried morning, with billowy white curtains blowing next to me like poetry itself, the air all around the camp has become an orchestra of whispers. It's the song of the grass blades bending under the rushing wind, talking to one another, telling secrets, hushing one another, sighing. I move my head closer to the window and listen, contentedly, for a long time.

I can see the wind, too. I watch as it moves in streaks and gusts across the grass, parting the blades this way and that, giving evidence of its exact whereabouts, signing its name. As if stroked by a giant hand, the grass bows down in long, quick columns, blades falling like dominoes and then bouncing back in swaths as long as city blocks. Other gusts are unruly, heading in one direction, then zigzagging from side to side, taking sharp turns as if avoiding invisible obstacles, while the grass, faithfully, records every move. Now and then exquisite swirls come to the grass, my favorite among the patterns. Little whirlwinds touch down and push the blades into imperfect circles, giving wondrous documentation to curlicue flows.

Judging by the sunlight, still gold-tinged and delicate on this faultless spring morning, the time must be around nine o'clock.

With satisfaction I think back to the great catch the night before. The skiff, tied to the wharf, sits low in the water, burdened by that great mass on board, the *grosse tallée*. Through my window I watch another skiff pass by, moving slowly along the bayou, headed to shore with gunwales equally low to the waterline, weighed down just like ours by last night's good fortune.

I see more shrimp boats in the distance, their engines too far away to be heard above the soothing hiss of grass. The boats follow avenues of water that are completely hidden by the lush growth, giving the vessels the appearance of floating on grass. The Louisiana marsh, often called a sea of grass, is never truer to form than when seen this way, plied by boats with no visible hulls, by wheelhouses and booms moving effortlessly through the cordgrass and oyster grass as if lighter than air. They look less like boats at such moments than wondrous land-based creatures wandering the marsh as gently and gracefully as the wind itself, apparitions in whitewash.

Those distant boats are headed to Pointe-aux-Chenes to sell their shrimp, something Papoose and I will do in a few hours. But now we laze about the camp, our reward for last night's supreme effort. Papoose is still asleep as I take a shower from the cistern's supply of rainwater, then make a pot of strong coffee, drinking it black, Cajun-style, the way I've come to take it after so many servings down here.

I've been awake a full hour before I realize my back isn't killing me. It's stiff and it hurts but it's nothing like the morning after shrimping with Knuckles and Rose. Maybe Lawrence's treatment had a positive effect after all. Given the gator episode and the smiles of that smoke-bathed baby, I'm certainly willing to grant Lawrence new credibility in the area of spinal rehabilitation. I test my back again, touching my toes, and decide I probably got my money's worth.

Coffee in hand, I head to a porch rocking chair and continue to take in the panoramic wetland world all around. There are muskrat dens in the distance and muddy new raccoon prints on the wharf. A dolphin rises in the bayou as a royal tern, its beak brilliant orange, flutters off to a distant nest. And was I dreaming last night or did I hear a coyote howling in the faraway grass?

A few miles from here there's a state wildlife preserve where bird-watchers and wetland enthusiasts from around the world come to lay eyes on these endless riches. Later, as Papoose and I catch speckled sea trout with rods from the dock, cleaning them with bowie knives to add to our lunch of crabs and shrimp taken from the boat, I ask him if we can go visit that wildlife preserve in his boat. "Why?" he says. "Nuttin' dere we don't have at dis camp. Nuttin' at all."

But if the area around this camp is itself like a giant preserve, sharing the wondrous diversity of the Louisiana wetlands, it also shares its woes. As I sit there in my rocking chair that midmorning, sipping my coffee, listening to the wind, my bright mood begins to change. That's because, in the distance, I can see the gaps. I can see the holes and tears in the marsh landscape.

Papoose, like all coastal Louisianans, has his stories. Cemeteries he's seen disappear. Whole forests wiped out. And there's the camp itself. Built in the 1970s, it used to rest atop a grassy bank, with a riot of green blades crowding around the edges and spreading out to the wharf. Now the camp rests completely over the water, having joined the bayou itself, suspended above a newly formed eddy while the grass has retreated fifteen feet to the camp's rear.

And Pointe-aux-Chenes, four miles away, has its own problems. Despite all those magisterial oaks running through the community, looking so mighty and eternal, the southern tip of the village, reaching toward the sea, is actually a tree cemetery, thick with the familiar skeletal trunks, dozens of them, part of a malignancy that's well advanced and poised to metastasize throughout the village body in the next few years. My goal of escaping to the deepest bayou country did not mean, in the end, escaping the hard facts of coastal demise, no matter how much I had wanted to believe otherwise.

As for the coastal Indians, the cultural implications of land loss are arguably even greater than they are for the Cajuns and Vietnamese. Like most Native Americans, the Houma consider burial areas sacred, so their loss to the incoming sea is a strike at the very heart of the tribe's identity. Then there's Lawrence, walking proof that the cultivation and gathering of herbs for medicinal and ceremonial use is still very important among many Houma. But as the encroaching tide contaminates more and more soil with salt water, wild herbs die and the cultivation of others becomes impossible. Entire communities discontinue the old practices; the cultural knowledge dies.

Add to this the coast's ever-increasing vulnerability to hurricane assault and it's no wonder growing numbers of Houma have begun giving up and moving inland, taking oil-company jobs in Morgan City and in the city of Houma to the north. But there aren't that many Houma Indians to begin with, so when lots of them begin leaving concentrated communities like Pointe-aux-Chenes and Dulac and Isle de Jean Charles, scattering themselves inland, living wherever they can find work and affordable housing, then it's easy to see how the whole Houma Nation might eventually disappear, killed by dilution, erased in perfect parallel with the land.

Alarmed by this growing wave of "environmental refugees," the tribal council of the Houma Nation has begun searching for an adequate parcel of land situated twenty miles or more back from the coast where the refugees might come together to live and own the property communally, attempting to keep the culture intact. A retreat, in other words, has begun in earnest. The goal now is to make it as orderly as possible.

It seems odd that there would be a connection somehow between this sad and terrible retreat and the fact that, right now, tens of thousands of shrimp lay jammed atop Papoose's boat—a connection between the disappearing land, in other words, and the staggering catch we had last night; or, put another way, between Louisiana's giant contribution to America's seafood supply and the fact that I can look down, right now, through gaps in the porch floor and see only water. But the connection exists, and it is this: the wholesale destruction of the Louisiana coast is a cruel stimulus to fishery production. The state, in a very real way, is being eaten alive. It's a basic matter of biological principles applied to an immense coastline.

These thoughts come to me there on the porch in part because of the continuing flow of the soft morning wind. It blows along the bayou, passing through the hanging nets of Papoose's boat, creating a dim, funereal whistle that deepens my conflicted feelings about the catch last night.

The fact is this: it takes a hell of a lot of grass to cover twenty-five square miles, the amount of land that Louisiana loses each year. Every day, another fifty acres slip a few centimeters too far below the waterline and the grass cannot carry out basic functions. The roots become waterlogged; the critical shallow-water periods during low tides, when dissolved oxygen reaches the roots, is cut too short or eliminated altogether. And so the grass grows stressed, stunted, and eventually collapses. Additional acres succumb to that other scourge: the battering effect of wave action along the state's ten thousand miles of eroding oil-industry canals and navigation channels. Still more acres are killed by saltwater intrusion into brackish habitats.

And when it happens, when the grass withers and turns a sickly brown, slumping finally into the water, decomposition begins quickly. A gooey film of bacteria and phytoplankton appears on the blades, unleashing enzymes and other chemical compounds that break down the basic cellulose structure of the plants, releasing nutrients locked in the stems and blades. So-called grazers—snails and tiny fish—soon feed on this thickening green film only to be eaten, in turn, by larger fish and foraging shrimp and crabs. These, in turn, are devoured by still bigger fish, crabs, waterfowl, dolphins, and, ultimately, people. As the grass rots further, turning to a mush of detritus scattered throughout the water, the environment becomes a kind of giant compost pile, rich with available nitrogen, phosphorus, and sulfur, the building blocks of organic life, stoking the food web further.

On the muddy marsh floor, tiny mollusks and worms and other invertebrates begin to thrive on the settling phytoplankton, as do many types of zooplankton, small animals such as the shrimplike copepod, a microcrustacean about the size of a pencil tip. These bottom-hugging creatures, now fattened and made plentiful by the decaying grass, are a favored food of Louisiana's brown shrimp. The water above the muck, meanwhile, has become a veritable brown tea, dense with algae and dissolved organic compounds, a paradise for "filter-feeding" oysters, clams, and small species of fish such as menhaden and anchovy which continuously trap the algae in their gills. These fish, again, are devoured by a wide array of larger species like speckled trout, redfish, and crabs. Then come the human beings.

The Louisiana coast, in this way, is transformed into a giant starter kit for marine life, hyper-rich with inputs, refueled every twenty-eight minutes by another acre of dying grass. It's a metabolic meltdown—a "systemic dieback," in the language of coastal biologists—that paradoxically stimulates new life, producing catches of shrimp and fish and crabs and oysters larger than they would otherwise be, catches which by definition cannot last forever, catches which might give way *any year now* to a steady and calamitous crash, according to expert studies. The wetland "host" will inevitably die, its body devoured completely. Then: no more food. No more habitat. No more nursery. No more fishery.

For fishermen, work along the coast thus becomes a form of living off the seed corn with no way of planting tomorrow. Other observers have cast the phenomenon in banking terms: instead of living off the interest of this long-held trust, the people of Louisiana are in effect spending the principal, cashing in on the great deposits left long ago by the Mississippi River, using up that principal faster and faster, hurtling toward bankruptcy.

Shrimp, among all the estuarine species, seem to thrive particularly well on this road to ruin. They gorge themselves on the artificially stimulated food supply. They profit, too, from artificially spawned shelter. The fragmenting blocks of grass created by subsidence, and the ragged borders imposed on those blocks by erosion, maximize the "edge effect" for shrimp, creating more edges, more avenues of escape, between the protective habitat of grass—where much of the food is—and the migration avenues of the open water—where the predators are.

Together these factors are a major reason why, in the year 2000, despite the loss of another twenty-five square miles of Louisiana land, despite more cemeteries gone and trees destroyed, more homes sandbagged with oyster shells and more GPS coastal maps abandoned for new images of destruction photographed from space—despite all of this, the 2000 shrimp season in Louisiana will be the second best ever recorded; a historic season. Papoose and I will have several more 1,000-pound nights together, adding to the best fifty-day run of brown shrimp he can remember. Dean Blanchard, on Grand Isle, will buy 4 million pounds of browns by the end of the season, easily besting his previous record by half a million pounds. And the state as a whole will ship to America's supermarkets an unprecedented 114 million pounds of shrimp (browns, whites, and others), an amount twice as large as all the other Gulf Coast states *combined.*

But a growing body of scientific data suggests that this same year—2000—may be the high-water mark, the last great hurrah. National Marine Fisheries Service biologist Joan Browder warns in a widely cited study that if wetlands loss continues at its current pace, "brown shrimp catches may fall to near zero in seventy-five years" across most of the coast. Using Thematic Mapper satellite images, Browder carefully plotted the trend of wetlands loss and the corresponding increase in brown shrimp harvests—due to the edge effect—over a twenty-eight-year period. By carrying that trend into the future, Browder forecasts a steady drop in shrimp beginning right around 2000, as the marsh habitat begins to disappear entirely.

All estuarine-dependent species—crabs, oysters, clams, redfish—will suffer similarly, though the rates of decline may vary. Most of these species—and the birds, reptiles, and mammals that feed upon them—will not disappear entirely from Louisiana, scientists say, but will survive in numbers a tiny fraction of their former levels. All told, a staggering 40 percent of America's total seafood catch, connected in some way to the Louisiana coast, will be at risk of decimation. Even the big-money bluefin and yellowfin tuna catches out in the deepwater Gulf stand to suffer significantly as the estuarine-dependent fish they prey upon—menhaden, anchovy, and others—drop dramatically.

So back at Papoose's camp, the morning after our excellent haul, the thrill of the catch begins to fade for me. I had learned months earlier that the destruction of grass was a pitiless and temporary stimulus to the state's fisheries. But somehow it only becomes real to me when I witness a monstrous catch myself; when, with my own hands, in a damaged land, I help pull half a ton of brown shrimp from the water on a single night, participating in the great Louisiana clearance sale, rushing Dunkirk-like to the water to bring in shrimp made fat by the drowning sea of grass.

And then, there on the porch, I hear it again. I hear the sound of the grass swaying in the breeze. I hear the voice of the nets—the same nets that snared all those shrimp—moaning as the wind passes through them, a low, whistling groan carried softly through the air. I hear Papoose waking in his room, ready to start another day in a life his newborn son may never know, a son who may instead live among refugees on land set aside for his generation a full universe away from the wetland world of his ancestors.

And surely those same Houma ancestors, pushed by European settlers for so many centuries, pushed to the end of the earth—surely they never imagined that the sea itself would become an enemy, coming with the same ruthless and unrelenting force, taking more and more land from the Indians—and more and more—until the tribe has nothing left at all.

# Ten

"It's gotta be around here somewhere," says Kirk Kilgen. "It's gotta be."

He stops his Boston whaler in the middle of Bayou Lafourche and, for the tenth time, pulls out a map. It's a big laminated photograph, actually, a Landsat shot snapped by a satellite of the wetlands around Leeville. Kirk pores over the tangled web of bayous and canals in the photo and shakes his head. "Dis marsh," he mumbles. "Boy, boy, boy. It can sure get you turned *all* around."

Kirk works for the Coastal Management Division of the Louisiana Department of Natural Resources. His job today is to transport ten mostly college-age AmeriCorps volunteers to a marsh restoration site west of Leeville. He's toting several big crates of mature oyster grass, too. The plan is to plant, by hand, as much of the grass as possible by late afternoon to offset at least a fraction of the marsh being lost across the state. I've come along as a volunteer, too.

But we can't *find* the restoration site, and Kirk, as our leader, is starting to look confused. "Okay," he says, running his finger along the satellite photo, "we went down that canal and it didn't go nowhere, and we tried this one over here and it was a bust. Hmmm."

It's my first time in the marsh with someone who doesn't know the marsh like the back of his hand. Kirk's got a desk in an office up in Houma and he doesn't get on a boat every day. My experience traveling the wetlands with numerous local fishermen has pretty much spoiled me into believing this maze of grass and water is relatively easy to navigate. In truth it can be maddeningly difficult, requiring both a decent knowledge of the land and damn good instincts if you get lost. Parts of the Louisiana marsh even today are so vast and complex that stories emerge of inexperienced people heading out into the grass and never coming back. They get lost, run out of gas, yell for help, get no response, try to walk, get stuck in the marsh, try to swim, don't quite make it. *C'est la fin.*

"Let's try this direction," Kirk says, pointing to a new area on the photograph. He throttles his 50-horsepower outboard and we're off again . . . only to get lost down yet another blind alley, burning up more gas, wasting more time.

At one point we come across the sadly submerging remains of the Leeville cemetery, passing in silence those doomed crosses and crumbling sarcophagi. Rudely, our boat throws a foamy wake up into those structures, crashing against bricks drowning with agonizing slowness, slipping farther into the water every day. Ginger Landry, the twenty-one-year-old Ameri-

Corps volunteer next to me, takes in the sight and asks me about cemeteries "up north." A Cajun like most of the kids in this bunch, Ginger grew up in a cypress swamp in Napoleonville and now makes her living singing rock songs at nightclubs in Houma while working for AmeriCorps saving the coast by day.

"What are cemeteries like up where you live?" she asks me. "I hear dead people get put *below* the ground. Is that true?"

I confirm the point.

"That's so *weird*," she says. "All that dirt, they just heap it on top of those dead people and then just leave 'em that way?"

I nod and watch her face contort with disgust. Yet somehow the shocking sight of the Leeville cemetery doesn't seem to bother her, so common are watery graves in South Louisiana, violated daily by tide and waves.

Kirk stops the boat once again and pulls out his satellite photo, and Ginger and the others roll their eyes. These volunteers are getting impatient, to be sure, but not just with Kirk. They're impatient with the whole pace of coastal restoration in Louisiana. Like lots of Louisianans, they've grown tired of watching little of substance actually get accomplished. They're tired of waiting for the governor and the state legislature and the U.S. Congress to wake up and declare an emergency along this coast.

Unable to stand it any longer and unsure *if* the elected officials will ever rouse from their slumber, many Louisianans have taken matters into their own hands. All along the coast, communities have come together to do what they can, no matter how small the project, ranging from building Christmas-tree fences that protect small patches of marsh, to erecting picket fences that build sand dunes along threatened beaches, to constructing artificial reefs from sunken boats to support marine life. Taken together, these actions are no substitute for the multibillion-dollar government plan needed to construct sediment diversions and make other large-scale plumbing changes to the coast, but at least it's something.

And then there's the dirtiest, yuckiest, most deeply satisfying restoration activity of all: jumping into the mud and planting new grass with your own hands.

Virtually everyone on this boat of AmeriCorps volunteers has tried to prepare me for what's coming. The *boue pourrie* (rotten mud) is going to smell bad, they say. It's going to grab my legs and take me in like quicksand. "So make sure your shoes are tied tight!" Ginger says. And forget about washing the muck out of your clothes afterward. Can't be done. And get ready for mosquitoes the size of hummingbirds. And for heaven's sake try not to get the "nutria itch," that bacterial skin infection carried via the feces of the nutria, a much hated grass-eating marsh mammal.

Such are the occupational hazards of front-line, hands-on restoration work in the Louisiana marsh. Dawn Bagala, at age forty, the only "elder" in this group of volunteers, still has poison ivy all over her body from a recent roadside trash cleanup just north of here.

So why do they do it, I wonder. Why postpone college and careers for work like this paying the handsome hourly sum of $3.60?

Laughing, volunteer Ian Richard (pronounced Ree-shard) is quick to answer. "The heroin market down here in Louisiana isn't what it used to be so I figured I'd save the coast instead. And after AmeriCorps," he continues, "I plan to go to med school, graduate with honors, then become a famous rapper."

But then he turns serious. "Why do this? Because our Louisiana culture is tied to this land and always has been," he says. "And if the land disappears, where will that leave us? Who will we be? I could get a job on an oil rig or shrimping, but at the end of the day you come home and you're not part of anything bigger. This coast is important to me. So I'm here."

It's this kind of outlook that made recruits easy to come by last January when AmeriCorps, a federally funded community service organization, opened an office on Bayou Lafourche inside an ex-tattoo parlor with wooden floors and creaky ceiling fans. Soon the office walls were covered with hanging shovels and rakes and posters of egrets and ducks, and the recruits came flooding in, ready to serve the program's basic mission of healing the coast with a balm of elbow grease.

"There it is! There it is!" Kirk suddenly yells from the stern, standing up and pointing, keeping one hand on the throttle. "Aha! Found it."

At last, up ahead along the water's edge, lies a narrow stretch of muddy land roughly a quarter acre in size. It's completely bare of vegetation, begging for cover. Kirk skids the boat up onto the bank and the volunteers and I jump overboard into a nightmare of goo. The mud is up to our knees. Walking becomes a matter of overcoming the extraordinary force of suction that resists each new step. You free one foot with a dull, gloppy pop only to fling it forward toward another disappearing act and more unnerving suction.

Dawn eventually abandons walking altogether. She lies down right on top of the mud, dispersing her weight, crawling around like a U.S. Marine commando slithering under barbed wire. The whole front of her body, from her feet to her chin, turns black.

Somehow we get the three crates of grass off-loaded onto the bank and Kirk, with decidedly suspect confidence, tells us not to worry. He's heading back to Leeville for more grass but he'll definitely be back. He'll *definitely* find us.

Then he's gone.

Chad Odom, a handsome long-haired volunteer from Minden, Louisiana, jokes that he has matches to light a fire for the rescue teams when our drinking water runs out. Chad adds with frustration that we were supposed to have two boats here today, the second one belonging to the Lafourche Parish Sheriff's Department. But a deputy sheriff, at the last minute, got called away to raid a marijuana field just up the bayou and so needed his boat to transport *that* grass.

Chad pulls out a bottle of all-natural lemongrass mosquito repellent native to Sri Lanka. "First things first," he says, slathering it onto his face and arms as he tells me in a gentle voice that he's a religious studies major at Louisiana State University. He dropped out of school to do this work, he says. He admits that his passion for spiritual and philosophical discourse makes him something of an oddity down here in the no-nonsense bayou region, as does his passion for gun control and the Grateful Dead.

Clutching bundles of oyster grass, Chad and I struggle through the mud like animals in a tar pit until we reach the far edge of the denuded bank. Planting the grass turns out to be very simple. "Just jam the root end right into the mud until the mud reaches about twelve inches up the stem," he says. "That's it."

The plants are about three feet tall, and the goal is to establish several rows in the shallow water right at the bank's edge. Given the right conditions, oyster grass *(Spartina alterniflora)* is famously hardy and prolific and will quickly seed itself farther out into the water and up onto the bank. The grass's presence literally holds the soil together, slowing the pace of subsidence and creating a buffer against erosion.

Soon the group has spread out all along the bank, everyone

settling into a rhythm, planting quietly in the hot, hot sun like peasants toiling in an Asian rice paddy, bent to their task.

I've finished a couple of twenty-foot rows when a lone tugboat chugs by, creating a disastrous wake. The waves pound my newly planted stalks again and again until the roots lose their grip and a quarter of the plants start to float, washing ashore like jetsam. None of the other volunteers' plants have suffered similarly. "You're not planting deeply enough, like I showed you," Chad says. So I redo all my work, my appreciation rising mightily for the very thin line between living grass and dead grass in this Louisiana mud.

The stretch of land we're working on was actually created a few months earlier by the Texaco oil company. The company received permission from the U.S. Army Corps of Engineers and other agencies to deepen an existing canal as long as the dredged muck—the so-called spoils—was used to create new wetlands nearby. So the spoils were spread out evenly along the edge of this existing marsh area, creating a tabletop-flat area which will soon settle below the water, stabilize, and become a platform for newly emerging wetland grass. The blades we're planting now will protect the edge of this new land area from erosion while speeding the spread of the grass across its entire surface.

In years past, oil companies could do whatever they wanted with dredge materials. The preferred method was simply dumping the stuff on-site, shovelful by shovelful, as the digging proceeded, thus forming a long straight row of excavated dirt running the length of the canal. These so-called spoils banks, literally walls of solid earth rising several feet above the water, today measure in the thousands of miles in Louisiana and serve to upset the natural hydrology of the marsh. They impound bayou water here, block the flow of tides there, and disrupt the growth of grass almost everywhere. The canal banks opposite these walls, meanwhile, erode profusely.

Thus, to the long list of restoration to-dos along the Louisiana coast, add this one: busting a million holes, like hammers put to the Berlin Wall, in the thousands of miles of spoils banks spread across this estuary system, allowing the water to once again flow free per nature's original edict.


"Kirk! Kirk! Over here, Kirk! Over *here!*"

The chorus of cries spreads down the line of muddy volunteers like a brush fire, all of us struggling to our feet in the muck, waving our muddy arms, trying to get Kirk's attention.

But he doesn't see us. There in the distance, piloting the Boston whaler, he's lost again, overshooting the mouth of this canal, heading west, passing right by us with that cargo of additional oyster grass.

"Oh brother," Dawn says, flopping back down onto the mud. "This could take all day."

She reaches for another fistful of grass from our dwindling supply, then does her belly crawl to the next area in need of planting. I've given up on walking too, having adopted Dawn's technique of lying prostrate atop the mud. I plant a few blades, then do the marine-commando crawl, then plant more. Cumulatively, perhaps one square foot of my body has not yet been covered with mud.

By eleven o'clock, the sun is starting to peak and there's not a stitch of shade to be found and we've run out of grass and Kirk's still nowhere in sight.

Ginger, the twenty-one-year-old nightclub singer, is smoking a cigarette with muddy fingers, taking a break along the water's edge. I plant a final stalk of grass and then sit beside her. Ginger's doing everything she can to stay cool, wearing a visor pulled low over her face and rolling up her T-shirt sleeves to the tops of her tanned shoulders. She has short brown hair and boyish good looks.

"Do you like Cajun jokes?" she asks me, perspiration dripping from her chin.

"Sure," I say. "Got one?"

To pass the time she launches into a joke about two Cajuns named Clarence and Boudreaux.

"These guys, they lived on opposite sides of a bayou, and they hated each other like you can't imagine," she says. "Boudreaux, he was always telling his friends that when the new bridge got built over the bayou he was going to walk across it and give that Clarence a real good thrashing.

"Then one day the bridge gets finished," Ginger says, "and all of Boudreaux's friends ask if he went over yet and whipped Clarence's butt." Here Ginger lays on a thick Cajun accent. "'Well,' Boudreaux says, 'don't you know I went up dere to dat bridge and I had my fists all balled up, me, ready ta fight, and den I seen dis really big yellow sign over de bridge and it says *Clarence: ten feet ten inches,* and I says, "Oh no, I ain't tanglin' wit' no Clarence dat big." So I run back home.'"

Ginger laughs as much as I do at this. "How's *that* for a dumb ol' coon ass?" she says.

Yet for all the self-deprecating humor, Ginger is fiercely proud to be Cajun and loves everything about her people—the food, the music, even the noses.

"See my nose?" she says. "I got that classic Cajun nose. Long and kinda slim with a certain curvature to the nostrils. I think it's a beautiful nose. Kinda sexy. I find that when it comes to men, I'm very attracted to guys with that handsome Cajun nose."

Like most Cajuns her age, Ginger can't speak French and I ask if that makes her feel, in some way, less Cajun.

"Not really," she says. "I can still sing the old French songs. I come from a family of musicians and my father plays guitar. Whenever the family gets together we play and sing the French songs.

"My grandfather, you know, he lived during a time when the schools beat you if you spoke French on the premises. The state wanted to stamp out our language altogether. So my grandfather was ashamed of his French and didn't teach my dad much so my dad *couldn't* teach me. Now we're all proud of our Cajun language and all but fewer and fewer people actually know how to speak it."

We're interrupted suddenly by another chorus of urgent, shouting voices.

"Kirk! Kirk! Here we are! Here we are! Over here, Kirk!"

Sure enough I look north and there he is in the distance, passing by this canal again, looking totally confused, heading back the way he came.

"Wait!" everyone yells. "Kirk! Wait! Come back!"

Had he turned just slightly to his right he would have seen a gaggle of far-off figures in blackened clothes, frantically waving muddy arms, hollering from sunburned faces, some futilely lobbing mud balls in his direction.

But he doesn't look and in a flash he's gone and we all slump back to our muddy seats, marooned and dejected but figuring he's bound to find us sooner or later. It's not time to swim or light fires. Not yet.

I take a drink from our shrinking supply of water, then ask Ginger how she came to join AmeriCorps.

"As a kid, I was always into nature and against littering," she says. "I loved rain forest stuff at school. But it wasn't until just a few years ago that I came to understand the crisis of our own wetlands vanishing right here in Louisiana. I learned about AmeriCorps in college and it seemed like a perfect way to get involved."

"But do you ever get discouraged," I ask her, "knowing that what you're doing is basically a symbolic gesture?"

I point, for example, to the work we're doing today on this quarter acre of land. If the grass holds and spreads over the next year or so, we will have preserved—for now, at least—a quarter acre of marsh while forty-nine and three-quarters other acres will die today. And across the coast, all restoration projects combined, large and small, from the Caernarvon freshwater diversion to the use of Christmas trees, are estimated to do nothing but *slow* the rate of land loss by 15 percent per year.

"You're right," she says. "This what we're doing now is nothing in the grand scheme. And I'm probably pessimistic about this estuary surviving. Seems like by the time we all realized what we were doing to our coast, it was almost too late to fix it.

"But," she continues, "our AmeriCorps group does more than just plant grass and build sand dunes. We have a goal of giving two hundred community talks a year—to schools and churches and places like that—on the importance of wetlands and their disappearance in Louisiana. Two *hundred* talks. I try to bring some of my stage skills to those talks and really get more people to think and care. And you know what? No one ever came to *my* school when *I* was a kid to talk about wetlands loss. So that's a difference. That's something."

The distant whine of an outboard motor suddenly reaches our ears, getting louder. I look up to see Kirk bearing down on us at last. A round of mock applause erupts among the volunteers. Kirk plays along, taking a bow after beaching the boat, enduring the ribbing like a good sport, and all is forgiven.

We unload the crates of fresh grass, and I follow Ginger to a distant stretch in need of planting, both of us struggling in the mud.

She stops, pulls out a single green stem from her bundle, then lowers it into the soil. "This," she says, pointing to the newly planted stem, "is an act of hope. That's all it is. We're not saving the coast with this, but by doing it I can keep on hoping. And maybe other people will pass by here and see the grass we've planted and they'll have hope too. And as long as we all have a little hope, the fight won't be over. Maybe a miracle can still happen."

"So you believe in miracles?" I ask her, busily tending to my own rows of grass.

"Sure I do. Don't you? I've *seen* miracles happen."

"Like what?"

She stops planting and thinks for a moment.

"When I was four years old," she says, "my family went to the beach at Grand Isle and I swam out a little too far. My parents were on the shore and they didn't notice at first. And then, out of nowhere, whoosh, a dolphin swam up to me and swam between my legs and carried me to the shallow water. Just like that, it carried me along until I was safe, and then it put me down."

"That really happened?" I ask.

"Yes, it did."

"I mean, a relative didn't tell you the story later? You actually remember it happening yourself?"

"It *happened*," she said. "I remember it. You've never been swimming off a beach and had dolphins come near you? That happens to lots of people. They just come near, sort of checking you out because if you're thrashing, even if you're just swimming fine, they think maybe you're in trouble. But this one time when I was four, a dolphin just comes under me and pulls me to the shore."

"Were you scared?" I ask, squatting next to her, both of us steadily adding more grass to the Louisiana coast. Ginger finishes her story, going on about this event, this miracle, and how such things happen sometimes when you need them most and expect them least.

"No," she says, "I wasn't scared. I mean, at first I didn't know what was happening. There was just a sudden gush of water and I was moving toward the beach, hanging on to the dolphin's back."

She stops planting just then and struggles to her feet. Her stance is wobbly in the soft soil. She looks down at me, her face wet with sweat, flecked with mud, the sun beating down all around us, hitting the water, bathing the marsh.

"And then the next thing I know I'm in shallow water, standing up just like this. I feel the sand under my feet. And when I turn around to look for the dolphin, it's gone. As quickly as it came, it went back to the sea. Totally vanished."

# Eleven

For weeks my luck meeting Vietnamese people along the bayous remains spectacularly bad. There's little change that sunny afternoon, north of Houma, as I head down Old Highway 90 trying to find the Buddhist temple. According to my directions, I should have reached the temple well before now. Frustrated, I press on, passing an odd mix of roadside junkyards and churches and gas stations and pawnshops until I see a Baptist preacher cleaning stained-glass windows outside his sanctuary.

"The *Vietnamese?*" the preacher asks, barely concealing his surprise. He clearly wants to add, "Why in the world are you going *there?*" But he resists, saying only, "You passed the temple already. Turn around and look on your right, about half a mile down." As I pull away, he adds, "And tell those people, when you find them, that they need *Jesus* in their hearts."

I nod, thanking him for his concern, and minutes later I see a hand-painted sign over a red set of double doors: "Công Dồng Phât Giào Viêt Nam tai Houma." Ironically, the "Vietnamese Buddhist Congregation of Houma" occupies a former American Legion hall, where old U.S. soldiers once gathered for beer and recreation. The building is a nondescript blond-brick affair, separated from the road by a concrete-slab parking lot. The lot is empty of all cars when I arrive and the doors are locked. Not a single soul can be found.

I frown, pausing briefly to admire the large lotus flower resting on the roof, above the front doors, sculpted from steel. It stands in stark contrast to the Confederate flag next door, flying high above a good ol' boy's red-brick house with junked cars out front and pens of yelping hunting dogs out back. I wander to the rear of the temple, where peaceful Bayou Blue flows quietly below a carpet of purple-blooming hyacinth flowers. I knock on the temple's back door, vainly hoping for an answer, but the place is empty. My luck's still rotten.

Then one evening everything changes. I spy a Vietnamese man outside a crab shed in Golden Meadow, unloading traps along Bayou Lafourche. His name is Tri Dong Phu, he tells me, and he owns this shed, buying crabs mostly from Vietnamese fishermen. But all of his men have gone home for the day, he says. It's almost sunset. "Come back tomorrow and I give you work. I help you work with Vietnamese cwabber," he says.

Sensing an opening at last, I tell Tri I'll definitely return. I try to solidfy the breakthrough by telling him I've actually visited his faraway country, traveling to Vietnam five years back and greatly enjoying the people and landscape.

But before I can say more, a forceful voice, directly behind me, intrudes on the conversation.

"*Where* in Vietnam you go?"

I turn around, startled, to see a short and skinny Vietnamese man with thick unruly hair parted to one side. He's smoking a Marlboro cigarette, the smoke rising in curls past pitch-black eyes on a reddish brown face, past thick eyebrows arched in a severe way.

"*Where* in Vietnam you go?" he asks again.

"This," Tri tells me, "is Phan Duc Nguyen. He one of my cwabbers."

"Hanoi," I say, answering the man. "I visited Hanoi and Haiphong and Ha Long Bay."

"Aha! All in North Vietnam!" says Phan Duc Nguyen, his eyes squinting through the cigarette smoke. "You don't go to South Vietnam?"

I shake my head no. "I was there for work. There was no time to visit—"

"So you like Communists?" he asks. "You like them? You only go to north? I don't like Communists. All they do is lie. Why you want to visit liars?" The tone of suspicion in his voice grows steadily stronger. "And why you want to talk to us now? Why you here?"

I'm dizzy from the speed with which this once promising situation has unraveled. Twenty-five years after its official end, I'm standing inside a crab shed in Lafourche Parish, Louisiana, being dragged into a lingering skirmish of the Vietnam War.

Before I can speak, Phan says, "Did you go to reeducation camps while you in North Vietnam? You see all those terrible camps? Was that part of visit for you?"

"They don't have those camps anymore," Tri interjects, correcting Phan. "They turn all reeducation camps into hotels. Big hotels for tourists now. And owners, they make big money. Everything in Vietnam, all for business now. My uncle, he sells gasoline wholesale back home and makes more money than me in America."

Both Tri and Phan are quick to tell me that things back in Vietnam are getting better in large part because so many Vietnamese-Americans like themselves have been sending money back to the country for so many years.

The men switch to their native tongue next, speaking rapidly, and I infer that Tri is explaining to Phan my desire to work for a few days on a Vietnamese crab boat. Given his initial suspicions, I'm surprised when Phan turns to me, speaking English again, and says, "Can you wake up five A.M.?"

"Sure," I say.

"Okay, I take you on my boat and show you that people from South Vietnam better than people from North Vietnam. Five A.M. Be right here. Don't be late. You cwab with me."

It's well past sunset now as I review my options: I could drive down and spend the night at Tim Melancon's camp in Leeville. But that's ten miles away and I'm afraid I might miss Phan in the morning. I ask Phan if he knows of an inexpensive hotel here in Golden Meadow.

"You need place to stay tonight?" he asks.

"Yes."

"You want, you stay with me. That way I wake you up so we not late for cwabs."

"Are you sure?" I say. "I don't want to impose."

"It's okay."

Tri, the shed owner, has already locked up most of the doors and put away his ledgers for the evening. He waves goodbye and disappears, leaving Phan and me alone inside the brick and tin-walled shed.

"So where do you live?" I ask Phan.

"Here," he says.

I'm confused. "Where?"

"In shed. I live in shed. You have luggage? I show you where to sleep."

I grab my backpack and Phan takes me past the main wharf and warehouse where ice is made and where the crabs are refrigerated before being transported to New Orleans. We then come to a small supply room cluttered with new crab traps, coils of rope, raincoats, and boots. In one corner sits a full-length lawn chair reclined into a crude bed. Next to it are a small TV and mini-refrigerator, both connected by extension cord to an outlet in another room. Phan opens the fridge and removes two cans of Budweiser.

"You want beer?"

I take one, then clear away enough supplies from the concrete floor to unroll my sleeping bag. The place smells of crabs and bait fish but the floor is mercifully clean and there's a window-unit air conditioner. On the bayou outside, a few final shrimp boats are heading out for the night and an oil-field tugboat blows its horn. Seagulls begin to settle onto nearby wharves for the night.

I wait till we've each finished a beer before asking Phan the question: "Why do you live in this crab shed?"

He smiles, a bit embarrassed. "It's long story. You want more Bud?"

He cracks open two more beers and says, "For twenty-five years I want to go back to Vietnam. I come here in 1975, right after war, when I was twelve, and always I want to go back. Now I'm thirty-seven, but I never go. Not once. So I change that. I save money now for trip home. Tri let me sleep in shed for free to save money for plane ticket. Then I never come back."

"You don't like living in the United States?"

"Here, I never fit in," Phan says, lighting another Marlboro. "I like it here, but the living style, I rather be in my country. Some Vietnamese say I have 'old head.' But that's what I feel. I like Eastern way more than Western way. Over here, love come and go so fast. People always divorcing. Even younger-generation Vietnamese make divorce here. But in Vietnam, more belief in God. Families closer. Respect ancestors. My grandparents buried in Vietnam. I must go be close to them."

I ask him if Louisiana's disappearing land and the growing predictions of a crash in the fishing industry are factors in his decision.

"This town, Golden Meadow, I think in five years, everybody going to live under the sea here," he says. "Land sinking fast. But that's not why I go. I need be with ancestors."

He unrolls a scarred eggshell mattress atop the flattened lawn chair and rests his head on a pillow of balled-up T-shirts. Watching this, I begin to think something doesn't quite add up about Phan's story. I can't put my finger on it, but there's something missing. As he lies there on his crude bed in the back of this crab shed, clad in dirty clothes and in need of a shave, he increasingly evokes images of a homeless person on the streets of New York City or Washington, D.C. And maybe, I ponder, those beers he keeps reaching for—there's nothing else in the mini-fridge—have something to do with it. Yet despite my growing suspicions, I'm shocked when Phan finally confesses. He seems almost pained by a need to make a clean breast of things, and this late-night conversation in the rear of a lonely crab shed with a complete stranger—me—apparently makes it safe to tell the truth.

"In Vietnam," he says, "no cwack cocaine anywhere. No cwack there. So that makes it better place for me, too."

"Crack?" I say, staring up from my sleeping bag. "Is that what you said? Are you a crack addict?"

"*Used* to be," he says. "Seven months now I don't use cwack."

"How did you get involved with crack down here?" I ask. I'd heard scattered stories of abuse among Cajuns and Indians, but not Vietnamese.

Phan tells me his story, the whole thing, stretching from his childhood in rural South Vietnam to his nine-year nightmare trapped in that most American of modern horrors: destitute and strung out on rocks of smokable cocaine.

That Phan ever made it to America twenty-five years ago is something of a miracle, I learn. His father, a fisherman in the coastal town of Phan Thiet, was killed in a boating accident in 1971. So when the Vietnam War ended in utter chaos in 1975, it was just Phan's mother and the eight children who set off into the vast South China Sea inside the family's twenty-foot wooden fishing vessel. It took the family two days, hungry and thirsty, surrounded by dozens of other refugee boats, to reach international waters where a battleship with the U.S. Seventh Fleet came into view. An armored personnel vessel steamed out to pick up the refugees.

"That boat reach us," Phan says, "and marines in helmets help us on board, and then we just push our little fishing boat away. I remember I watch our boat, empty, floating away and I always wonder what happen to that boat? Where did it go? We say goodbye to Vietnam when we push that boat away."

Next, in the custody of the U.S. armed forces, the family made the long journey to America via the Philippines, then Guam, then Fort Chaffee, Arkansas, then Breaux Bridge, Louisiana. A monastery in Breaux Bridge provided emergency lodging for the family in the same facility that housed a dozen monks clad in brown robes and rope belts. Phan's mother found work at a Texas crab-processing plant a few months later. But uncertain how she would support so many children in a strange new land, she decided to leave Phan in the good care of the Louisiana monks. They raised him, loved him like a son, taught him English, and educated him. At age seventeen, however, he decided to strike out on his own, running away and eventually finding work down Bayou Lafourche as a deckhand on a Vietnamese tuna boat before settling into crabbing.

Everything was pretty much okay and he was prospering nicely like most Vietnamese when a Cajun fisherman friend, about nine years ago, after a few beers, asked Phan if he wanted to smoke something that would make him feel really good.

"After that, I lose everything," Phan says. "All my money go to cwack. But I never steal or rob people to buy. I always got on boat in morning and I get my cwabs to pay for cocaine."

He says he bought from crack houses up the bayou and somehow never got arrested, narrowly escaping several dramatic police raids. But now he's seven months clean and says he feels great. He's clear-headed enough to know he wants to go back home to Vietnam.

It's nearly midnight and the beer's all gone when Phan finally turns off the naked lightbulb dangling from the shed ceiling and we settle into our beds.

Before we drift off, Phan lights a final Marlboro in the dark. His Asian face glows with a faint orange hue as he says, "I think, you know, I'm like special eel in Thailand or salmon in Alaska. Many years go by and I travel far from home and I grow up and now, much time later, I make long trip back, thousands of miles back, to place where my life began, to place where I was born."

---

It's still dark out, well before 5 A.M., when Phan leads the way out of the shed to his nineteen-foot fiberglass crab boat moored along Bayou Lafourche. We tuck the cuffs of our jeans into white rubber boots and then wrestle a box of bait fish onto the boat. Phan starts the 200-horsepower outboard, switches on the running lights, and steers us down the dark and sleepy bayou.

We've only gone a short distance when we see a Cajun shrimper just back from a night's catch. Phan pulls over and buys a couple of pounds of fresh browns from the man.

"Why'd you buy shrimp?" I ask.

He points to a couple of rods and reels stowed toward the back of the boat. "Maybe we do sportfishing later. Catch sea trout for lunch. This swimp for bait."

He places the bag of shrimp on the boat floor. "Plus," he says, "this good breakfast."

He promptly peels several of the raw, fresh-from-the-water shrimp, then pops the meat into his mouth.

"You eat it raw?" I say.

"Sure. Just like sushi. You never eat sushi?"

"I love sushi," I say, reaching for a handful of shrimp. I peel one and take a bite. The taste is wonderful, the meat exceptionally delicate, still salty from the water, as fresh as can be.

"I always wonder," Phan says, "why Louisiana people don't like eat swimp this way. No cooking. Good, good taste. Good sushi. Very strange they don't like."

So that's how we head down the bayou that morning, Phan at the wheel, me sitting on the box of bait fish, both of us devouring raw shrimp the Vietnamese way, tossing the shells overboard, popping the tails into our eager mouths as the first traces of rosy light creep into the eastern sky.

It's a clear, calm day, with very little wind; the sort of day that magnifies that ancient sense of expectation and hopefulness that permeates every fisherman's early morning heart. But the feeling doesn't last very long. At least not for me. Just south of Golden Meadow, enough light emerges from the rising sun to illuminate a scene I first saw twelve months ago from the deck of Papoose Ledet's whitewashed trawler. It was then, on that very first ride, that I saw these very same telephone poles before me now, sticking out of the water along two-lane Route 1, weirdly upright and lonely in the bayou current, standing where healthy marsh had once flourished. And on that first boat trip I saw those oak trees in the far distance, dead and slowly rotting with nothing but water all around them.

Time is a force we often think of as making things better, able to heal all wounds. In Louisiana the opposite is true: since that day a year ago when I first tossed my backpack onto a shrimp-boat bunk and walked happily barefoot across the decks, the state has lost 17,845 more acres of land.

And now, just like Phan's, my time in Louisiana is winding down. My travels along the coast are almost over, and the sadness that comes at the end of any meaningful journey is now compounded by the very real possibility that I will never pass this way again. Not because I don't want to, but because the place won't exist. It might be gone. In all my travels around the world I've never had to say goodbye to a place in quite this manner. I've never even imagined such a place could exist. The *traveler* is supposed to go away, not the destination.

Up ahead, faint veils of blue mist come into view, hovering over the bayou. Beyond the mist, a mile away, the morning lights of Leeville emerge, brightly twinkling against a soft and pink horizon. It's still a very beautiful morning, still full of promise, and so I try to push back the somber thoughts for a while, wanting only to enjoy this trip with Phan, one of my last into the Louisiana wetlands.

Phan steers the boat toward the east, away from Bayou Lafourche, and I pull out a map, following our course. For the next hour we chart a perfectly byzantine route through the grass, passing through Lake Pierre, Fisherman's Bay, Oaks Bay, Bay L'Ours, Hatchet Lake, Bayou Casse Tete, and finally Barataria Bay before reaching Phan's traps near Bayou Ferblanc.

Unfortunately, though, there's no reward at the end of this passage. Phan puts on a pair of gloves and brings his boat to a halt and lifts the first crab trap out of the water just as the sun breaks through a thin bank of clouds to bathe us in a flood of fragile gold.

"Ha!" he yells as the trap breaks the surface. "We should have stayed home!"

There's just one crab in the rectangular three-foot-long cage, and it's a small one. It scurries rapidly around the cage, seeming to mock Phan, showing off just how much room it has to roam, unimpeded by company.

Phan predicts a very bad day even before reaching for the second trap, which holds nothing at all except the rotting remains of bait fish. He tells me the crabbing has been mediocre to bad all year long. South Louisiana's prolonged shortage of rainfall, now in its third year, is to blame, he says. Rain is needed to wash oxygen into the water, without which the crabs cannot easily molt and grow big.

"If only more raindrops come, then cwabs get some meat on their bones and come to my traps."

Phan checks only a few dozen traps that morning, gathering enough crabs for a nice meal later that day but with no hope of enough to sell. I'm amazed at how fast he works. He motors up to a new buoy, pulls furiously on the rope, raises the trap out of the water, opens it, empties the crabs, opens the interior bait box, rebaits with three pogy fish, closes the bait box, closes the trap, drops the trap in the water, and motors to the next buoy two hundred feet away. He does all this in less than a minute. I time him.

Normally, he says, he checks all 250 of his traps each day, five or six days per week. That's his life. Trap after trap after trap. He's a crabber.

With a couple dozen nice eating crabs in the boat, Phan calls it quits and reaches for the fishing rods. We bait up with shrimp and begin casting along the marsh's edge, eventually hooking several plump redfish and speckled trout.

As we fish, I can't help but stare at Phan's face, narrow and beautifully brown, wrinkled by the sun in a way which, despite past mistakes, makes him look exceptionally wise for his thirty-seven years. All around us, for miles and miles, there's nothing to remind us we're in America. Just grass and water. Just the marsh all lit up with morning sunshine, serving as a backdrop. The grass frames that tough and hardened Vietnamese face, giving it an eternal look, making it perfectly possible to imagine Phan back home, crabbing in the Mekong Delta or trawling in the Red River Valley, rejoining that ancient line of fishing people from which he is descended, no longer a lost spirit wandering the backcountry thickets and cultural pitfalls of faraway America.

My mind strays from fishing as I ask Phan if he has any fears about beginning life all over again in Vietnam.

"Only one fear I have," he says, casting his line and squatting gracefully, Asian-style, his backside fully at rest atop his calves. He's at the bow of the boat, watching for a strike. "People in Louisiana, they say Vietnamese steal jobs. They say we take swimp and cwabs and fish from Cajuns. But I know Vietnamese who go back home and they hear same thing in Vietnam. People at home say we left country when things bad. Now we come home when things better. We steal jobs from people who stayed home whole time and suffered all those years. I just hope when I go to my village people don't say I come to steal job. That's big hope I have."

Just then Phan lands another two-pound trout, our fourth, and he says, "That's enough. We go home now and have feast."

He starts the motor and we head back through the marsh. A stiffening wind is blowing from the south. The sun is directly overhead. It's lunchtime. I hand fistfuls of raw shrimp to Phan while he drives. Then I sit on the bait box, peeling and eating my own shrimp, one after the other.

When Phan was a boy back home in South Vietnam, he had a friend named Hanh Van Nguyen. Hanh was a neighbor living with his large family inside a mud hut just two hundred feet from Phan's own mud home. The boys fished and played together until Hanh became old enough to join the South Vietnamese army as a platoon radioman. Still a teenager, Hanh left the village and Phan never saw him again.

With the fall of Saigon in 1975, as Phan was at sea fleeing toward an uncertain future in Louisiana, Hanh was dismissed from his disbanded army unit and fled home to his village. Life was hard for former South Vietnamese soldiers. Hanh spent three years in Communist reeducation camps before finally fleeing in 1978 in his fishing boat, making it to Thailand, sadly leaving behind his extended family.

After two years in a Thai refugee camp, an American church group brought Hanh to the United States, where he struggled with English while working different jobs, including that of a garbageman in Indiana. What he really wanted to do, though, was return to the water and fish again.

Which is how in 1986, after more than a decade apart, Phan

Duc Nguyen, already an established crabber down along Bayou Lafourche, walked into a pool hall in Larose, Louisiana, and who should be standing at a pool table hitting a seven ball into a corner pocket but Hanh Van Nguyen. The two men embraced like long-separated brothers, each figuring the other had been killed in combat or lost at sea. Now they were together, friends again, exiled in a land they never even knew existed as children back in Vietnam.

So it is to Hanh's house that Phan takes me upon our return from the marsh that morning, bearing gifts of fresh crabs and sea trout. Amazingly, Hanh lives in Golden Meadow, right across the bayou from the crab shed where Phan now resides, a distance of maybe two hundred feet, about the same distance that separated the boys' huts as children in Vietnam.

Phan ties up his boat among some willows along the bank, just below an aging mobile home propped up on cinder blocks. From the trailer emerges a woman in a conical straw hat and black Vietnamese-style pantaloons, looking like she just stepped out of a Mekong Delta rice paddy. She's Thoa, Hanh's wife, an extremely shy woman who says almost nothing. She takes the fish and crabs and quietly disappears just as Hanh comes out of the trailer.

Hanh, too, is somewhat shy, quietly greeting us before offering chairs in the shade of a hackberry tree along the bayou, not far from where the family cultivates a plot of lemongrass for soups and other dishes. Hanh, who's a crabber like Phan, has a wide smile and thinning hair and carries in his pocket a key chain with Pope John Paul II's picture on it. Both Hanh and Phan are Catholics, not Buddhists.

Phan, who has no family of his own in Louisiana, tells me he comes to this leafy, bayou-side spot along Hanh's backyard most afternoons after work to relax and socialize and mend crab traps. Hanh's mobile home is set among others owned by Vietnamese fishermen along a dead-end gravel road. It's a relatively secluded spot, set apart from the rest of the Golden Meadow community, perched opposite the bayou from where most of the local Cajuns live.

There under the hackberry trees Hanh lights a butane cooker and Thoa, who's been cleaning the fish along the bayou in her conical hat, pours in the crabs when the water begins to boil. This shaded place is sort of an outdoor room for these Vietnamese people, where they cook and eat most of their meals and spend much of their free time.

Phan lies in a hammock between two trees and tells Hanh of our bad luck that morning. Hanh reports a similarly bad outing and says he's praying daily for rain. Hanh needs a particularly good catch this year since his son Hung, the eldest of five children, will begin college at the University of New Orleans in September.

I ask Hanh if he'll be shorthanded gathering crabs once his son leaves.

"Oh no, I never let my son on boat," Hanh says. "Cwab work too hard. I don't want my kids grow up and do this. Sun too hot every day. Money not so good. One day catch cwabs. Next day nothing. My kids go to school and study hard. No fishing work."

His answer surprises me, given how many Cajun and Indian children regularly contribute on their family boats. Upon reflection, though, I realize I've seen virtually no children or teenagers working on Vietnamese vessels.

"So what work do you want your children to do?" I ask Hanh.

"Doctor, engineer, lawyer, president of America, president of world. Anything but catch cwabs or fish," he says.

Speaking of crabs, they've finished cooking and Hanh pours them in a big pile on top of a steel table under the trees. He then throws several medium-size box wrenches onto the table, leaving me confused until he picks one up and begins cracking a crab's shell with it. I grab a ¹³⁄₁₆-wrench and do the same, my mouth soon full of succulent white meat barely two hours out of the water.

To join us, Phan needs help getting out of the hammock. That's because the hammock stretches over the bayou water itself, hung between two trees being gobbled up by the ever-widening stream. Hanh walks over to a tongue of land and pulls the hammock and Phan toward the bank.

"Two years ago," Hanh tells me, "this hammock over land. Now over water."

To combat the constant sinking and erosion, Hanh dumps oyster shells along the bank every week. Bag after bag after bag. I now notice, in fact, that a large part of the "land" here is nothing but oyster shells. The shells stretch a good six feet inland from the water.

"If I don't put down oyster shells, water take my trailer," Hanh says. "My home go away to ocean."

There's a calm, matter-of-fact tone to his voice when he says this, not a scintilla of discernible panic. I ask Hanh if he's concerned that he'll eventually lose this battle with the water and that both his home and career will be swept away.

"No, I'm not concerned," he says. "No worry for me."

Just then Thoa comes out with bowls of "Vietnamese gumbo" for everyone. She hands me a steaming portion consisting of a brown lemongrass broth with noodles and sliced tomatoes and cilantro and exceptionally delicate portions of sea trout minced and shaped into balls. It's a complete delight. We need spoons and chopsticks to eat it.

I put down my wrench and settle into my soup and ask Hanh, "*Why* aren't you worried about the land disappearing?"

"Because," he says, taking his own bowl, "there's enough land here for me to finish my life as cwabber. Maybe fifteen more years I need work. After that, if land all gone, my kids take care of me. That's why they go to school now and don't fish: so they get good jobs and I don't have to fish later."

Everything about his long-range strategy makes perfect sense, but the underlying significance makes me shudder. Unlike the local Cajuns and Houma Indians, the Vietnamese are mostly unburdened by any emotional ties to this land, free to walk away since the region is not and never has been truly "home." Indeed, some Vietnamese, like Phan, are packing up and preparing to leave already. The "promised land" most of these immigrants came here looking for, I now realize, was the America of wealth and education and freedom, and not necessarily the beauty of the grass and the bayous and the visual splendor of blue-winged teal flying down each autumn.

South Louisiana's unparalleled treasure, this huge estuary system of the Mississippi River, this Mekong Delta of America, has in one generation allowed thousands of poor Vietnamese refugees to extract enough wealth to launch their children into stable careers—with white-collar salaries and status—that free those kids forever from the hard burden of fishing. Simultaneously, all dependence on—and vulnerability to—the vanishing land is eliminated. For the Vietnamese, thanks to a grand accident of history, this coastline has become something of a disposable commodity: Use it and walk away. It's like a bridge to another life that disappears behind you the moment you cross it. And for those Vietnamese who *do* continue fishing, many now own and operate their own longline boats capable of going virtually anywhere on earth in search of tuna and swordfish. Some

Vietnamese captains already leave the Gulf for the Caribbean Sea or steam through the Panama Canal to fish the California coast, returning "home" to Louisiana only now and then.

"My son, he never miss one day of high school," Hahn tells me, his chopsticks reaching for more noodles. "GPA 3.75. He got part scholarship to UNO."

I eat my own gumbo with chopsticks and stare across the bayou at the land on the other side. I see the docks and the Piggly Wiggly in the distance. I see a new car dealership and a barbershop and the State Bank and Trust Company. It's America over there, while over here, under the hackberry trees of this outdoor room, it's neither America nor Vietnam. It's something else, something in between, something temporary, like a fragile Gulf cloud that rolls in and changes shape and moves on. Too soon it's gone completely, a product of wind and chance, sad somehow for its fleeting existence.

I put down my chopsticks, having eaten my fill, as Phan squats Asian-style on the dirt floor, smoking a postmeal cigarette. He rises next and walks over to the hammock, pulling the netting toward the bank with a stick. He puts one leg in, then steps free of the bank and lies down, and the hammock swings softly over the water.

# Twelve

I never thought I'd live long enough to travel to the moon, much less see—firsthand—the miracle of human settlements spread across faraway galaxies. Maybe my son, three years old, projected to live to the year 2070, would have that chance. But for me, a journey through outer space to colonies where people live and work in a hostile and exotic environment, clad in special suits and helmets and boots and gloves, their every tool, their every drink of water and bite of food, ferried to them aboard special vessels from distant supply stations—for me, that journey would never come.

Or so I thought . . . until one afternoon, in the most unlikely of places, it happened. I hitched a ride on a boat just east of Morgan City, Louisiana, along Bayou Black, and rode straight out into the Gulf of Mexico. Out there in the Gulf, in the vast space of the open ocean where humans are forever visitors, forever vulnerable, Louisiana's immense and fantastic colony of offshore oil platforms came into view. Those platforms, stretching nearly 150 miles from land, form a full-blown city of futuristic towers and space-age technology as alien to life on earth as any sci-fi novelist's most far-out concoction. Out there, in the Gulf, travel to another realm happens every day.

But I knew none of this on that night weeks earlier in Golden Meadow when I attended a Cajun dance, a *fais-do-do*, and an oil-industry executive handed me his card. "Call me," he said, sipping ice tea after a waltz, "and I'll get you on board one of my supply boats headed to the Gulf. No problem." Out there amid the platforms, he promised, I'd catch a glimpse of the grand and bountiful future of Louisiana's coastal economy.

And so a month later I make the call and I take down directions to an offshore supply yard along Bayou Black. Within an hour I'm standing in a world scaled to giants. The place is loud and intimidatingly busy. A flatbed 18-wheeler rolls up with tons of steel cable on spools the size of small houses. In the distance, a ten-story-tall crane loads ten-ton sections of pipe onto a ship the length of a football field. The security fence surrounding this yard stretches for miles in several directions, rising up to a height of ten feet. At the big front gate, two security guards in hard hats keep watch below a sign as big as a billboard whose message is written in two-foot-tall letters: "J. Ray McDermott— Western Hemisphere Operations." McDermott International, Inc., a multinational energy giant headquartered in Houston and specializing in the construction of offshore platforms, is so large it can only make sense of itself in hemispheric terms, it seems.

A crew member of the supply boat *Leah Callais* meets me at

the security gate, signs a piece of paper, and hands me a hard hat. I follow him to the boat, moored nearby. It's 160 feet long and 40 feet wide, its gunwales lined with huge jet-aircraft tires serving as bumpers. On board we climb two sets of stairs to the upper deck, a perch from which the enormous supply yard comes into full view. It's a checkerboard of industrial-size pipes and I beams and valves of every imaginable sort, all neatly stacked and segregated like the playthings of some fastidious titan. Trucks carry these supplies to waiting boats while more trucks bring more supplies through the front gate. Helicopters buzz overhead, just back from the offshore colony, the pilots landing on scattered helipads, talking through headset microphones inside bubble cockpits. Boats heading back out to the colony crowd the wharves: crew boats, supply boats, utility boats. Everything the offshore city needs, the boats bring. Here they line up for water, there for fuel, there for passengers, there for food.

I meet the captain of the *Leah Callais*, a remarkably diminutive thirty-five-year-old named Tee Brud (little brother) Griffin. He's a Cajun who grew up shrimping until he parlayed his small size—he weighed only 105 pounds at age twenty—into a seven-year career as a thoroughbred racehorse jockey. Now retired, he captains a considerably larger beast: the *Leah Callais* weighs 392 tons and is powered by two 3,508-horsepower Caterpillars. Having received his day's cargo of water, mail, some pipe, and a photocopy machine—all destined for an oil platform 140 miles away in the Gulf's "South Timbalier Block 49" area—Tee Brud pulls free from the wharf and the journey begins.

We head first down Bayou Black for a mile or so, then turn east onto the Gulf Intracoastal Waterway. This man-made east-west navigation channel serves as an inland superhighway for boats, especially the tugs, barges, and supply boats of the oil and gas industry.

While this is my first trip by boat out into the Gulf of Mexico, it's by no means my first ride among oilmen. In fact, industry vessels are so common along the bayous, canals, and lakes of South Louisiana, ranging from 300-foot-long oil barges to 20-foot Boston whalers manned by roustabout crews, that it's relatively easy to thumb a ride almost anywhere you want on their decks. The vessels very nearly rival the Louisiana fishing fleet in total number, revealing just how great oil's contribution is to the local economy.

It's rare, in fact, to find a fisherman who hasn't worked at least part of his life in the oil business, and rarer still to find a coastal family without at least one member whose entire career involves drilling or pipe fitting or welding or working as an offshore technician. Such jobs lack the romance of traditional family fishing, but they offer lots that fishing can't: a guaranteed paycheck most years and, often, health benefits and a pension.

So while I've not yet been out into the Gulf, I've traveled easily among men whose job it is to maintain the estimated three thousand oil and gas wells spread across the wetlands inside the barrier islands. I've traveled with "gaugers" who roam daily from well to well, making sure pumps are working properly and nothing is overheating and nothing is close to bursting from too much pressure. Maintenance is achieved by monitoring various gauges and manually turning delicate valves—*very* carefully—trying never to turn the wrong valve in the wrong direction and so ignite an explosion that hits you before you even know there's a problem. I've traveled with "mop rag" crews whose job it is to stop leaks and clean up minor spills, their skiffs full of the tools of apparent torturers: hacksaws, duct tape, crowbars, pliers, blowtorches. And I've traveled on the deck of a 10,000-ton oil barge heading slowly up the Mississippi River to a refinery north of New Orleans.

In all these travels, the oil-industry people I've come to know have stressed two major points. First, in a clear case of self-interested denial reinforced by bad "facts," they say the oil and gas industry has in no way contributed to the rapid disappearance of Louisiana's coastal lands. Second, they say this same region of interior wetlands is now almost entirely empty of oil and gas reserves. The fields have been pumped dry, they claim. Hence the much maligned oil-extraction business won't be around much longer—at least not on this shore—for the conservationists to kick around.

As concerns the first point, of course, the oilmen are dead wrong. Study after study has shown that at least a third—and probably more—of Louisiana's land loss stems directly from the erosion and altered hydrology caused by the industry's ten thousand miles of pipeline canals and navigation channels. As for the second point, however, the workers are dead on the mark. After seventy years of boom times, the inshore oil and gas reserves of the Louisiana coast are rapidly running out. They're a shadow of their former selves. All across the region, wells and tank batteries have been abandoned, the hulking equipment rusting and falling apart, waiting to be carted off as scrap metal. The large companies—Exxon Mobil, Chevron Texaco, BP Amoco, and others—are rapidly selling to smaller outfits that squeeze the last few drops from dwindling reserves, then shut down those wells too.

So the retreat has begun. It's a scramble, in fact, a veritable stampede, everyone eager to be done with this old and dying coast, this depleted shoreline, free instead to turn to the vast reserves just beyond the horizon, there in the fathomless sea. Out there, along the ocean floor, lies the new frontier. Out there, the amazing colony of oil platforms grows larger each day, rising up in a habitat unnatural to human occupation yet thriving thanks to twenty-first-century can-do technology.

Out there is where Tee Brud, captain of the *Leah Callais,* is now taking me on this windy and clear afternoon. Like the industry as a whole, we're fleeing—running away from the shoreside stench of nature's death, away from the embarrassing million-acre monument to man's engineering mistakes, and toward, instead, a brave new realm of fresh ingenuity and stubbornly unrepentant human pride.

But it's going to take a while to get there, Tee Brud tells me. We're still several hours from the Gulf, farther still from our designated platform. So Tee Brud's small jockey's body is perched casually atop the driver's stool in the wheelhouse, relaxed for the long haul. He steers the *Leah Callais* with his feet, like many fishermen I know, guiding the wheel lazily with the sole of a brown steel-toed work boot.

"You want a pork chop?" he asks me out of nowhere, keeping his slate-gray eyes on the traffic before him while extending the usual Cajun hospitality. "We got a whole mess of pork chops and gravy down in de galley. Go get ya a plate."

I'm fine for now, I tell him, content just to sit up here in the wheelhouse and watch the barges go by, listening to the crackle of captains' chatter over the radio.

Tee Brud tells me he's a "28-14" guy. He works twenty-eight consecutive days on this boat, then gets fourteen days off. It's the same for the other three crew members: a second captain, engineer, and general deckhand. To make the monthlong hitch bearable, the boat's superstructure includes a fully equipped kitchen, walk-in fridge, washer and dryer, showers, TV and VCR, and enough bunks to sleep sixteen people.

But the boat itself never sleeps, Tee Brud tells me. Hence the need for two captains working alternating twelve-hour shifts. Tee Brud guides the boat around a slight bend in the channel while explaining that in the rush to tap new reserves out in the Gulf, there's simply no time to be idle. The offshore colony never shuts down, never stops drilling and pumping oil, and so the platforms need to be fed and supplied twenty-four hours a day. We won't reach our particular oil platform until 3 A.M., for example, after which we'll head straight back to shore for more supplies for another platform, he says.

A half hour has passed when Tee Brud decides to turn the *Leah Callais* in a new direction. Maintaining a running speed of 12 knots, he points her down a relatively obscure bayou, thus avoiding the traffic of the Intracoastal Waterway while giving us a more direct course to the Gulf of Mexico, forty-five miles away.

Soon after this change in direction something remarkable happens: we're all alone. There's not a single boat in front of us and none behind us. More amazing, we've been swallowed whole by a wilderness swamp. All around us lies a landscape dense with trees; a mazelike, watery forest stretching seemingly forever in every direction. Century-old bald cypress trees, veiled with Spanish moss, line the bayou banks and continue without interruption into the murky swamp water beyond. The interior is beautifully dark and forbidding, full of flared trunks and weird shadows and the occasional splash of a lonely water moccasin or snapping turtle or bullfrog.

"Pretty itn't it?" Tee Brud says, adjusting his sunglasses and pulling a cup of coffee toward his rugged, unshaven face. "Dis is Bayou Chene [pronouced Shane] one of de prettiest bayous you'll ever see in Louisiana—and believe me, I seen 'em all. Not too many boats come t'rough here. And de only people live in swamp camps scattered here and dere. It's like a secret passageway to de Gulf here."

I borrow Tee Brud's binoculars and slip outside, onto the deck, walking toward the bow. With a slight breeze jostling my hair, I look down at the boat's hull cleaving the lazy olive-green water, then I gaze up at the winding, somnolent, sunlit path of the bayou itself, etched in utter contrast to the dark and brooding swamp beyond.

Up ahead, a glossy ibis rests atop a fallen log, nonchalantly grooming its wings. Tee Brud and other Cajuns call this bird a *bec-croche* because of its lovely crooked bill. Behind the ibis, water lilies the size of manhole covers decorate the hems of cypress trunks while scattered willows perfume the air with their fading yellow blossoms.

Tee Brud gave me only one instruction when I fled the wheelhouse. "Keep your eyes peeled for gators," he said. "You'll wanna see one. It's like de New York City of gators out dere."

Eventually, to port, a subtle rolling wake breaks softly against the "knees" of several cypress trees, proving Tee Brud right. I spy the alligator's head, an armored triangle with raised knots for eyes. It's gliding slowly toward some new killing spot no doubt, a place to stop and blend in and ambush, with ferocious patience and lightning speed, a passing otter or careless heron. The gator's body trails behind, unseen below the water, so I zoom in with the binoculars and do the standard calculation: for every inch of length between those knobby eyes and the tip of the gator's snout, the gator's body is at least that many feet long. I gaze at the head for a long time, then lower the binoculars, clean the lenses, and gaze again. No illusion: this one's got to be at least twelve feet long.

I return to the wheelhouse, giving Tee Brud the news, whereupon he tells me that when he was a boy in the 1960s there weren't nearly as many gators—big or small—anywhere along this coast. They'd been hunted nearly to extinction. It was a story I already knew well. Ruthless exploitation, stretching back to the Civil War when hides were used to make Confederate boots, had by 1962 reduced the Louisiana population to barely 100,000 or so. But when the state wisely banned all hunting and introduced a hugely successful stocking program, the gators came roaring back. By 1981 controlled hunting once again was permitted all across the state and today there are no fewer than 1.5 million gators here, one for every three Louisianians. It is, quite simply, one of the greatest comeback stories ever for a species recently near extinction. It's a powerful case study, if any more were needed, that natural systems in steep decline from human impacts can be brought back to life—quickly and spectacularly—when human beings lend a careful, restorative hand.

I try to keep this point in mind as I look out at all those cypress trees spreading arm in arm across this majestic swamp, their limbs touching softly and silently like delicate fingertips pressed sensuously together. In thirty years all of these trees will be dead, I know, killed by subsidence and coastal erosion, turned into sorrowful stick figures, contortions of lifeless, standing wood, and added to the countless other tree cemeteries already spread across this battered state.

No dose of magic is needed to stop this forest from dying, of course. No grand leap in human knowledge or applied science. The lifeline just needs to be made bigger, that's all. The merciful lifeline tossed forty years ago to the homely, prehistoric, awe-inspiring Louisiana alligator—it just needs to be stretched out a bit and laid carefully across this entire 400-mile-long shoreline, pulling the whole of coastal Louisiana back from that same dark place of extinction.

I finally take Tee Brud up on his offer of pork chops down below, then rejoin him in the wheelhouse, asking what's the most difficult part of his job.

"Dat's easy," he says, still steering with his boot. "Finding good crew. Now *dat's* hard. In de oil business here, t'ings are pretty good right now, so everybody needs crew. Dat makes good hands really hard to come by.

"Den," he continues, "dere's de fog. Lots of fog. From December to February, it can get so bad along dese swamps and shore areas dat you can't see even de bow of your boat. But you can't exactly drop anchor and kick back. De offshore rigs don't quit working just because you're having a little fog trouble. De best you can do is slow *way* down and travel by radar, completely by radar, till you get to safety. You might have forty t'ousand gallons of diesel fuel on board or a million dollars' worth of drilling equipment, and you're totally blind except for dat gadget telling you where you're going in de pea-soup fog."

The afternoon sun has fallen lower in the sky, giving warm tones to pockets of cattails and maiden cane growing along the banks. Eventually the cypress swamp begins to yield to a brackish marsh of widgeon grass and scattered scrub trees while, in the distance, a couple of tar-paper marsh camps come into view, flanked by duck blinds made of cane. Yet we've still not seen an actual human being out there along the banks, and only a couple of boats have passed by in the last two hours, pushing slowly upstream.

An hour before dusk we finally emerge from this wetland frontier to enter the powerful, surging, wide-open current of Louisiana's second-largest river: the Atchafalaya. The contrast couldn't be greater. From the brooding confines of serpentine Bayou Chene, we're suddenly swept along by an avenue of water half a mile wide, its girth so great that whitecaps frost the river's surface from bank to bank, kicked up by a stiffening wind from the approaching Gulf.

We'll follow the Atchafalaya another twenty-five miles to the sea, Tee Brud tells me as I reach for the binoculars again. I slip outside to do some more bird-watching, noticing that the green hue of Bayou Chene has given way here to a brown water the shade of pale chocolate. It's a shade I immediately recognize, having seen it before, in the water of the Mississippi River just south of New Orleans. The similarity is easily explained: it's the exact same water. One hundred miles north of here, a portion of the Mississippi's flow turns south, away from the master stream, to form the Atchafalaya, the largest "distributary" of America's longest river. Though short in distance, the Atchafalaya carries no less than 150,000 cubic feet of water per second at its mouth, every drop full of the same sediments and nutrients of its parent, collected as runoff from across two-thirds of America and parts of Canada. But unlike the Mississippi River, which is forced to flow in an unnaturally fixed way out to sea and over the cliff of the continental shelf, taking with it all of its land-building silt, the Atchafalaya takes a more natural course to the Gulf, thus bringing *natural* consequences—both benefits and headaches—to the coastal area we're about to pass through.

Peering off the bow, I can now make out the floats of crab traps sprinkled liberally across the river's larger eddies, signaling the water's turn to a saltier state. The familiar presence of oyster grass, meanwhile, begins to dominate the marsh as far as the eye can see. Near the river's mouth several tiny islands appear, each covered with gnarled and stunted black willows. The islands are rookeries for an extravagant profusion of egrets and roseate spoonbills. The birds not only cover every square inch of the island surface, packed in like Manhattan subway passengers, but they crowd wing-to-wing along the flimsy, sagging branches of the trees themselves, looking somewhat ridiculous, their legs precariously balanced, leaving one to wonder how many precious nests below will be flattened when that first bough breaks.

Here, near the mouth of the Atchafalaya, the bird life is par-

ticularly prolific thanks to the undisturbed quality of the wetlands all around. Unlike the rest of the coast, the marsh isn't
fragmenting and vanishing here. Ages ago—or so it now
seems—I saw this area from the cockpit of a plane with Kerry
St. Pé, listening as he explained how this miniature Serengeti of
wetland grass, extending unbroken for miles, not a wound or
scratch upon its body, was nourished and maintained by the
natural flow of sediments from the Atchafalaya.

For the rookeries we just passed that means lots of protective habitat, of course, and ample food not only now but guaranteed into the future for those tiny chicks just now tapping the
dark interior of fragile eggs with their beaks, ready to become
the newest link in their species' multimillion-year chain of life.

Indeed, instead of dying and disappearing like the rest of
the coast, the land here is actually *growing,* a phenomenon that
brings great aggravation and hassles to Tee Brud and thousands
of other boat captains.

The sun has started to set off our starboard deck as the
mouth of the river finally spits us out into the wide expanse of
Atchafalaya Bay. Immediately Tee Brud looks down and begins
paying very close attention to his depth finder. The instrument
was reading a depth of 40 feet (beneath the keel) back in the
river, but now it drops quickly to 20 feet, then 15, then 10. This
despite Tee Brud's strict adherence to the channel markers guiding us out to sea.

"You wouldn't *believe* how hard dey work just keeping dis
channel open," Tee Brud tells me. He's sitting upright in his
chair now, looking much more serious, steering with his hands
for the first time all day and casting repeated glances at that
depth finder. "You need an army to keep dis channel clear."

He's not exaggerating. So great is the silt pouring out from
the mouth of the Atchafalaya River—100,000 tons per day—

that giant mechanical dredge ships work almost constantly in this bay, scooping up the soil and spraying it out—in wet, arching, mucky streams—away from the channel's crowded line of boat traffic. But within days new silt barreling out of the river's mouth begins filling the channel again.

In the distance, meanwhile, beyond the chain of oil and fishing vessels heading out to sea, myriad small islands and sandbars dot the water, new ones popping up all the time, every few months, like mushrooms after a rainstorm. From the deck I watch a trio of brown pelicans, way out in the middle of the bay, plop down on a raft of sand, waiting for the next school of channel mullet to bring supper.

Each year, in a wonderful and rare reversal, nearly two thousand acres of this bay simply disappear, turning to *land*. The bay is getting smaller and smaller.

And the boats keep right on struggling.

"Uh-oh!" Tee Brud says, suddenly staring down with disgust at the depth finder. "We're about to skim bottom."

The gauge, incredibly, reads only 1.3 feet! Then it goes blank. Just like that. Nothing on the screen at all. At the same moment, the boat begins to shudder and vibrate noticeably. It begins to slow down. We've hit bottom all right. Part of the hull is actually in mud, plowing through it. Most amazing, we're a full ten miles from the river's mouth now, entering the Gulf itself, surrounded by wide-open water. Such is the reach of the Atchafalaya's flow. Gradually the meter edges back up to 5 feet and the boat picks up speed and Tee Brud lets go a sigh.

"You definitely don't want to get stuck out here," he says. "You have to call a tug, and it can eat up half your day. Believe me, if dey didn't dredge all de time, it'd get so bad out here it'd shut everyt'ing down completely. Nobody in or out. Everybody stuck in de gunk—like a giant car wreck."

I, too, begin furtively watching the depth meter now, simultaneously wondering what the good people of Leeville, Louisiana, wouldn't give for a car wreck like the one Tee Brud just described. And what of the folks in Golden Meadow and Pointe-aux-Chenes, Chauvin and Grand Isle—and New Orleans too? The Atchafalaya River is creating a glorious mess of new land here, efficiently guarding one small portion of the Louisiana coast, offering a daily reminder of the power of the Mississippi's sediment load while, beginning just a few miles away, 90 percent of the rest of the state's coastline continues to melt away. For all those communities on the brink of drowning, where water—hour by hour—draws a tightening noose around what little land is left, the idea of sediment buildup so thick it inconveniences boats while throwing up pesky sandbars and new islands between shore and sea—for such communities, a problem like that is the very definition of salvation.

But I guess, deep down, I'd never been a true believer after all. Not really. Not until I floated down the Atchafalaya River and out into Atchafalaya Bay aboard the *Leah Callais.* In my own hands I had held the plans for Woody Gagliano's Third Delta Conveyance Channel, that vision of a man-made river, huge in scale yet rooted in feasible physics, designed to divert a third of the Mississippi's flow and scatter it along the Louisiana coast. But those plans were mere sheets of paper. Just words and drawings and gradient ratios set in print. It wasn't until I sat at the head of the *Leah Callais,* watching that depth finder rise and fall like a pinball, watching the boat's hull labor through the stifling muck, its propellers actually churning up the silt and filling the air with a rich scent not found elsewhere in Louisiana, a smell like mud and musk and seaweed and salt water and hope all mixed together—it wasn't until then that I truly believed. Down in the galley I could actually hear the hull skidding across hidden mud and sandbars, making a *sssssssshhhhhhh* sound. And up on the deck I can almost reach down, it seems, and scoop up big, wet, heavy handfuls of earth with my own fingers.

Yes, I believe now. With a slight turn of the tap, with a careful redirecting of just part of the Mississippi's flow, with a surgical precision that brings that sediment-rich water into the areas that need it most, much of Louisiana's worst land loss would stop. Communities all along Bayou Lafourche and large areas to its east and west would be saved. Smaller diversions, like the one at Caernarvon, would help protect New Orleans in a very big way.

Never mind the paralyzing bickering over the cost (as if further delay were actually an option), the strategy itself is overwhelmingly simple: *Arrêtez la chute.* Stop the waterfall. Stop the Niagara-like flow of American soil over the precipice of the continental shelf, ushered there by the levees of the Mississippi River. Put that water to work. Let it save something truly worth saving.

It's almost dark as Tee Brud grabs another cup of coffee and we continue our slow journey out into the Gulf's wide-open water. Suddenly, for the last time, the depth meter plunges—12 feet, 10 feet, 8. It halts at 6 feet and stays there a while, and I look out through the wheelhouse windows at the amazingly shallow water all around us, so far from shore. And for a moment I swear I can almost see it down there. Despite the waning light, despite the dark color of the sea itself, I think—no, I'm sure—I can see the bottom. I can see land trying to rise up, pushing and pushing toward the surface, almost to the top, almost there, trying, with all its might, to catch a breath of air.

"You wanna steer?" Tee Brud asks me, rising from his stool and pointing to the boat wheel.

"Sure," I say, having asked for this privilege a while back and now happily taking the helm as he stretches his legs a bit. A velvety blue-black sky has blanketed the whole of the Gulf of Mexico now, extinguishing the last pink whispers of dusk.

I grip the polished wooden wheel, keeping an eye on the compass that marks our southward course. And then I see it. In the distance, bright white with floodlights, the first oil platform of the evening comes into clear view, getting closer and closer. This had been our destination all along, to reach this vicinity of the Gulf and travel among these mammoth man-made structures. But after so many hours in the company of migratory birds and swamp frogs and wild-eyed alligators, floating through a forest ideal of cypress trees laced with moss, the transition to 3,000-ton towers crowned by helicopter pads, all garishly plunked down in the middle of the sea, is a shock to the senses.

That first platform in the distance has the weird, hybrid look of a giant mechanical giraffe landed somehow from outer space. Its legs are long and straight, made of riveted steel and set atop concrete pedestals for feet. I squint at those legs as they rise dozens of feet from the water to an enormous body, a half acre in size, where the beast's vital organs lay exposed inside an outer skeleton of strut work. The torso holds humming diesel generators and throbbing electric pumps and vibrating heating tanks, all crisscrossed by pipes and various ducts and exhaust vents running everywhere like blood veins.

The boom of a fifty-foot-long crane serves as a tail for this mammoth creature, extending far over the water. At the other end, above the front legs, rises the lofty neck: a three-story-tall dormitory for workers. It's made taller by the radio antennae and satellite-TV dish and foghorn and hazard lights shining bright to warn off ships and low-flying aircraft.

Before we get much closer, the recognizable shapes of several other offshore structures come into view, each brightly illuminated against the dark night sky. The size of the platforms differs from edifice to edifice, as does the arrangement of equipment on board, but they all have that same look of four-legged creatures landed from another world, far too large to have been made by men. The structures dwarf even the largest passing ships, striking a vaguely aggressive pose with those hulking metallic bodies atop great concrete legs. They look down on passersby like the top-heavy titans in H. G. Wells' *War of the Worlds*.

There in the captain's chair, I survey this unfolding scene, my head turning from tower to tower. Eventually I start counting: one dozen, two dozen, three dozen. We've barely entered the Gulf of Mexico and already I count more than *forty* offshore platforms spread before us—enough to equal a decent-size town. Still more structures appear every minute, their twinkling lights floating over the horizon, a dim smudge at first, then getting bigger and brighter, gradually closer, making room for more lights behind them.

From the corner of my eye I suddenly see a different kind of light. A series of strange white explosions occur to the southwest. The explosions are silent, too distant to be heard. They mysteriously come and go, bursting into the air, then disappearing, eerily painting the sky each time with a blue-white afterimage that leaves me baffled. Finally I realize what I'm seeing: it's a blowtorch. A man maybe two miles away, standing on a platform one hundred feet above the ocean, is busily welding, his work sending bursts of weird light racing across the vast, dark Gulf.

Equally eerie are the gas flares that roar high atop most of the platforms, burning off excess natural gas released as part of the production process. The flames shoot ten or fifteen feet into the air, looking oddly primitive amid all the complex machinery on space-age stilts; looking like the ancient torches of lost sailors alone far out to sea.

Having let me sample the captain's chair for a while, Tee Brud retakes the wheel, keeping us on the same steady southward course. Soon we reach and begin passing the first of the oil platforms, drawing within a few hundred yards of some of them. Most of these offshore structures tap into multiple pockets of oil, Tee Brud explains, thanks to a technique called "directional drilling." Widely adopted by the oil industry in the 1980s, this method allows rigs to drill diagonally and in more than one direction, thus penetrating several pools of oil scattered in different directions and at different depths below the ocean floor. As a result, the average platform along the Louisiana coast today is connected to at least three or four different wells. The crude fuel is drawn toward the "parent" structure where the oil and gas are separated from water and then pumped to shore via underwater pipelines.

Tee Brud says that platform workers generally work seven days on, seven days off, putting in twelve-hour shifts. It makes for long and lonely stays at sea, a hardship softened somewhat by air-conditioned dorm rooms and hot showers and satellite TV and twenty-four-hour cafeterias. Some platforms even have pool rooms and weight-lifting facilities tucked in amid the tight fit of machinery, everything suspended high above the rolling waves of the Gulf.

A "platform" should not be confused with a "drilling rig," Tee Brud tells me. Platforms are the finished product of the offshore process, equipped to clean up and pump away—with factory efficiency—the oil and gas already tapped in proven fields. As a result, the supplies these structures require from boats like Tee Brud's are limited mostly to food and water and diesel fuel and various replacement parts.

A "drilling rig," on the other hand, is a high-maintenance creature. Though constructed of the same steel and concrete legs rising up to a tabletop structure supporting men and machines, a drilling rig is by definition a busy, material-hungry place. Many times more men are needed during this phase of the offshore process, beginning with the rig's construction—piece by piece—from the ocean floor, where every nut, every I beam, every box wrench, every sack of cement must be ferried out from shore. And once the drilling begins, a constant supply of new drill pipe—several miles of pipe—must arrive right on time, without delay, to follow the drill's foot-by-foot progress toward its targeted field. To haul so much equipment, supply boats like Tee Brud's are designed like big nautical pickup trucks, with the wheelhouse and living quarters pushed far to the front and the entire rear deck—three-quarters of the boat's length—left flat and open for cargo.

Drilling rigs, I also learn, require hundreds of thousands of gallons of a strange concoction called "liquid mud." Tee Brud's boat is designed to hold no less than 63,000 gallons of liquid mud, stored below deck in a double-hulled steel hold. When hauling this substance, Tee Brud ties up to the receiving rig and radios up to the drill foreman, who pumps the watery brown mud up to the top of the rig where it's then poured down into the drill pipe. This helps seal the area inside the pipe and around the drill stem, neutralizing the tremendous underground pressure constantly pushing up and threatening to send oil gushing dangerously up and all over the rig. Several onshore companies make liquid mud by mining a special volcanic clay and mixing it with water and other minerals to achieve the precise composition required for drilling. Then, in an odd twist of symmetry, it's ferried out to sea, many miles away, and duly put back into the earth, injected thousands of feet below the ocean floor.

It's an hour past sunset now and we're thirty miles offshore and I make a 360-degree scan of the horizon. For more than an hour they've kept coming—and coming and coming—beginning as mere pinpricks of light on the horizon and drawing closer, five and ten at a time. Now, wherever I look, through every wheelhouse window, I see only oil platforms and drilling rigs. They stretch away, all around us, enveloping us, interrupted in the distance only by the curvature of the earth. I step out onto the boat deck and try to count them, but it's nearly impossible. I give up, guessing there are several hundred—at least—within view.

Every few minutes another of the ten-story structures passes by—here to starboard, there to port—sometimes close enough for me to hear the work going on. I hear the clang of drill pipe fitting into place, the roar of diesel-engine cranes lifting supplies, the bang of hammers. I see work crews in hard hats communicating with each other in shouts, some crews bringing up oil from established fields, others drilling down to new fields.

After each of these rigs passes by, I turn away and look around and blink my eyes all over again at the endless maze of other platforms in the distance, one after the other after the other, each a replica of what I've just seen up close, more men doing the same work, hundreds and hundreds of teams together in a great choreography of furious effort, getting the oil up from the seafloor.

I float through this world now almost in a daze, standing there on the deck, barely comprehending the busy, noisy, lamplit forest of mechanical towers all around. I watch the growing number of gas flares high atop those towers, so many now they form a forest of their own with trunks of urgent orange flames dancing wildly toward the black sky. Distant welders, meanwhile, three and four at a time, work all across this man-made milieu, sending scattered explosions of lurid blue-white light into the darkness. And then comes the rare night-flying helicopter—like a blinking rocket ship in the darkness of deep space—buzzing overhead and landing on a distant platform while, just below, supply boats by the dozens, just like ours, meander among all the giant concrete legs, delivering vital rations from the far-off world of earth and trees.

For the first time in my life, I realize, I'm in a city, a full-blown metropolis, set in a universe all its own, utterly divorced from land and the earthbound realities of human existence. It's a city, too, that never sleeps, just as Tee Brud had mentioned. Midnight or noon, it's all the same. The work goes on—no interruptions, no slowing down—like a space colony without seasons or sunlight to break up the days.

Like most Americans, I had no idea it was like this out here. No *idea*. Who in his right mind would ever conceive of such a vast ocean tract so utterly transformed in appearance and function? I had always thought of offshore oil platforms as relatively rare creatures, kept few in number by their fantastic size and immense complexity, hovering offshore in quantities approaching perhaps a few dozen, maybe even a few hundred, but certainly not more than that—not even in the oil-rich provinces of the Gulf of Mexico or the offshore fields of California. But here, before my eyes, at this one spot in the Gulf, I see more platforms than I previously thought existed in all of America.

The sheer scale of this artificial world makes me glad, a few minutes later, when I look up and notice that the sky has grown darker and a beautiful starscape has emerged across the cloudless night canvas. Intensely bright despite the light of the platforms, the stars are the only thing familiar to me at that moment, the only thing I can make sense of. They offer a comforting tether as I stand there on the deck, immersed in this journey, moving deeper and deeper into this strange and disorienting ocean milieu.

But soon I notice something: the spacing and proportion are just about right. The oil platforms, brightly lit and spread more or less evenly across the sea, look unmistakably like reflections of the stars above. The celestial light is coming down and bouncing off the water, it seems, one star for every platform, so great is the presence of oil in the Gulf of Mexico.

"You're not that far from the truth," Tee Brud tells me back in the wheelhouse. There are, he says, no fewer than four *thousand* platforms and drilling rigs off the coast of Louisiana, servicing a grand total of thirty-five thousand wells. His comment seems preposterous on its face until I glance out the cabin windows again at the ceaseless expanse of lights. Every year, he adds, as more and more oil is discovered, this staggering number of platforms grows larger. Eighty percent of *all* offshore platforms in the United States are found right here off the Louisiana coast, so vast and deep is the hydrocarbon reservoir right below our hull, an ocean below an ocean.

"Here, I want to show you something," Tee Brud says.

He leaves the wheel for a moment and returns with a nautical chart rolled up in his hands. In the soft lamplight of the cabin, he unfurls the paper to reveal a depiction of the Gulf of Mexico south of Louisiana. It covers the whole coast, from the Texas border to the Mississippi state line, and extends a good two hundred miles offshore. But the chart seems unconnected to reality, its features dominated not by coastal land and the salient blue of ocean water, but by thousands of small black squares spread across the Gulf. Some of the squares are bunched together in dense clusters. Some are spread evenly across large stretches of water. Some sit far out to sea, all by themselves, like the lonely outposts of an overreaching empire.

"Every one of those squares represents an oil platform or a drilling rig," Tee Brud tells me, running his hand across the full breadth of the map. "This is what Louisiana's offshore oil patch looks like to a boat captain like me."

That this nautical chart also looks like a galaxy—like a map of the stars—is unmistakable. Those multitudinous black squares, just like stars, appear infinite and uncountable. And like stars, they arrange themselves here and there into odd shapes, deepening the illusion of outer space.

"See down here," Tee Brud says, moving his finger to an area a few miles off the coast of Port Fourchon. "See how all these platforms just happen to come together in a way that looks like a rabbit? See? It's like a constellation. A rabbit. See?"

There it is: the long pair of ears rising up from a round rabbit face. It looks like the Playboy Bunny emblem. Only this one's sketched entirely by those tiny black squares, hundreds of them, each in reality a tower of steel and concrete and living quarters and pool tables and bad cafeteria food set high above the ocean waves—yet on this map, collectively, a rabbit as discernible as the Big Dipper or the Southern Cross. It's an image that suggests order amid chaos, the same phenomenon that inspired the first celestial maps of the ancient Greeks so many millennia ago.

And like the ancients, Louisianans, in their own way, navigate by these stars.

"There might be a lot of boat traffic heading out while I'm heading in," Tee Brud explains, "so I tell all the other captains I'm just east of the Rabbit Field and we stay clear of each other that way. Or a platform foreman might need me and says he's in the ear of the rabbit and I immediately find him on my chart."

Tee Brud then points to other constellations—the Barbecue Pit, the Hole in the Wall, the Circle Field—their shapes equally recognizable, especially when viewed on radar.

"And here," he says, switching to still another section of the Gulf, "is where we're headed tonight."

There in the semidarkness of the cabin he moves his finger along the chart, passing through miles and miles of stars like a spaceship navigator plotting his trajectory. He stops at a cluster of black squares far off the state's central coast. "Right here," he says. "This is the place. We should be there by three A.M."

Tee Brud gets a call on the radio just then and heads back to the wheel while I continue examining the chart, poring over every last nook of the galaxy. How is it possible, I wonder, that this implausible mass of offshore construction is not as famous as the Sears Tower or the Grand Canyon? While Louisiana's coast continues to implode, creating the fastest-disappearing landmass on earth, the story of its demise remains stubbornly unknown to most Americans. Likewise, what's happening out here in the Gulf, just beyond that same shore, goes almost entirely unnoticed. Thousands of acres of new "land" are being brought into existence here, literally built above the water, a mass of solid structures so huge that if they were stacked end to end they'd stretch from Washington, D.C., to Philadelphia. Instead of saving one place, we're creating another, developing the largest artificial mass of offshore property ever conceived. It's just too bad that drills and dorms and pumps set atop pillars of steel and concrete can't nurture juvenile shrimp or save New Orleans from the hammering blow of hurricanes.

And every year that offshore world gets bigger and bigger. More platforms are built farther and farther out to sea, now reaching the deep water of the outer continental shelf—almost 150 miles out—where the newest fields are being discovered.

Out there, I learn, some platforms sit in water a mile deep, with crews lowering drill bits all that distance, then drilling another five miles *below* the ocean floor. Fittingly, the Shell oil company now refers to its deepwater rig farthest out in the Gulf as the "Mars Project."

Deepwater extraction like this wasn't even feasible until ten years ago, when an evolved version of a technique called "dynamic positioning" came into use. Declassified by the U.S. and Soviet governments at the end of the Cold War, advanced dynamic positioning was developed to allow nuclear submarines to remain perfectly still while firing underwater. A sophisticated onboard computer interacts with several thrusters (high-speed propellers) spread evenly across the sub's outer shell to constantly assess and compensate for waves and underwater currents. This same technique now allows oil-drilling rigs, whose legs could never extend a mile to the ocean floor, to literally float in the Gulf of Mexico, hovering almost perfectly motionless and so not upsetting the vulnerable drill stem. In this way, dynamic positioning has allowed the offshore oil boom to keep right on rolling, shattering the old barrier of deep water and opening up a whole new realm of the offshore galaxy. These rigs can even survive hurricanes thanks to special longline anchors that secure them to the Gulf floor.

Weeks ago at that Cajun dance where I first got invited to travel offshore, an oil-company executive had told me I'd see the future of South Louisiana's economy out here. And so I have. And what's clear to anyone who journeys this far out is that a lot of coastal people will continue to make a lot of money off this boom. Peter Callais, the owner of this very boat, started out as a small-scale operator with just two boats in 1993 and today he has twenty supply vessels plying the oil patch under his name. He coordinates their activities from his fifteen-room office complex in Golden Meadow where his own desk is flanked by a putting green and practice cup.

Thousands of other ex-fishermen like Tee Brud now work on supply boats or punch clocks on the offshore rigs. Many thousands more will soon do the same as coastal land loss eventually brings the seafood industry to the point of collapse. Gone will be the old life of trawling with sons along bayous running a few feet from people's homes. These men will instead spend their lives, months at a time, away from their families, sleeping out here in cubicle dorm rooms and watching satellite TV after twelve-hour shifts "slinging" drill pipe or pumping liquid mud or monitoring monotonous gauges amid the lonely ocean waves.

There aboard the *Leah Callais*, meanwhile, as I roll up the nautical chart and head outside to the deck for a final walk before bed, the question comes to me: What will come next? Offshore oil has become increasingly important to South Louisiana's future in part because the *onshore* world is dying and disappearing, a major subtraction from the local economy. That coastline is dying not because anyone wanted it to die or consciously made it happen, but because of the unintended consequences of human engineering and technology. First came the mammoth leveeing of the Mississippi, then the giant mechanical dredgers digging up a highway system of canals through the wetlands.

And now, as I walk along the deck that night, surrounded again by the freakish spread of brightly lit platforms stretching to every horizon, I can't help but wonder what will be the unintended consequences of such aggressive oil exploitation, of so many new platforms made possible by dynamic positioning and directional drilling, technologies now as important to modern, oil-thirsty America as levees once were to the survival of colonial Louisiana.

But I already know the answer. The nonstop quest for oil—

not just here but across the globe—will soon bring Louisiana to the rest of the world. An avalanche of scientific studies now tell us the world is warming rapidly and that the burning of fossil fuels is the cause. Yet just like the ironclad science produced by Woody Gagliano thirty years ago showing that the Louisiana coast was sinking and disappearing, the phenomenon of global warming has been met worldwide with denial even as the situation gets worse, the symptoms more obvious.

Leaving aside the impacts on agriculture and the rapid spread of human diseases, global warming's projected handiwork of up to three feet of sea-level rise will dramatically affect more than two billion coastal people worldwide. Whether the land sinks (as in Louisiana) or the oceans rise (as in the rest of the world), the effect, after all, is the same: saltwater contamination of drinking water, battered barrier islands, the death of coastal forests and wetlands, damaged roads and homes, and vast populations put at risk of injury or death from hurricane storm surges. If you want to see what will consume the energies of Miami and New York, Shanghai and Bombay, fifty years from now, come to Louisiana today. The future really is here.

But it doesn't have to be *that* future. There's still enough time on the clock. We could just as easily use our love of big tools and grand engineering schemes to repair what's broken along the Louisiana coast and so show the rest of the world how to care for an ailing planet. We could do that—or we could stay the course, building more and more contraptions like the oil platforms around me now, insisting that everything heel before our ambitions, following the same old story, defiling larger and larger realms of the only planet we have to live on.

And then, when that mission is finally complete, when there's nothing left to upend and undo, it really will be time to make the long, cold journey to the stars.

———

I like to think I had wonderful dreams that night, lying on my bunk bed aboard the *Leah Callais*. I like to think that, in my sleep, floating through the Gulf, I remembered in vivid detail all the best things I'd experienced in Louisiana before waking at 3 A.M. to experience some of the worst.

Perhaps I dreamed of music that night, of the accordion player in Houma, for example, playing "Jambalaya" to a two-stepping crowd at the Jolly Inn, his seven-year-old son keeping rhythm on an old steel washboard. Perhaps the food came back to me, too—the gumbo (Vietnamese and Cajun), the crawfish and corn on the cob, the hot venison sausage and hardtack, the shrimp boulettes. Well fed, perhaps I floated next to my favorite fishing boats, hauling ice and swapping stories with grizzled fishermen, so immersed in the flow of Cajun dialect that *tempête* and *paupière* and *boue pourrie* come naturally to my own tongue as I hoist that last net and pick with my bare hands one more *grosse tallée* of shrimp. And then I rest in my dream, sleeping late in a far-off camp, surrounded by endless waves of grass, waking up to catch speckled trout for breakfast atop a wobbly dock before meeting, by chance, an Indian healer who cures my sore back on his way to saving a baby's fragile health. And then, reluctantly, I head back to shore, leaving this place, following a group of happy, diving dolphins whose glistening backs arch regally below a flock of laughing gulls and above that great school of menhaden they chase. And on an oyster boat I hitch one last ride, helping out with the catch before my hatchet opens the biggest shell of all and I tip it toward my tongue and shudder at the salty magnificence of pure heaven. And that's when the rain begins, falling softly on my face, landing all across this old wooden vessel even on this sunniest of sunny days. I look around, confused, until I see the Catholic priests, dozens of them, gathered along the banks, dressed in flowing white robes, wind-caressed and smiling, blessing every boat that passes by with delicate showers of holy water, offering mercy and protection.

But then, in my deepest sleep, in the tight embrace of these sensory joys, a voice intrudes. It's a loud and insistent voice, a shouting voice, trying to wake me up. It belongs to a tattooed deckhand on the *Leah Callais*. "Come on! Come *on!*" he yells. "Get up! If you want to see it, get up! We're here."

I moan from my bunk. "What time is it?"

"Three o'clock," he says. "Tee Brud said to wake you up when we reached our drop-off point. So get up!"

I pull on some clothes and stumble up the stairs to the wheelhouse. At first I'm puzzled as I look out the windows, rubbing sleep from my eyes. We've left the Gulf and returned, unexpectedly, to shore. Now a huge building complex at least four acres in size is right in front of us. To its right stands something else, something I would describe as a crane except it's far too big. It's a virtual skyscraper, a massive pointy-topped, black-painted tower of strut work seemingly designed to launch Saturn rockets or to serve as a bulked-up radio tower of some kind.

"Nope," says deputy captain Mark Dismuke, seated behind the wheel, when I express my puzzlement. "We're still in the Gulf, and that's *definitely* a crane you're looking at."

I stand next to Mark, who relieved Tee Brud hours ago, and I stare out the windows again. Sure enough, there's ocean water all around, filled with the same forest of man-made structures as when I went to bed. But this building before us now is so huge, so obviously off the charts in every way, that for the next twenty minutes I feel as if I never woke up, as if I'm still in bed, still dreaming. Shapes and sounds, distorted and unreal, float all around me, bearing no connection to the waking world.

Mark is talking again, cigarette in his mouth, long side-burns running down his face. But he's not making much sense. Did he just say that this four-acre edifice of steel is really a giant barge, a kind of floating factory? And is that really a seven-story dorm over there, as he claims, one that houses the two hundred men who do the work on board, who use tools as big as train cars to lay pipe and build platforms and deploy drilling rigs, all of it achieved with assembly-line quickness and efficiency? Yes, that's what he said. And now he's pointing to that strange tower over there, that Goliath crane rising up from the barge deck. It is, he says, one of the largest cranes human beings have ever built. Only a handful are bigger anywhere on the planet.

But how, I wonder, could such a crane exist out here, in the middle of the Gulf? How could it *float* this way? I press my face closer to the window and tilt my groggy head way back to see the crane's lofty top, lit up by lamps like a famous monument presented for night viewing. I hear Mark's voice again, floating across the dark wheelhouse as if from a faraway place. "It takes," he says, "five *miles* of cable to make that crane work. And the cable, it's as thick as your wrist. By itself, this crane can lift four thousand tons! It can lift the whole body of a new offshore rig. Just lift it up and set it down on its legs. Gonna do that very thing here in a couple days."

Hence the busy scene of preparation on the barge deck. I go outside for a closer look. A chilling wind has kicked up, prompting me to wrap my arms around my chest as I look out at one hundred men busily organizing materials, stacking pipe, driving transport vehicles with bulldozer-like tracks for wheels—the whole place lit up as if by klieg lights. Another hundred men lie inside the dorm, awaiting their next shift, sleeping despite the Allison nine-cylinder diesels roaring away on board, turning massive turbines that create the electricity that runs this factory, that powers this crane.

The wind has turned the water choppy, and the *Leah Callais* bobs and sways. But the barge, miraculously, doesn't move an inch. A gazillion gigabytes of computer brainpower speak every half second to four thrusters spread along the hull, keeping this factory almost perfectly still, the crane almost completely free of sway.

"DP," Mark says when I come back to the wheelhouse. "Dynamic positioning."

Unknown to me, this floating factory has been our destination all along (instead of a platform), and we've brought lots of supplies to feed her: tools, pipe, a copy machine, 40,000 gallons of fresh water. But I'm too worn out to watch the off-loading of the cargo. I just can't absorb much more. Mark wants to keep talking about the jumbo crane, meanwhile, a tool he's proud of in some sort of industry-patriotic way. "She can lift, this baby, the equivalent of one hundred eighteen-wheelers," he says. "Picture that. One hundred Mack trucks! And if you were to take . . ."

I'm not sure I ever fully woke up during that 3 A.M. visit. That the visit took place I have no doubt. I just remember it as if through a mist. So it's easy, afterward, back on my bunk bed, to slip into a deep sleep again, falling back into the realm of dreams. And what went through my mind the rest of that night is something I recall with utter clarity, no question about it, because it has come back to me many, many times since, both day and night, awake and asleep.

It's a dream where the fear and the loss and the ceaseless regret, so long a part of this coast, finally ebb and fall away like a retreating tide, washing out to sea. It's a dream where the factory-like roar out in the Gulf begins to soften and wane, growing fainter and fainter each day until it stops completely, never to return. Then comes a new sound, from the other direction, a rumble that's deep and powerful yet calming somehow, recognizable by its ancient tone. Louder and louder the sound grows, spreading across the coast, the voice of the Great River itself, emerging from its banks, flowing back to the land, branching and flowing and branching again, creating miles and miles of streams like roots probing deeper into the terrain, holding everything together.

And then the grass—you can almost hear it too, a great eruption. It grows and grows as it once did, stretching far and wide, waist deep in nourishing water, a placid green-gold wilderness large beyond understanding, cloaking with its swaying blades those old wounds left too long bare upon the land. Gradually the grass becomes just as it was when those first French Cajuns arrived centuries ago, on foot and on boats, persecuted and exhausted, exiles in a strange new land only to be welcomed and taken in by the great realm of the river, the rescuing Mississippi, munificent giver of life.

Which is why, in this dream, one not yet finished, Louisianans return the favor, for themselves and a grateful nation, using gentle hands to restore a natural place until, at long last, the old debts are repaid. And the cycle is complete.

## Epilogue

Predictably, the ecological unraveling of coastal Louisiana continues to accelerate. But the bayou people hang on.

After Tee Tim Melancon graduated from South Lafourche High School, his mother, Phyllis, moved back down the bayou to resume living and shrimping with Tim Sr. in Leeville. Young Tee Tim now has a permanent job at a big shipyard up in Larose, specializing in building and repairing large ship engines. He hasn't baited a crab trap in three years and has no intention of ever doing so again.

Meanwhile, Lawrence Billiot, the Houma Indian *traiteur*, fell into a two-year stretch of appallingly bad luck that almost ended his healing career. In twenty-four months his house caught on fire, he was in a serious car accident, he developed "diabetes sores" across his ample abdomen, he painfully passed several kidney stones, and Leah, his fifty-year-old common-law wife, amazingly got pregnant and then sadly miscarried. But thanks to the power of prayer, herbs, and his own healing touch, Lawrence has managed to reverse his fortunes and has at last returned to his healing ways full-time, curing snake bites, baby colic, and sunstroke all along the bayou.

Phan Duc Nguyen, the Vietnamese crabber in Golden Meadow, finally realized his goal of returning home, having saved enough money from crabbing to buy a plane ticket to Vietnam. Before leaving, he told his Vietnamese bayou friends that he wanted to find a good Vietnamese bride and settle down in his ancestral town, never to return to America. He was still drug-free as he headed for the New Orleans airport.

The small area of marsh grass I helped plant near Leeville with ten AmeriCorps volunteers has turned out to be a success. The grass took hold nicely and has expanded rapidly in the past two years, covering nearly half an acre. It's not that much in the grand scheme of things, but the grass is strong and healthy and still salutes passing boats like a beacon of hope.

Unfortunately, the marsh almost everywhere else along the coast continues its rush to oblivion, with land still disappearing at the astonishing rate of 25 to 35 square miles per year. As if this wasn't enough, a new threat has emerged. Fishermen and biologists have begun to notice huge areas of previously healthy green marsh suddenly turning brown and dying all along the coast, not from subsidence or erosion but from some new and mysterious ailment. Dissection of grass samples under a microscope revealed no disease, yet hundreds of thousands of acres continued to die in what has become known as the "brown marsh" phenomenon.

Even now there is no scientific consensus as to the cause of the new decline, though one theory is that the changing climate of North America, including the Gulf coast region, is at least partly to blame. A nationwide drought plus greatly reduced snowpack formation and spring melt in the Rocky Mountains—thanks to unusually warm winters—kept the Mississippi River at record or near-record low flows for much of 2000 and 2001. This has limited the amount of water getting to the coastal grasses. During this same period, the tides were unusually weak along Louisiana's shore, owing in part to a great decrease in strong southerly winds, which normally help push Gulf water up into the marsh. The weather has been exceptionally strange, in other words, leaving coastal grasses, especially those in the interior portion of marsh areas, with insufficient water depth to survive. Or so the theory goes.

Whatever the cause, vast and sickening new swaths of marsh began to die at such a rate that Louisiana Governor Mike Foster, an avid duck hunter across the wetlands, finally became alarmed. Foster organized an event that restoration activists had been seeking for years: a summit of state business leaders, conservationists, scientists, civic leaders, and government officials designed to fully commit the entire state to saving the coast. Foster emphasized his own determination by saying he planned to wage *jihad* against the land-loss problem.

The governor's office is now gathering concrete recommendations to include in an historic Everglades-scale piece of federal legislation—likely involving more than $14 billion in state and federal money for restoration—which Louisiana leaders hope to see passed on Capitol Hill as early as 2004. To muster broad support for the bill, the state launched a nationwide media campaign—financed largely by the Shell Oil Company—

to inform average Americans of the threats to national security that will come from lost oil infrastructure, hurricane protection, and seafood production if the coast continues to collapse.

Yet despite these new efforts, the nation remains almost totally ignorant of Louisiana's plight, and securing billions of federal dollars may prove impossible from a White House and U.S. House of Representatives openly hostile to almost everything having to do with environmental protection. But the paramount preoccupation of these same Washington leaders with protecting the health of the U.S. oil and gas industry, plus the fact that no one—no matter what political stripe—wants to see New Orleans disappear, may make Washington sympathetic to the enormous rescue plan. Only time will tell.

One small part of the rescue effort *has* become reality. A second artificial diversion of the Mississippi, this one twenty-three miles up the river from New Orleans, has become operational. Similar in size to the Caernarvon diversion south of the city, the new diversion—called Davis Pond—is reintroducing millions of gallons of freshwater full of nutrients and sediment to the stagnating and salt-threatened estuary system. This project by itself is expected to directly preserve 33,000 acres of marsh.

But many more diversions are needed—including the massive Third Delta Conveyance Channel—before the coast can hope to reach a level of healthy sustainability. Just how vulnerable the region still is was made terrifyingly real in September and October of 2002 when two major Gulf storms slammed into south Louisiana. The first, Isidore, was a deadly Category 4 hurricane, with 145 mph winds, and was heading straight for Leeville and Golden Meadow before miraculously weakening at the last moment. It came ashore having been downgraded to a tropical storm, but still dropped fifteen inches of rain in twenty-four hours all along Bayou Lafourche and New Orleans. Flood-water sloshed through low-lying homes, motels, and businesses, in some places rising more than four feet high in bedrooms and kitchens, especially on Grand Isle and in Houma. Scattered tornadoes flipped RVs like rag dolls. Fields of sugarcane were flattened. Tens of thousands of people lost electricity, and in New Orleans a main evacuation route was inundated and rendered impassable, reinforcing fears that the low-lying city's inhabitants could drown en masse when the Big One hits. But this wasn't the Big One.

Just seven days later, a second Category 4 hurricane, Lilly, was bearing down on Louisiana, completing a bizarre one-week, one-two punch of storms the state had never seen before. But Lilly, like Isidore, dramatically weakened just hours before hitting, coming ashore near New Iberia as a Category 1 hurricane. Mighty oak trees fell and splintered, transmission towers snapped like twigs, football goalposts twisted and bent, and an 18-wheeler toppled like a toy. About 350,000 people lost electricity and many more fled their homes. But this, too, could have been much, much worse. Louisiana got lucky. The storms together produced no deaths and only a few injuries, and caused about $700 million in damage, still enough for President Bush to declare the coast a federal disaster area.

The biggest damage, of course, was inflicted on the marsh, a subject totally missed by the national media. Tens of thousands of acres of already declining wetlands were torn up and tossed about over hundreds of square miles, creating yet more open water where protective grasses had once stood. The sinking barrier islands also took a terrible beating. One beach on Isles Dernieres retreated an amazing 300 feet in just one week.

But what concerned emergency management officials most was the unusually high surge tide that reached populated areas across the coast for such relatively weak storms. In Golden Meadow, the tide climbed more than six feet against the protective hurricane levees for both Isidore and Lilly. In the 1950s, a Category 1 hurricane would have brought only about half that much water to this inland town. But fifty years ago there was twice as much marsh to absorb the tide between the Gulf and the town. Thus, the question persists: What *will* this coast do when a Category 4 hurricane finally *does* come ashore with almost nothing to stop its surge tide, which is likely to be in the neighborhood of eighteen feet? The water will furiously topple all levees in its path and go and go and go, all the way to the outskirts of Baton Rouge, like a liquid bulldozer, flattening everything it meets, and hundreds of thousands of people will be at risk of drowning.

But again, that didn't happen this time. Two Category 4s somehow took mercy on the state and came ashore more politely. Governor Foster called it divine intervention: "I know some people don't believe that. But we have had divine intervention, in my opinion."

Maybe. But Louisianans better keep the prayers coming and coming.

# Index

*About the Author*

Mike Tidwell is the author of four previous books, including *In the Mountains of Heaven, Amazon Stranger,* and *The Ponds of Kalambayi.* A former National Endowment for the Arts fellow, Tidwell has published his work in *National Geographic Traveler, Reader's Digest, Washingtonian,* and many other publications. His frequent travel articles for the *Washington Post* have earned him four Lowell Thomas Awards, the highest prize in American travel journalism. He lives near Washington, D.C., with his wife, Catherine, and their son, Sasha.